The Return
of the
Great Britain

Richard Goold-Adams

The Return of the Great Britain

Weidenfeld and Nicolson   London

© Richard Goold-Adams 1976

Weidenfeld and Nicolson
11 St John's Hill, London SW11

ISBN 0 297 77144 2

Printed in Great Britain by
Cox & Wyman Ltd,
London, Fakenham and Reading

Contents

Illustrations

Preface

This is the story of the first eight years of the British effort to save the SS *Great Britain*. It is also a personal story. I felt that it should not be lost and that no one else was quite so well placed to witness what was going on. I have been the chairman and in effect the managing director of the SS *Great Britain* Project throughout. While I have thus been responsible for a good deal that has happened, I am also the only person who has really known the full facts about most of the rest. No doubt several books could be written about these years by those who have taken part. But this one is mine. And a feature of the story it tells is that life with the *Great Britain* has never been dull. Indeed, much of it has been exciting, tense, and to my mind altogether astonishing.

Having said that, let me also make it clear that I was neither the originator of the idea of saving the *Great Britain* nor the architect who showed how it might be done. That was Dr Ewan Corlett. His letter to *The Times* of 7 November 1967 started the ball rolling in this country, and he has given to the enterprise untold hours of costly time and professional acumen as a naval architect. Between us we have perhaps contributed the lion's share of the voluntary effort. But that effort has sprung from many sources. Besides our immediate colleagues on the Project Council, it has come from all those whose support has qualified them to become Governors, Members, or Friends of the Project, as well as from our loyal and very helpful staff, whose contribution has always exceeded their reward. And for my own part I am deeply aware of how much I owe to the forbearance as well as the backing of my wife, Deenagh.

There have been a good many pitfalls to avoid in writing this account, and I hope I have managed to find my way around most of them. I have tried to tell the truth without being libellous or irritating or discourteous – not always an easy task. I have attempted to show up some of the absurdities without being unkind. And above all I have sought to explain how some of our best-known difficulties arose without thereby reopening old wounds.

In this last respect I think almost everyone who has followed the story of the ship knows that, when we brought the *Great Britain* into Bristol, this action had no more than the official consent of the authorities concerned. Many people have naturally been puzzled ever since by all that has happened. And now that the story has had a happy ending, and we have most gratefully received a rent-free berth in perpetuity from the new city council, I feel that some explanation of the course of events is both possible and necessary.

It was not only the local political situation which caused the Project more problems than one might have hoped. The timing of the salvage happened to coincide with the nation's approach to a politico–economic watershed that I certainly feel is more serious than any other for three hundred years. Money-raising is a forbidding task at the best of times, but with unprecedented British inflation and the fundamental changes taking place in the economy, particularly in the private sector, the going has got steadily harder.

The essence of the Project's challenge, however, has always been that there is no easy way. And by writing this book I hope that the facts may speak for themselves, in showing both what has already been achieved and what we are still striving to accomplish. Certainly it has been no part of my purpose to spell all this out merely in order to enlist further aid. But there do seem to me to be two messages combined in it. One is that the *Great Britain* really *has* now become established as a national treasure. The other is that, although no one can say in present circumstances how long it may take to complete restoration, this unique vessel in her drydock in Bristol is already of absorbing interest to more and more visitors every year. With each step forward this can only increase, and obviously the more help we get the more effective we can be in finishing the job.

One of the questions I am always being asked about the Project is how much of our finance comes from public funds. And most people, including all foreigners, are astonished when I have to tell them: none. Up to the time of writing every penny of hard cash has been derived from private or industrial sources – if one does not count, that is, help from the nationalized industries as being from what is normally meant by 'public funds'. Although this question is referred to in the final chapter, I feel that a brief word should also be added about it here.

No one could appreciate more deeply than I do how much the *Great Britain* owes to those who have contributed to what has been achieved so far, either in the form of finance or as gifts in kind – many of them from the companies concerned. With the outstanding pre-eminence of Jack Hayward, who financed the salvage, their generosity and support have made everything worthwhile, and all of us involved in the Project are very grateful indeed. But I am also clear that in this day and age it is no longer appropriate to the national significance of the *Great Britain*, that people and businesses like them should be expected to continue to shoulder the burden alone indefinitely.

The principle of grant-aiding private initiative and effort has become widely accepted as a means of preserving our national heritage. State funds, that is, then at least match pound for pound any money raised privately. And although in these harsh times the last thing one wants is to add to government expenditure, to stick rigidly to out-dated priorities is a policy of despair. In recent years there has been a very worthwhile trend towards a more general popular understanding of modern society and therefore of its origins. This has brought an altogether fresh importance to industrial archaeology. It would therefore seem to deserve not only a possible reallocation of existing funds, but also a reassessment of overall priorities in terms of both educational and tourist expenditure. While many millions are spent, for instance, on the preservation of old buildings, all but nothing goes on our maritime heritage – and this for a nation which above all has lived by means of the sea! The *Great Britain* is now a symbol of this dichotomy. And I believe – almost as much as I hope – that the day must come when the position will be corrected. The role of the *Great Britain* both in this country's history and in the worldwide development of marine engineering has been such that her future warrants support from the public as well as the private sector of our now mixed economy.

To return to the personal aspect, and the question of charities, I do not think that anyone who has not been directly involved in a charity can really picture how difficult it is to get things done. Inherent inertia is one of the greatest forces in human affairs, fed in part by people's natural caution about change, understandable laziness, and sometimes instinctive suspicion of the motives of others. In charity work nobody can ever be pushed into doing anything they are unwilling to do. With the *Great Britain* all these factors have played their part in slowing us down. Thus, while proud of what we have achieved in spite of it all, I am also constantly dismayed by the fact that we have not accomplished more in the time.

Would I do it again? When people ask me this too, the answer must depend on what they mean. There are really three different questions and therefore three different answers – though each is covered by the same reply. If they mean, as some people do, whether I would start out again and try to rescue any other single ship, the answer is emphatically 'No'! Enough is enough. To go through the gamut of experience I have had with the *Great Britain* is something which happens once in a lifetime, and once only. On the other hand, they have introduced me to the whole range of wider problems involved in preserving the records of the past and presenting them to the public. And these I am sure I shall always find fascinating.

If the question means, secondly, would I have dropped out earlier on, if I had known what it would all entail, the answer again of course is no – though in a different sense. At each stage the next one became unavoidable, and the whole was implicit in the original decision to see the thing through.

Lastly, however, if the question is really whether I regret having devoted so very much time and effort over the past few years to the cause of this great ship, then again the answer is no. As with others, when I went into it at the start, I neither knew nor cared how forbidding the problems would prove to be. There was one simple fact. The *Great Britain* represents a tiny but vital part of the development of man's genius and so of the evolution of civilization as we know it today. Thus, with each step that we have taken, her significance and historical importance to this and future generations have seemed to grow. And now that the process of restoration appears to be firmly established, the fight has been worth it every inch of the way.

Richard Goold-Adams
Hampshire 1976

Historical Introduction

There are two main reasons why so much effort has been put into the salvage and restoration of the SS *Great Britain*. One is that she was the very first propeller-driven ocean-going vessel ever built. The other is that her salvage in 1970 when she was 127 years old became an epic of the sea. That she should have survived for so long in the circumstances that she did was very remarkable. But what added a whole new dimension was the timing and method of the operation itself. To be brought home on a huge pontoon, she was raised from her lonely beach in the Falkland Islands at very nearly the last possible moment, in view of her accelerating rate of disintegration. Thus, the fact that we have the *Great Britain* in Bristol today is something of a miracle.

The *Great Britain* was designed by the great Victorian engineer, Isambard Kingdom Brunel, and built in Bristol between 1839 and 1843 in the very same dock in which she now lies. She was launched by the Prince Consort on 19 July 1843, and she completed her fitting out late in 1844.

I. K. Brunel was born in Portsmouth on 9 April 1806, and died at the early age of fifty-three on 15 September 1859. He was half French and half English. His father, who later became Sir Marc Brunel, was an almost equally brilliant engineer and had arrived in England at the age of thirty in March of 1799 as a refugee – via America – from the French Revolution. His mother, Sophia Kingdom from Plymouth, had first met his father when she was learning French in Rouen. They married in London on 1 November 1799, eight months after Marc Brunel's arrival in England. Isambard Kingdom Brunel was their only son. Sir Marc died much honoured at the age of 80 on 12 December 1849, only ten years before his son, and well after the *Great Britain* had made her first historic screw-driven voyages across the Atlantic.

The background to the ship herself was one of immense boldness and enterprise. Brunel's first ship, the *Great Western*, a wooden paddle-steamer of 1230 gross registered tons launched in Bristol on 19 July 1837 – in a yard now marked only by a plaque near the old Prince Street swing bridge – had also made history. Although she lost the race to the *Sirius* by only three and a half hours to be the first vessel to cross the Atlantic under steam, she was the first to make regular voyages carrying passengers. She ended by running for ten years between Southampton and the West Indies before being broken up in 1856. Like the *Great Britain* she was at one time used for trooping in the Crimean War.

When Brunel had turned from his railways and bridges to ships, trade on the Atlantic was dominated by the Americans with faster and better sailing ships than the world had ever seen before. So the second ship to be built by him and his associates in the Great Western Steamship Company, the future *Great Britain*, was intended to be a big leap forward which would set a new standard for Atlantic travel. And it was conceived metaphorically as another extension from Bristol of the splendid new Great Western Railway line from London.

Brunel poured new ideas and new principles into his *Great Britain*, but two in particular stand out. He had found with the *Great Western* that for size she was about as far as one could go with wood, if the novelty of steam was to be fully applied to marine engineering. So the *Great Britain* would be of iron, now only just beginning to be used and so far only adopted at sea for small and experimental vessels. She was also to be far larger than any previous ship, because of the shattering new principle which he proceeded to enunciate, and which was to apply for ever afterwards to all waterborne – and indeed eventually, on its own terms, airborne – traffic. Brunel had discovered that, in his own words:

> The resistance of vessels in the water does not increase in direct proportion to the tonnage. The tonnage increases with the cubes of their dimensions, while the resistance increases at about their square, so that a vessel of double the tonnage of another, capable of containing an engine of twice the power, does not meet with twice the resistance. Speed, therefore, would be greater with the larger vessel . . .

Alternatively, at the same speed the larger vessel would be more economic.

As first planned, when her keel plates were laid down in her present drydock on 19 July 1839, the big new ship was to be of 2936 gross registered tons, and a paddle steamer. She was expected to be called the *City of New York*. And it was only during her actual building that Brunel gained enough knowledge about the revolutionary new technique of screw propulsion to make the tremendous decision to adopt it for his great ship. Plans were switched, the existing engines were to be swung round at right angles to drive a propeller shaft – another piece of pioneering machinery – and the name was changed to that of the country itself: *Great Britain*. Other features to make history included the first watertight bulkheads, first virtual double bottom, and first balanced rudder. This was in fact to be among the dozen most significant ships ever built by man, even to this day.

The cost of the vessel in round figures was £117,000, with an additional £53,000 spent on constructing the special drydock and setting up an engineering shore establishment capable, in particular, of building the engines on the spot. The total of £170,000 in 1843 would be equivalent to at least £2 million in 1975. Brunel established a management committee to organize the building along with himself. His three famous colleagues were William Patterson, whose shipyard had handled the *Great Western*, Captain Christopher Claxton, a retired naval officer who was Quay Warden in the City Docks and became the managing director of the Great Western Steamship Company, and Thomas Guppy, a wealthy Bristolian engineer whose enterprise and spirit were natural partners to Brunel's own.

The *Great Britain* left Liverpool for New York on her transatlantic maiden voyage on 26 July 1845, and did the crossing in poor weather in just under fifteen days at an average speed of 9·4 knots. Taking a different course out of New York on 30 August, she returned in fifteen and a half days at an average of 9 knots. Although modifications were required with changes of the propeller and a different sailing rig, she completed three more round trips during the next few months before disaster struck on her fifth outward voyage, when she ran hard aground on the east coast of Ireland at Dundrum Bay in County Down on the night of 22 September 1846.

To this day there is no wholly satisfactory explanation for the stranding. Though the night was dark and wet, the weather was by no means stormy. Emily Brontë, writing of the summer that year, put it in verse:

> July passed on with showers and dew,
> And August glowed in showerless blue . . .
> Week after week, from noon to noon
> September shone as bright as June . . .

Captain James Hosken appears to have missed the southernmost light on the Calf of Man and to have left his turn to the North too late, the ship making more speed than he evidently calculated. While navigational arrangements on board seem to have been poor, so does Hosken's own record in this respect. Nevertheless, seconded from the navy, he returned to it and eventually became an admiral. As for the *Great Britain*, although no lives were lost, she was refloated only with great difficulty the following year, and this was the end of the original ship as Brunel had designed her. It broke the Great Western Steamship Company.

Sold, re-engined and again re-rigged with three masts instead of the original six, however, the *Great Britain* was now to enter the main period of her extensive service life. Built originally as a steamer with auxiliary sail, she was converted to being more of a sailing ship with an auxiliary engine specifically for the long voyages to Australia, going out by the Cape of Good Hope and back by Cape Horn. Between 1852 and 1876 she made thirty-two such passages between Liverpool and Melbourne, except that on the initial one she came back via Capetown. She called at the Falkland Islands for the first time in January 1854, on the first of her round the world voyages.

Some say that the *Great Britain* had a sister ship. But this was never true. What happened was that in 1855 (16 years after the *Great Britain* had been laid down) a vessel of somewhat similar size called the *Royal Charter* was bought, while still half built in North Wales, by Gibbs, Bright and Company, the new owners of the *Great Britain*, in order to double their capacity on the Australia run. The myth may have gained a certain additional credence in that William Patterson was called in to complete the building, and in some respects he applied lessons learned with the *Great Western* and *Great Britain*. But near the outset of her career the *Royal Charter* was in any case the victim of a disastrous shipwreck off Anglesey in October 1859, with the loss of 454 passengers and crew.

The *Great Britain* became a popular ship. She was comfortable by the standards of the times, and reliable in that she could use her propeller when the wind dropped – which she did a great deal. She carried up to 600 passengers; and about a quarter of a million modern Australians probably have forbears who came out on her. She averaged around sixty-five days for each leg of the voyage, and her fastest run was fifty-four days. Her Australian voyages were interrupted to carry troops from England at the time of the 'Indian Mutiny', as well as for the Crimean War, and twice for special voyages to New York. By 1876 after thirty years at sea she was withdrawn from passenger service and laid up, pending a possible sale.

The hull was still so sound that by 1882 she had been sold for a second time. Her engines were removed, heavy timber was bolted on the outside to strengthen her old iron plates, and she put to sea again as a cargo sailing ship, carrying coal from South Wales to California. She made two long slow voyages, each lasting nearly a year. On her third, in 1886, she was partly dismasted off Cape Horn and put back to Stanley in the Falkland Islands, never to sail again. But even now she still had half a century ahead of her, afloat in Stanley harbour as a storage vessel for the Falkland Islands Company until nearly the very end. Only by 1933 had she at last become uneconomic. Then finally in April 1937, in order to dispose of her – it was thought for ever – she was towed three miles out of the harbour and beached in the remoteness of Sparrow Cove, the haunt of terns, shags and Gentoo penguins. She remained on the sandy shingle, open to the tides, for thirty-three years, until salvaged and brought home in 1970.

Brunel had died during the ship's Australian period, at a moment in September 1859 when the *Great Britain* had just returned, as it so happened, from one of her rare visits to the port she was originally designed to serve – New York. He died worn out by his exertions on his huge, third, and last ship, the famous *Great Eastern*. First conceived in outline in 1852 at the time when the *Great Britain* had passed out of Brunel's control and before her Australian voyages, the *Great Eastern* was originally designed with that same destination in mind. Applying his principles of size she was to be of 19,000 gross registered tons, with paddles as well as propellers, and large enough to steam all the way to Australia without refuelling.

Here at the end, however, his luck at last ran out. The boldness of his design for the *Great Eastern* was too much for the technical abilities of the day. She was to stick at her launching in Millwall on the Thames from the first attempt on 3 November 1857, till ultimate success on 31 January 1858. No ship has ever had a more inauspicious start, and, although she was to last for thirty years until sold for breaking up in November 1888, the *Great Eastern* never ran successfully as a passenger ship. Instead, she has a special place in the history books as the ship used for laying the first transatlantic cable, as well as other cables all over the world – off India, Aden and the Red Sea, France, the United States. No one built another ship as large as she was until the end of the century. But if Brunel had finally overreached himself with the *Great Eastern*, the long life and success of his intrinsically far more important *Great Britain* won him immortal fame in the annals of marine engineering.

1. How it all Began

Now that so much has happened to make the SS *Great Britain* an accepted part of the national scene, the story of how it all began seems to stretch back into another age. But to those of us involved at the time the events were as dramatic as any that have taken place since. And in this personal account of the Project I shall attempt to show how the long battle to save the *Great Britain* developed, and how it was gradually won.

From the early 1950s research about this famous ship had been quietly going on on both sides of the Atlantic. In America it centred around Karl Kortum, who as Director of the San Francisco Maritime Museum greatly hoped to see the *Great Britain* brought safely in one day under the vast span of the Golden Gate Bridge. And he was actively supported by certain of his trustees. In Britain the naval architect, Ewan Corlett, had become a walking encyclopedia on the subject ever since acquiring a print of Brunel's ship in 1952, his interest being fully understood only by the National Maritime Museum at Greenwich.

By 1968, however, the year in which the salvage effort was started in earnest, the Americans reckoned that they had spent nearly $100,000 on their work, including two visits to the Falkland Islands in 1966 and 1967 – where the ship was beached. And Ewan Corlett in the true spirit of Brunel himself had begun to inspire a small circle of enthusiasts with his ideas. The catalyst had been his letter to *The Times* of 7 November 1967. In this he had drawn attention to the existence and historical importance of the hull of the second and most successful of the three epoch-making ships designed by the great Victorian engineer, Isambard Kingdom Brunel; and he had asked that efforts should be made to save and restore it for future generations before the winter storms of the South Atlantic finally broke it up in the next few years.

All this was quite unknown to me personally at that time, when one weekend in February 1968, my eye was caught by a photograph in the *Observer*. It was taken I believe by Karl Kortum, and showed the *Great Britain* with her three masts beached about a hundred yards off shore against the curving outline of Sparrow Cove in the Falkland Islands – down in the South Atlantic some four hundred miles from Cape Horn. The caption indicated that by a series of miracles, the hull of this very old iron ship had survived, and that suggestions had been made to salvage and return it to England in view of its outstanding importance in maritime history.

Another fact also arrested my attention. This was the ship's name. Although I knew a certain amount about Brunel, the names of all three of his ships did not spring readily to my mind that February morning as I sat and looked out into the garden and watched the thin branches of the trees swaying in the winter wind. A few days later, when I came to look them up, I was reminded that the original one had been the *Great Western*, the wooden paddle-steamer launched in 1836. The next was the *Great Britain*, the first propeller-driven ocean-going ship in the world, launched in 1843, and the third the huge ill-fated *Great Eastern* of 1858, a ship of 19,000 tons, too unwieldy and too far ahead of her time. Indeed, until our recent resurrection of the *Great Britain* I think it was the *Great Eastern* that most people remembered from the history books. What struck me now, however, was the importance of the name of the ship in the photograph. No other ship in modern times had carried the country's name. And she had done so for well over a century. If she was worth saving, she was the more worth saving for that.

What was I to do about it? I felt I could not just let the matter drop. Who were the people who were suggesting salvage? How far had they got? What were their plans? It seemed really incredible that a metal ship launched in 1843 should still survive out on a lonely beach in the South Atlantic, and from the photograph it seemed still very much a ship. And how, moreover, had Brunel's historic hull come to be down there anyway? I determined to find out.

Instead of ringing the *Observer* straightaway, I felt that the first thing to do was to talk to someone who actually knew the *Great Britain* and had seen her in Sparrow Cove. So one day soon after seeing the photograph I looked up 'British Antarctic Survey' in the London telephone directory and rang their offices in Gillingham Street. I knew that they operated at least in part from the Falkland Islands.

The telephonist was helpful about my strange request and put me on to 'our Mr Salmon', who had recently been based at Stanley, the capital of the Falklands. Salmon told me exactly what I wanted to know. He was familiar with Sparrow Cove and had been on board the *Great Britain*. He described the state of the hull. He also knew quite a bit about her history. And he gave me an outline of how she had come to be beached in Sparrow Cove in April 1937, after lying in Stanley harbour since 1886 and having been used until 1933 as a storeship. It was all fascinating. He ended with a note of caution and some good advice.

'The *Great Britain* has become a local landmark,' he said, 'and everyone in the Falklands is proud of her. But if you want to know more about the ship I suggest you ring the people at the Falkland Islands Company. They have an office in London.'

So I did. And this was where fate took a hand.

The Falkland Islands Company is the major trading organization in the islands. It owns thousands of acres of sheep stations, runs the central export and import business in Stanley, and at that time operated the only regular link with the South American mainland, the SS *Darwin*. I was put on to Mr F. G. Mitchell, then the company secretary – he has since become managing director. After he had confirmed what Salmon had said, he told me that, as it so happened, there was shortly to be a meeting at the company's offices to discuss the future of the *Great Britain*.

'Would you like to come? If so, I'll find out whether it would be all right and ring you back.'

He did, it was, and I came. And that was where I first met Dr Ewan Corlett. The meeting was at 10 o'clock on 5 April 1968 in Pall Mall. One of the directors of the company, Mr J. H. Yorath, was in the chair. But what I did not know was how small the meeting was to be. I had pictured quite a few members of the public being there and my own presence passing unnoticed. When I reached the second floor and entered quite a small boardroom at the back of the building, I felt slightly embarrassed to find only four others there besides myself. They were Yorath and Mitchell from the Falkland Islands Company, Ewan Corlett and Basil Greenhill, the Director of the National Maritime Museum. With the early spring sunshine pouring through the window we all sat round the central table and were given cups of coffee. Then the proceedings began.

It was, I think, one of the most absorbing mornings I have ever spent. Maps, plans, reports, and other documents were produced. There was detailed talk about the condition of the *Great Britain*'s hull and its exact position on the gently sloping shingle of Sparrow Cove. I also gleaned a bit about her history – though I did not like to ask anything that was so patently obvious to the others present. But they were extraordinarily tolerant of my ignorance. And I began to feel that, if I had come into the room a free man and uncommitted, I would not be able to leave it so. By the time we had finished I had crossed the Rubicon and henceforth the *Great Britain* was inexorably to become part of my life.

Some of the technical language being used I did not at first understand. A key word of this kind was 'hogged', and I took a moment or two to guess its meaning correctly. The question that was argued back and forth that morning was central to the whole concept of salvage. It was whether the *Great Britain* was so much down at each end, 'hogged', that she had broken her back. This question arose from the fact that the ship was known to have a serious crack in her starboard side at the upper deck level, and it was possible to see from the several photographs available that the third mast, the mizzen, was slightly out of alignment with the other two. This meant she was a little down at the stern, that is somewhat hogged, as well as having a very slight twist to port – which was also indicated by the mis-alignment of the masts. But the view was adamantly expressed that the evidence, so far is it was known, was nowhere near enough to suggest that the ship had broken her back. If she had, of course, the task of refloating and salvaging her would have been too great.

In all this the leading part was taken by Ewan Corlett, who was con-vinced from a professional point of view that salvage was technically possible. I remember feeling that Basil Greenhill took the same view, though he did not claim that his own researches were as exhaustive as Corlett's had clearly been. Nor was he by profession a naval architect, having been only recently appointed to the National Maritime Museum after a career in the civil service – though he had written a certain amount about ships and the sea. Yorath, I think, was as impressed as I was by Corlett's knowledge and assurance. His Falkland Islands Company came into the matter because it had owned the *Great Britain* from 1886 to 1937, surrendering her officially as a 'Crown wreck' in that year, when she had been towed out of Stanley harbour and deliberately beached three miles away in Sparrow Cove, as being no longer economic even as a store-ship.

'The question then is,' Corlett summed up, 'what do we do now?'

I was crystal clear that a real effort should be made to save the *Great Britain*, and I was delighted to find that two lines of action lay open to us, both of which we would take. First, we must make direct and personal contact with the Americans and find out exactly how far they had got and what their plans were. Both Greenhill and Corlett knew that they had been fairly active for at least three years already. Secondly, we must make common cause with a number of people in the Bristol area who, I learned, were arranging a meeting on 4 May at which everyone interested in the *Great Britain* could get together and assess the situation.

Before our own meeting closed, Corlett, Greenhill and I agreed that we would invite William Swigert to come over from San Francisco and join us in Bristol. Swigert was the moving spirit among the trustees of the San Francisco Maritime Museum interested in the *Great Britain* and the millionaire who had put up the money for the American effort. He had already visited London with Karl Kortum to pursue his enquiries, and they had each separately been to the Falkland Islands. In the event, he accepted and came – at his own expense.

For myself, as I walked down the stairs and into the street with the traffic pouring out of Trafalgar Square, I reflected that I had come a long way since I had first looked up 'British Antarctic Survey' in the telephone book. And it hardly struck me as odd that I would in fact now be travelling to Bristol in a month's time to see what I could do to help float an old ship off a lonely beach somewhere down near the Antarctic.

Earlier that year a number of enthusiasts in Bristol had launched a new group which they called the Brunel Society. Its object was to promote wider knowledge of the engineering achievements of Isambard Brunel and also of his distinguished father, Sir Marc Brunel, an immigrant into Britain from the French revolution. While the Brunel Society naturally included the *Great Britain* and the other two steamships in its interests, I came to understand that its emphasis lay quite as much, if not more, on the building of the Great Western Railway with its bridges, tunnels, track and locomotives.

I mention this because the fact that the meeting in Bristol was held under the auspices of the Brunel Society led eventually to a certain amount of misunderstanding and indeed friction – without which, however, one gradually finds in life that few worthwhile things ever really get done. And certainly that May morning when we all assembled at the Bristol City Museum to discuss practical plans for the *Great Britain*, all systems seemed to be go. Neil Cossens, then Director of the museum, had made a large room available in which, when I arrived, I found that something like thirty-five or forty people had gathered. The chair was taken by Robert Adley, one of the founders of the Brunel Society, and himself a keen railway enthusiast; at that time he had not yet been elected to parliament as he later was, first for Bristol North East and then for the Christchurch and Lymington division of Hampshire. He handled the meeting with youthful vigour, briskness and lucidity. Afterwards I joined the Brunel Society and have remained a member ever since.

A good deal of the ground which we had covered in London four weeks earlier was gone over again. Corlett gave his views about the practicability of salvage; and Greenhill, as well as George Naish who was also present from the National Maritime Museum, outlined some of the problems which had been met and overcome when dealing with other historic ships. There were in addition a number of people present who had personal knowledge of the *Great Britain*, including a man who had done some practice diving in Sparrow Cove. But although bringing a certain rugged realism to the discussion, he was not all that good with words and in effect could do little more than confirm what Corlett and Greenhill at least already knew or suspected about the famous crack in the starboard side.

The star visitor was William Swigert from the United States, a reserved, close-cropped, youngish middle-aged man, who quickly showed that he knew a very great deal about the *Great Britain* and in particular about her current condition. We plied him with questions so that at one stage he did most of the talking. And I remember thinking how his researches and invaluable first-hand knowledge were being taken tremendously for granted by everyone present, as if, instead of having just flown six thousand miles from San Francisco especially for this interrogation, he had merely driven over from Gloucestershire.

For myself I soon came to see two things. One was that the dominant element in the meeting, those who were making the running, had little to do with the Brunel Society as such, except perhaps for Robert Adley. And the other was that a steering committee of some kind would have to be formed if action was to be taken to follow up the views and conclusions expressed at the meeting. This would involve something more limited in aim than the Brunel Society. In its existing form so far as I could make out, the Society was too generalized and as yet too embryonic to be a suitable instrument for raising the kind of money that would be needed, for negotiating contracts and organizing the salvage, and then indeed for conducting the actual restoration. Nor was there any inherent reason to suppose otherwise.

There remained the American position. And here Bill Swigert, sensing the practical and determined bent of some of those present, wound up by clearing the air.

'I think I can speak for all of us in San Francisco,' he put it, 'when I say that we feel that the right place for the *Great Britain* is here in England where she was built.'

There was a moment's silence as he held the attention of the room.

'If a serious British effort is going to be made to salvage this ship, therefore, we in America will stand back and wait for you to go ahead.'

Then he added on a personal note: 'I myself have already sponsored a great deal of work collecting information. It is all at your disposal if you want it. I will help you in every way I can.'

Although I realized at the time, and heard it confirmed later, that the Americans had not in fact got to the point of being ready to go out to the Falklands and salvage the ship, Bill Swigert's attitude was a generous and helpful one by any standard. I felt it important nevertheless to be as precise as possible.

'When you say you will stand aside and wait for us to mount a salvage attempt from this country,' I asked, 'how long will you give us?'

Swigert thought for a moment. 'As long as necessary.' Then he added: 'Well, let's say a year in the first instance. And then it would depend on how you were getting on.'

It was only some years later, when I went to see him in Oregon, that I really appreciated how deeply involved he was in spirit with the *Great Britain*, and how much it had cost him emotionally that day to say what he did. I believe he never regretted it. But I also think that for ever afterwards he was sad about it. For several years he had set his heart on bringing the *Great Britain* to San Francisco.

At the time we all expressed our gratitude and then pressed on to form the steering committee. Seven people were nominated. Corlett of course was the central figure. Naish was put forward by Greenhill, who declined for himself in view of his official position. Adley came in as a prime mover and chairman of the meeting. Sid Urry from Brunel University and at that time Secretary of the Brunel Society was included. C. H. Miller, Vice President of Bristol Technical College, was named as someone from that city. I was invited to join, partly I think because I had had some previous experience of fund-raising. And at my suggestion Swigert himself was put on the list, a step which I was glad he accepted.

That, then, was the nucleus from which everything else has sprung.

One of the extraordinary aspects of our saga, however, was that the whole of this little group never actually met as such. Quite apart from Swigert's absence in America we never even met as the remaining six. Instead, in a very British way we kept in touch by telephone and letter, and by some of us meeting two or three together when we could. After a few months as things got going, we added to our number and in effect re-formed the committee. But the fact remained, as almost anyone with practical experience will bear witness, that success or failure depends more on the individuals concerned than on any committee as such. A camel, it is often said, is a horse put together by a committee – but few committees are so useful. Or, to use the words of that great but temporarily discredited British poet, Rudyard Kipling: 'It is always one man's work, always and everywhere.' While dealing with the *Great Britain* has never been precisely that, the principle holds good of its having been only two or three at any given time.

After the meeting in the Bristol Museum had broken up that morning, Neil Cossens and Basil Greenhill gave me an introduction to the nature and character of the ship with which I was so inexorably linking my life. Downstairs they showed me the museum's excellent four-foot model of the *Great Britain* and then opened up some of the great drawers in the archives in which lay coloured prints of the ship and a good deal of miscellaneous information about her. Meanwhile some of the others had gone out to have a look at No. 2 drydock in Charles Hill & Sons' shipyard, where the *Great Britain* had been built and where it was suggested she might now be brought back at least for the first stages of restoration. Afterwards the main party met again in the museum canteen and we all had lunch there together. As I drove out of Bristol that afternoon, I realized that a turning point had been passed and that some things would never be quite the same again. I could not have been more right.

During the summer of 1968 the two people I mainly worked with over the *Great Britain* were Ewan Corlett and Robert Adley. I was still engaged in a number of other commitments: I was on the boards of three companies and active in all of them, as well as being chairman of an international institute with a membership in fifty countries. At first I had little extra time that I could devote to our enterprise. Corlett for his part was in the full flood of his career as a naval architect, a partner in his own firm, and with a growing professional reputation. Adley was heavily committed on the sales side of a large firm, as well as nursing a parliamentary constituency – for which he became the member in the 1970 general election. Nor were we normally centred in any one place. Corlett's offices were at Basingstoke, Adley commuted between London and Bristol, and I was based in Hampshire. Of the original committee members, Naish was at Greenwich, Miller in Bristol, and Urry at Acton just outside London – with Swigert of course in California. But between us we managed to keep things moving forward.

Our problem seemed to me to present itself in a number of steps, some of which could be taken together, though others were necessarily consecutive. The key one was to establish for ourselves, and then beyond reasonable doubt in the eyes of anyone who might back us financially, that the hull of the *Great Britain* out in the Falklands really was in good enough condition to be salvaged at all. Assuming that it was, we had to solve the fundamental question of how to raise enough money for the purpose. Allied to this was whether we could get any substantial help from the Admiralty, or from shipping interests, in terms of man-power or equipment. We also had to decide exactly where the *Great Britain* would be taken when she arrived in the British Isles, and what would be done to her in terms of restoration. And in order to progress on each and every one of these points we had to start rallying supporters immediately wherever we could find them, not least in high places, as well as building up a public relations organization to develop our image as we went along.

To call all this daunting would, I suppose, be an understatement. The only points in our favour so far as I could see, were that a mixed group of people, some of them quite expert and level-headed in their own fields, had decided after very careful consideration that this venture was worth a good try, and that those of us now committed to leading it certainly meant to be stopped by nothing except the impossible. And, as time went by, I found that my own reaction to anyone who raised objections was to let him get them off his chest and then, if he was still willing, to start discussing the real problem.

The world being what it is, we made a start at once in trying to enlist wider support. And in doing so I learned of several MPs who had already expressed some interest in our aims, among them Sir Peter Kirk, David Owen, and John Smith, at that time still in the House of Commons as Member for Westminster. Through other contacts I was also able quite early on to go and see the then Minister for the Royal Navy, Maurice

Foley. And while there was nothing he could do for us on his own, he expressed a valid interest and asked us to keep him in touch with developments, so that the Admiralty might be able to help at the appropriate moment – which in due course it did.

It was obvious that we needed the right sort of publicity as soon as we could get it. While there had already been a little in the press about our ideas, no coherent story had yet been told and the facts about the *Great Britain* herself had barely been touched on. I volunteered to my colleagues to explore the possibilities of finding someone suitable to handle our public relations professionally. Through friends I thus very soon met an enterprising Australian who ran a small office overlooking Fleet Street and who was said to know his way around. All of this attracted me, since it was just the kind of individual approach I felt we needed. His name was Adrian Ball and he has been with us ever since. Curiously enough at that time he also had a subsidiary office in Bristol. His initial advice was basic: 'You don't want to come out with anything until you are really ready. Then, when you are, you want to make as much impact as possible.'

The result was that we agreed to work towards holding some form of press conference in the late summer or early autumn.

Meanwhile, I was, of course, increasingly conscious of the overriding need to raise some money. We were already beginning to spend it even though we did not have it. Robert Adley and I accordingly made a first – and abortive – attempt to interest a firm of professional fund-raisers in assisting us. Towards the end of June we had our second meeting with the hard-headed individual who ran it. Our first meeting had been exploratory. This one was to try to reach some positive arrangement, and I remember well his summing up. After suggesting quite genuinely a number of lines along which we ourselves might proceed – which was advice helpfully given and gladly taken – he ended by declining to involve his own firm and saying: 'If you are really thinking seriously of going on with this scheme, my advice quite simply is "Don't".'

While we naturally ignored his advice in general, we did decide to postpone any formal fund-raising until our own organization had taken on rather more shape. This immediately called in question four aspects of it – having a chairman, an honorary treasurer, a tax-free status as a charity, and a readily recognizable name. As to the chairmanship of our little group, it was not at first clear what the best course would be. But Basil Greenhill from his established, yet by now slightly detached, position as Director of the National Maritime Museum discreetly initiated a move. In a roundabout way he had sounded out my own views quite early on, adding his own dry comment. 'Somebody,' he put it, 'is going to have to spend an awful lot of time on this thing, if it is ever to get off the ground.'

Ewan Corlett, we all knew, was the obvious person. But it was not long after this that he rang me one day and himself suggested that I should become the chairman of our steering committee. If I agreed, he would sound out the other members. I replied that, before anything of that kind was done, it must be made perfectly clear why he should not be chairman himself. I could almost hear him shrug this off on the telephone. 'Honestly,' he said in that tone of voice one uses when one really means it, 'I am far too busy.'

So I accepted and that was that. What the chairman would do, how his role was to be defined, whether in fact it would amount to anything at all specific, these questions were never exactly asked and certainly never answered. Again, the whole thing in its way was terribly British. But the move did provide the organization with a bit more shape, and I also knew that it would help my own position when trying to enlist support and help outside.

It was Greenhill who then once again stepped into the breach over an honorary treasurer, almost casually as it seemed to me at first. I was asked if I would like to go down to Greenwich on a day in June and sit in at the annual general meeting of the long-established Society for Nautical Research, which normally meets on museum premises. My only previous experience of Greenwich had been to lecture about international affairs on a number of occasions at the Royal Naval College. But now, as a newcomer to the exclusive world of those who go down to the sea in ships, I welcomed this fresh approach. Immediately after the meeting the plan unfolded itself. In his office Greenhill made two telling points to me.

First, he felt strongly that it would be necessary at least for a time for our newly formed committee, which nobody had ever heard of, to be affiliated in some way to a recognized charity, if we were to go out at once and ask people to give us money. And the obvious body for this purpose was the Society for Nautical Research (SNR) which, as he put it, he had reason to believe would be entirely willing to accept us. When I agreed that this seemed a good idea, he quickly made his second point.

'In that case,' he said, 'probably the best thing would be to see if the Honorary Treasurer of the SNR would be willing to do both jobs. He is as a matter of fact outside and, if you like, I will ask him to come in. His name is Eric Custance.'

So began a long and pleasant relationship that saw us through the early years and lasted until he was succeeded by a Bristolian, John Gordon. Custance, a senior Lloyds Bank manager, had had a good deal of experience of voluntary bodies. And he piloted us into that world with skill and a great eye for detail, aided very actively by his wife, Margaret. As Honorary Treasurer he became the first addition to our original committee.

My own first act as chairman was to resolve the question of our name. As firmly as I dared, I urged that we should call ourselves the 'SS *Great Britain* Project'. The word 'Project' was not so commonly used at that time as it has become since. And maybe we helped in a small way to foster a trendy fashion for it. 'Project' seemed to me to have a touch of glamour, a hint of new frontiers and the unknown, something faintly Elizabethan about it. I recognized that it might slightly confuse those with a purely pedestrian approach, but they would not care much for our enterprise anyway. And I successfully fought off the use of the word 'Committee' after it. All this being agreed to, we thus became in our own minds at least and to many people outside quite simply 'The SS *Great Britain* Project'.

During that summer of 1968, once we had organized ourselves, we were able to take fresh stock of our position. And the truth was that, although not a finger had yet been lifted out in Sparrow Cove itself, a prospective salvage operation on the *Great Britain* had begun to seem a far more realistic possibility than it had the previous winter. While keeping an eye on the vital need to get one of us out to the Falklands as soon as possible to conduct a preliminary reconnaissance on the spot, we applied ourselves with a new sense of purpose to clearing our minds about two or three other questions, which would arise the moment a possible salvage expedition looked like being successfully mounted.

The basic one, I felt, was where we would take the ship once we had got her back to England. And here two elements in the problem seemed obvious. First, so far as I was concerned, I found that an understanding already existed whereby the *Great Britain* would initially be put in Charles Hill's shipyard in Bristol for restoration. Then, secondly, it was an entirely separate question where she would end up once the work had been completed. She might stay where she was or she might be moved. At this early stage I accepted the supposition that the directors of the shipyard would agree to have the ship during restoration, together with the assumption that the *Great Britain* herself could physically be got into the proposed dry-dock. But I resolved to meet the chairman of the dockyard myself as soon as I could and to explore the possible arrangements with him direct. What I had not the faintest inkling of at the time was the local furore which was to be caused by the concept of our bringing the ship into Bristol in the first place, and then again by the question of her final destination once she was in there. This in the end led to a far rougher ride than the whole drama of the actual salvage itself.

Another factor, to which Ewan Corlett rightly drew attention, was the great desirability of securing a good film record of the salvage, assuming it ever took place. We cast about in various directions to see whether anyone would be interested in sponsoring such a film. If they would, we could give them an exclusive assignment to make it, and we hoped that this could be a noticeable financial help to our funds. We recognized from the start, however, that exclusivity would be hard to define, since Sparrow Cove, though remote, was a public part of the high seas and we could not possibly prevent anyone else going there who wanted to do so.

In the end the most obvious course looked the most viable. The British Broadcasting Corporations BBC 2 programme, *Chronicle*, proved to have two people on it keen to take us up. The late Paul Johnstone, the producer, was a member in his own right of the Council of the Society for Nautical Research, and I soon learned that one of his directors, Ray Sutcliffe, had already established contact with Ewan Corlett in order to make a television programme based on the latter's researches.

When Ewan and I discussed the position, we agreed that, as no alternatives seemed to be particularly good runners, we had better abandon our grander ideas and settle with the BBC. But we did ask for two undertakings by the Corporation which were duly given – or at least so far as we understood them. One was that the Project should be provided for its own use with a free copy of whatever main film came out of the operation. The other was that we should receive any left-over material that was not required for the BBC's own purposes. Unfortunately, when it came to the point, neither of these propositions was interpreted as we had supposed them to be meant. And this too eventually caused the Project more harm by denying us a film for fund-raising and me more personal anguish than anything I dreamed of at the time.

Another aspect of our immediate position that summer which I felt needed going into was our relationship with certain plans that I knew were afoot to create a 'National Maritime Trust'. Very shortly after the original photograph of the *Great Britain* had attracted my attention in the *Observer*,

I had noticed a short news item in the press. It concerned a meeting at which the Duke of Edinburgh had presided over a discussion about the circumstances surrounding the hulls of four notable British ships. The first three were warships – *Warrior, Unicorn, Belfast* – and the fourth was the *Great Britain*. I accordingly got in touch with Prince Philip's private secretary and then his treasurer, who was at that time Rear Admiral (later Sir Christopher) Bonham-Carter. I told them what we were doing and made sure that, perhaps unknown to us, other parallel steps were not being taken in regard to the *Great Britain*, which might lead to a general mix-up and waste of effort. I received an explicit assurance that the formation of a Maritime Trust was still only at a very early stage and much encouragement to press on with our own plans as vigorously as possible. Thus was started an association which was to prove very helpful to the *Great Britain* over the years.

During this period I used to have many long telephone conversations with Ewan Corlett, occasionally running to nearly an hour – something we could not have afforded later on, as inflation began to bite. We talked over everything that we were trying to do. And as we came up towards our proposed press conference, now to be in September, when we would announce our existence publicly and seek wider help, we both felt we ought to bring the Americans fully up to date. So I put a long-distance call through to Bill Swigert in California. When he came on the line and heard our news, he was clearly both glad and sorry. We left it that we would keep him in touch with the more substantial developments we hoped for in the autumn.

He then, however, repeated his offer of help and suggested that one of us might visit San Francisco to go through the material in Karl Kortum's possession. As things turned out, Ewan Corlett was in fact able to take him up on this only a few weeks later and was with them both on 11–12 October. He found it 'extremely useful'. I, too, managed a similar visit, but not till very much later on. The Americans also sent us fairly soon after this an immense and fascinating tome of press cuttings, photographs, and copies of other records which they had painstakingly collected at the San Francisco Maritime Museum. At first on loan, it was later given to us and now forms part of our own archives.

Early in September I had to go to New York on business, spending only one night there before flying back – an exhausting and unwelcome experience. But while over there I had lunch with the head of the Ford Foundation, McGeorge Bundy, since they were major donors to the International Institute for Strategic Studies of which I was chairman. And I could not help thinking, as I sat out the hours over the Atlantic, how nice it would be if some one institution or wealthy individual like that could help us save the *Great Britain* with a really significant single gift. Though I could not know it at the time, this was to happen some ten months later.

2. The Ship is Surveyed

We would really have preferred to hold our press conference announcing our existence and future plans after Ewan Corlett himself had had a chance to visit the Falkland Islands. But in spite of various attempts to arrange such a trip during the summer of 1968 this proved unattainable. The problem was one of time rather than cost, though naturally both were involved. In those days the only regular commercial link was the SS *Darwin* which plied between Montevideo in Uruguay and Stanley, the Falklands capital, a distance of about a thousand miles. Nor did she simply go out and back. When she was in the Falklands she usually went round the islands as well.

The net result was that – although we sometimes managed it later on – one could not count on making a round trip from London back to London in less than five weeks, even flying of course out to Montevideo and back. And that was if berths were available at the right time each way on the *Darwin*, which was by no means always the case as there was a seasonal flow of Falkland Islanders themselves going on leave. The reason why there was no flying was that no flat space could be allowed to be available in the Falklands, in case an airborne invasion was launched from Argentina to seize the islands; a group of unofficial extremists had in fact landed a twin-engined machine on the racecourse shortly before this. For similar political reasons, based on the permanent Argentine claim to sovereignty, there was no short seaborne link either, though the nearest Argentine port was only some four hundred miles away. After 1974 an easing of the political situation led to the introduction of a weekly air service.

I remember that in the summer of 1968 amongst the many contacts and possibilities that Corlett and I were exploring was the idea that we might charter a flying boat. This was partly because there was a chance at one moment that either the BBC or the *Daily Telegraph* or both might put up some money to take a share in such a scheme, with a view to covering the first professional survey of the *Great Britain* in Sparrow Cove. Although the BBC was later to spend many thousands of pounds on its filming of the ship, those concerned became discouraged about this particular scheme because no one could find a suitable aircraft to charter from anywhere within reasonable distance in South America itself. We had heard that there was one ex-world war American Catalina flying boat in Chile. And this could have been very suitable. But for one reason or another no deal was ever clinched.

In selecting a site for our press conference in London, Adrian Ball cast round for an appropriately maritime setting. At Corlett's suggestion, we approached the Honourable Company of Master Mariners and they kindly let us use their headquarters, the *Wellington*, moored at Temple Stairs alongside the Victoria Embankment. We adopted just a touch of the cloak and dagger approach before the appointed day, Monday 16 September, since we hoped to achieve a better impact if people did not know what it was all about before it happened. They were thus only invited to hear 'an important maritime announcement'.

We had prepared a hand-out of a dozen widely spaced type-written sheets giving the nineteenth-century history of the *Great Britain* in some detail, our grounds for calculating that she could be salvaged, a statement about ourselves and our aims, and an invitation to the public to send donations to a special '*Great Britain* Account' at the SNR. Contrary to previous irresponsible findings our confidence about the condition of the ship, we indicated, had recently been reinforced by a survey carried out by the local detachment of the Royal Marines at the request of the Governor of the Falkland Islands, Sir Cosmo Haskard, as well as by a series of close-up photographs which we had specially commissioned. We also reported the sympathy for our ideas which had been expressed by the Minister of Defence, Denis Healey, and the Under Secretary for the Navy, David Owen (who had now replaced Maurice Foley). We estimated the cost of getting the ship to Bristol as up to £150,000, and (perhaps a little optimistically in the light of later events) said that the Port of Bristol Authority 'would support' the plan 'of refitting the *Great Britain* and setting her up as a maritime museum' there.

What we were nearly beaten by was the weather. During the preceding weekend the heavens simply opened all over South East England. By the Monday morning railways as well as roads were flooded, embankments washed away, and routes cut which had never been cut before. Not only did this become the great national story next day, taking up columns of space in the newspapers at the last moment – which is precisely what one always hopes will not happen when one holds a press conference – but many people failed to reach their destinations until the late morning; journalists were among them, and so, to my consternation, was Ewan Corlett. The main line into Waterloo was cut at Winchfield, and he spent most of our vital press conference sitting in a train on the wrong side of it. Without the authority of his professional expertise, I could see us playing *Hamlet* without the Prince.

Robert Adley and I, however, took the meeting together and in spite of everything it went with quite a swing. Ewan arrived just in time to meet some of the journalists while they were still drinking the coffee we gave them afterwards. We had representatives there from all the main papers and agencies, and some television coverage was given by means of interviews shot on the deck above. The following morning Adrian Ball told me he was delighted with the results.

There were ninety press notices up and down the country and two days later *The Times* ran a leader about us. While obviously not read by the masses, it was nevertheless a great encouragement, particularly in terms of helping us in those circles from which we hoped to draw immediate practical and financial support.

'The attempt to bring back to Bristol Brunel's famous ship, the *Great Britain*, deserves success,' *The Times* editorialized. 'The time has passed ... when only ancient country homes were thought to be worth preserving, and it is now accepted that outstanding examples of Britain's industrial development, particularly from the Industrial Revolution, should be retained also ... The same kind of arguments apply equally to ships. ...'

Liverpool's *Journal of Commerce* of 21 September went further, declaring: 'The *Great Britain* was one of the most important ships ever built by a British shipyard – and if the name she bears still means anything she should be brought home. The Government should be generous ... There is no reason why the Government should not make a cash grant or provide an interest-free loan to cover part of the restoration work. If the vessel were to be made into a maritime museum, part of the income could be used by the Bristol City authorities to pay off such a loan – or perhaps Bristol could put up the money itself.'

This was heady stuff, as well as a little confusing. Neither Bristol nor shipping circles as a whole were to see everything quite like that. And over seven years later not a penny had been given or loaned to us from any public fund. All the same, we were grateful and very much cheered by the first reactions to our cause – and the government did have it in mind to help us in ways other than financially.

On 7 November Gordon (later Lord) Campbell MP – whose wife, Nicola, is a direct descendant of Brunel – elicited in answer to a parliamentary question to the Minister of Defence a reply from the Parliamentary Under Secretary for the Royal Navy stating on behalf of the government, cautiously but hopefully, that:

'Subject to public money accountability and operational requirements we have agreed to help this venture in any way we can.'

Behind all this, of course, there had been a good deal of contact and continuing discussion. Denis Healey, who I had known well for a good many years, had told me that the opportunity might well arise for Ewan Corlett to be offered transport to the Falkland Islands in HMS *Endurance*, though both he and David Owen regretted that the Admiralty could not help us, as had also been suggested, with a naval tug to tow the *Great Britain* if she were ever floated.

Thus it was that later in the same month, November, our chance suddenly came. The occasion was the mission headed by Lord Chalfont, as Minister of State at the Foreign and Commonwealth Office, to explain the Labour government's point of view to the Falkland Islanders about negotiations with Argentina, and to solicit their reactions. This had become necessary because of the widespread distrust in the Falklands of London's attitude. It was felt there that, in return for the population's intense loyalty to the mother country, they were being sold down the river. Chalfont was to make a quick trip from the mainland in HMS *Endurance* and stay in Stanley for five days. This was ideal from our point of view.

HMS *Endurance* was an ice patrol ship with a helicopter platform and two helicopters, which maintained contact with British outposts in the South Atlantic and Antarctic peninsula. Although well-known in Stanley, she rarely came straight out and went straight back again. I was also happy that the politician concerned was Alun Chalfont since he had been a colleague of mine from earlier days, and I felt this could be a help.

Ewan Corlett left London by air for Rome on 17 November, catching the Alitalia plane from there to Montevideo, where he embarked in HMS *Endurance*. During the four-day voyage to Stanley he was able to give a lecture about the *Great Britain* and our whole Project to the assembled ship's company. The result was that they were ready to volunteer to a man, to give him all the unofficial help they could over his survey in Sparrow Cove; and this proved to be of enormous assistance.

He had four clear days in and around the *Great Britain*, which was just right. The naval help meant that he could be dropped off there each morning and picked up each evening in a naval launch and thus wasted no time. There were also invariably some off-duty volunteers who stayed with him. Not only were they extremely useful in taking measurements and generally aiding the many observations to be made, but they were an important safety factor. The big old hull of the *Great Britain*, half under water, its deck mostly rotten, and the corrosion of its beams uncertain, was no place to fall and be seriously injured on one's own. Finally and by no means least, the officers carried out a survey exercise in Sparrow Cove. This charted the various depths of water and proved the valuable point that it would be possible to bring up a deep-draught vessel to the port side of the *Great Britain*. All the information about the depths was of great value later on when the actual salvage came to be put into operation. In addition, because of the political topicality of the main mission, the BBC had sent out a camera team and some preliminary footage was shot of the *Great Britain*.

Corlett was also able to take the temperature of Falkland Island opinion about the ship and to meet the Governor. What he found was not reassuring, though Sir Cosmo Haskard was always confident that, so long as people were given all the facts, they would be willing to help us. As I had been told when I made my own first enquiries earlier in the year, local opinion started from the point of view that the *Great Britain* was a treasured possession of sentimental value to the settlement and should not be moved. Nor did most people consider for one moment that she could be. They were thus opposed to our plans and extremely sceptical of our chances of success.

HMS *Endurance*, with the Chalfont party on board, sailed back to the mainland, not North over the thousand miles they had come, but on the shortest sea route westwards to Punta Arenas on the Chilean shore of the Straits of Magellan. From there Corlett flew back via Santiago and reached England on 3 December, having given up just two weeks of his own time. We had to reimburse the Treasury at a modest rate for his sea passage, and my own contribution had been his air ticket. But the Project had taken a great leap forward. For now we really knew what the ship was like. We were no longer working in the dark.

When I talked to Ewan on his return, I could see at once that he felt we were vindicated. He was confident the job could be done. And he sat down straightaway to write a solid technical report about the condition of the ship and his proposed method of refloating her, both to clear his own mind and for the historical record. This has never been published, though it was made available privately to anyone suitable who was interested. It constituted the first and only professional naval architect's view about the facts and possibilities and was able to give the lie to some of the sillier rumours, a number of which had already been thrown at us, while others were to come later. The most inaccurate was that the ship had no bottom since its underwater plates had disintegrated with rust. In reality, as anyone can see today in the Great Western drydock, the lower plates are thicker and in better condition than the ones higher up.

What we needed to do next was to publish a popular summary of the findings. But, as the Christmas period was not a good one in which to achieve any public attention, we postponed this until the new year – 7 January 1969. And, since the idea was to get the survey report into lay-man's language, it was I who took the great work home and wrestled with it all through Christmas. I found the task at once both arduous and fascinating.

There were two main findings about the hull itself. On the question of general wastage through rust and other factors, the report was able to be specific, since Corlett had taken immense trouble to make measurements on a scientific basis with an ultra-sonic thickness tester all through the ship. He had found that quite enough of the hull was in fact left to be strong and usable. The main longitudinal members of the ship from the keel upwards were in good order, and the many frames were more than enough to maintain her transverse shape. The iron plate work itself was fairly un-even, parts of it being virtually intact. On this vital point his survey stated:

'In general, once the thick layers of rust and scale had been removed, clean white iron surfaces were exposed. The thickness of the metal mostly varies between a quarter and a half inch, except in one or two places where it has eroded through. As the bulk of the plating was originally 9/16 and 5/8 inches thick, the ultra-sonic thickness tester showed there has thus been a wastage of some 40 to 50 per cent in places. What is left, however, is substantial, and in those parts where the plating is depended upon for flota-tion there is about 3/8 of an inch of iron, which is fully adequate.'

Secondly, the state of the crack about a third of the way along on the starboard side was such that, while still ostensibly manageable, there were far-reaching implications. Corlett himself had done some skin-diving under the ship, though he had found it extremely difficult to penetrate as far as was desirable owing to the great masses of kelp, or seaweed. Thus the crack which started by being some 7 inches wide at the upper deck level tapered down to much less under water and, so far as could be judged, to a hairline and then nothing as it neared the starboard decking keel. At the deck, however, there was a 5-inch difference of level between one side of the gap and the other, the after section being higher than the forward. As was superficially confirmed by the misalignment of the mizzen mast, this indicated that the stern of the ship was very slightly twisted downwards to port.

Part of the survey dealt with the state of the woodwork, that is to say essentially the weatherdeck and the three masts. The deck which was largely rotten did not matter very much, except that if it had been sound the timber would have constituted an additional strengthening factor for the hull as a whole, since that was how Brunel had designed it.

The masts, however, were another matter. While they seemed to be in much better condition than we had altogether expected, they were sufficiently loose in their sockets to present some danger of falling in a heavy sea. And as the foremast and mainmast each weighed nearly twenty tons, this could wreak fatal damage to the weakened hull. Before any attempt at salvage could be made they would clearly have to be removed. This would be a difficult but by no means insuperable task with the limited equipment likely to be available in such a remote place. They were not in any case the masts of the original Brunel ship, but probably dated from the last major rearrangement of the steamer's rigging in 1857, and had then been re-located when the engines were taken out in 1882.

From the survey it emerged that the key to the chances of successful salvage lay as much in the nature of the beach, on which the *Great Britain* lay, as in the immediate state of the ship herself. She was not in any danger of sinking into soft sand. She was on a gently sloping beach of hard sand and small stones. If she could be made watertight and pumped out, she could therefore be floated off quite easily. And the surveys done by the team from HMS *Endurance* showed that there was sufficient depth of water for her then to be fairly readily drawn out stern first from the position in which she had been beached thirty-one years earlier.

What was ominous, however, was the action of the tide underneath the stern. The crack had developed at a point where the structure had been weakened by an entry port, cut to facilitate access during service as a store ship in Stanley Harbour. The reason for the crack was the scouring of the tide, which by now had left the actual stern suspended over clear water and not resting on the beach at all. Unfortunately, this process was still going on. And as the scouring took away more and more sand, the downward stress on the after section of the vessel increased. Although the sag was so far very slight, it was enough in itself to increase the scouring effect. The process was thus developing at a compound rate, and the *Great Britain* was in fact literally digging her own grave. It was obvious that in a very few years, perhaps five at the most, she would split in two. We had come on the scene only just in time, and speed was now of the essence.

These dramatic findings were in fact borne out by measurements which we arranged to have taken at the crack at certain intervals after Corlett had left. The jagged and broken edges made it difficult to be too precise. But, in general terms from 7 inches in November 1968 the gap did widen to some 13 inches by early 1970, just before the actual salvage took place. And the difference in level on each side of the crack virtually doubled, showing that, as well as sagging, the stern was also twisting increasingly to port.

When we published our assessment of the situation on 7 January 1969, we also issued a covering statement outlining our proposals about the method of salvage and the problem of getting the ship home. Corlett calculated that, although 'not entirely without hazard', it was practicable and feasible to straighten the hull before it left Sparrow Cove. The estimated 430 tons weight in the stern produced a downward moment aft, he said, of 35,500 tons-feet. By fitting two extra bag tanks, pumping out, and timing it to make the maximum use of a rising tide, a lifting moment could be produced of about 74,000 tons-feet. At the same time it was estimated that any fractional adjustment of the lateral angle, which might prove necessary, could be dealt with by means of winching from the shore.

I was greatly intrigued by the concept of these bag tanks. which it was felt would play a major role in keeping the *Great Britain* afloat once she had reached the open sea. Made of rubber and filled with air, they were to be attached to the hull below water level. For the lifting in Sparrow Cove they would be outside. But as an additional source of buoyancy, if the ship were to leak badly when under tow, they would be down inside. And the calculation was that, with the weight of the ship taken as 900 tons, thirty bag tanks giving an aggregate buoyancy of 1500 tons would be sufficient to keep her afloat, even if fully waterlogged.

This was in fact a recognized modern salvage technique and, with Corlett's adoption of it in mind even before the survey was made, I had already had a talk with the Chairman of Dunlop, Sir Reay Geddes. He had put me in touch with their appropriate division in Manchester and, a month before Ewan had left for the Falklands, I had had a definitive meeting with them to discuss our possible requirements and the extent to which the firm might be able to supply us with the necessary equipment on loan or partial loan. It was a stimulating contact with people who seemed to me to see life as we did.

In the event bag tanks were never required because the actual salvage a year and a half later took an altogether different form. But Dunlop did come to our aid for the final docking of the *Great Britain* in Bristol in 1970, when they lent us free of charge a vital sausage-shaped rubber 'dracone', which was placed in the bow and filled with fifty tons of water in order to trim the ship. By this means we got the bow down and the stern up by the few crucial inches that were needed to cross the sill of the drydock. We were deeply grateful.

In our announcement about the survey and its findings, we filled out the message by saying that we would take the ship to Bristol, though 'appropriate arrangements have yet to be made for her reception there'. We declared that, while everything depended on raising enough money, we hoped to commission a salvage team during the course of the year (1969), so that it could spend the two months probably needed to prepare the *Great Britain* for sea, as soon as the Falklands summer arrived – the equivalent of winter in the northern hemisphere.

We also stated our intention to widen our own committee membership and to 'create an appeal organization'. Money had in fact begun coming in slowly after our first announcement in September. This time we again had quite a good coverage in the press and on the air and it stimulated a few more small donations, though nothing approaching what was required. However, we were henceforth able to emphasize that anyone thinking of helping financially should do so in the knowledge that we had done our homework.

From the beginning of 1969 in fact our whole organization took a step forward, became more formal and detailed – as it had to in some ways – and presented a wider variety of pressing problems than one had imagined possible. But before giving an account of these unavoidable aspects of life at that time, absorbing and curious though some of them also proved to be, something must first be said about the circumstances we now had to explore to receive the *Great Britain*, if and when she really did reach England. Having done our homework in Sparrow Cove, we now had to do our homework in Bristol. By that I am not for the moment referring to the complex political issues in Bristol into which we eventually found ourselves drawn – that will come later – but the nuts and bolts of getting the ship into the drydock itself.

There were two aspects of the problem: first, relations between the Project and the company which ran the drydock, Charles Hill and Sons Limited, and secondly, the physical question of whether the *Great Britain* was or was not too big to be got through the actual entrance. One of the most extraordinary features of our whole saga has always seemed to me that this particular drydock should have been available at all at that particular moment – give or take a year or so. The magic of it was that this was the very dock in which the *Great Britain* had been built by Brunel, Patterson, Claxton, and Guppy a century and a quarter before. And now, drawn by the apparent suitability and availability of it, we had slipped into assuming that this was where we would go with the ship when she first came home, and irrespective, as I have said but would like to repeat, of where she might eventually end up.

It may be wondered why there should have been any doubt about getting her in physically, when she had been built there. But there were in fact several good reasons for such doubts. Brunel was known to have needed an extra high tide to get her out in the first place. No one quite knew from the records whether and what alterations had been made to the entrance of the dock since those days. And the rounded hull of the ship herself had now been made wider by several critical inches at each of the significant deck levels through having a substantial shield, or cladding, of heavy timber bolted on in 1882 outside the original iron. She might, in addition, be floating lower in the water if the hull remained even slightly hogged, or indeed for other possible reasons, such as mud and junk in the hold.

On the question of relations with Charles Hill and Sons, I realized that from my own point of view I knew nothing at first hand, and it was obviously essential that I should, since we had no binding agreement with them of any kind. And it would be nothing short of disastrous if we suddenly found that we could salvage the ship but then had nowhere to put her. Though part of a larger group with a stock exchange quotation as a public company, namely Charles Hill of Bristol Ltd, the original family, the Hills, still held control. And the new chairman both of the group and of Charles Hill and Sons Ltd, the subsidiary which ran the dockyard, was

Richard Hill. I therefore decided that the time had now come to meet him and discover for myself how the land lay.

We first met, quite briefly, on Thursday 16 January 1969, at the Grand Hotel in Bristol. And I think it is true to say that this was one of the most tightly packed and in its way significant conversations that I ever had in the whole *Great Britain* story. It was clear to me within the first few minutes that here was someone with whom I shared a common language. What developed from the occasion was a sense of confidence between us which has endured from that day to this. I knew that Richard Hill would stand by the Project – sobering though he already was in his warnings of the difficulties we would face. And I think he accepted at once that we were serious people. What I could not know immediately was how very much the *Great Britain* was to come to mean to him personally, or how extensively the company was in fact to help the Project financially.

Both for him and for us there have been some rocky paths to tread during these past several years, sometimes foreseen but sometimes unforeseeable. Through a period of unprecedented change Charles Hill and Sons have had their own interests to watch and we have had ours. These have not always been the same. Nor has there ever been – as some observers at one time appeared to believe – any undisclosed agreement between us to do anything other than pursue the interests of the ship. But from the very first we started on the right foot together and, in spite of all kinds of problems, we have shared a common purpose. The Project owes a great deal to this fact.

It was settled, then – as I saw it – that the *Great Britain* would be accepted in Brunel's old dock, the yard's No. 2 drydock, when she was ready to come. But would she get in? I knew that Corlett had already started making expert calculations, based both on his own researches and on drawings received from America. And I knew that he was optimistic, if not indeed confident, that she would. But there were in fact two unknowns, not just one. If the precise size and draught of this old ship caused hesitation on one side of the equation, there could be nothing positive on the other until the most precise and up-to-date measurements of the dock entrance itself were also known. And the obstacles here included any possible underwater obstruction which might have developed just outside. The only certainty was that it would be nip and tuck.

After I left Richard Hill that day I went down to his shipyard for the first time. There I discussed the prospects with the man in charge of the drydock, Alastair Peck. And I detected that the feeling in the yard was that the ship would not in fact go in. A few days later I sent on to him an extract of the ship's lines, which Corlett had produced to the scale of one eighth of an inch to the foot. This was a definitive drawing of the mid-ships cross-section. From it Peck would make up a full-scale wooden template, which could be placed physically in the dock entrance as a test and then photographed.

We awaited the verdict with considerable interest. When it came on 10 February it was not quite as final as one had wished. Peck, a very cautious man, was optimistic all right. But the key to this problem was the fact that the bulbous shape of the *Great Britain* meant she could go through only with the upper parts of her sides projecting over the stonework of the entrance. Thus, everything depended on the level at which she would float in the water. Besides the wooden cladding, there was also the question of the extra wooden keel, which had been added externally since she had originally passed through this same dock entrance in 1843. Although an extraordinary amount of information was available about Brunel's original ship, she had been modified several times in her life, and now over recent years the hull had been severely strained by wind and water.

'Have we *really* got the accurate measurements,' Peck asked, 'of the ship *as she is now*?'

It was a critical question. I was in Bristol again four days later. And obviously what we needed was that Ewan Corlett should be with us, but unfortunately he could not be there. However we both talked to him on the telephone, and this made us feel rather better. For myself I came away with the conviction that on balance all would be well, and that, if almost any single one of the factors which mattered were to show any improvement on further examination, we were – literally – home and dry!

As the next few weeks passed, both Corlett and Peck did indeed check and re-check. The template was fractionally modified, until on 10 March, when a second positioning in the dock entrance took place – and was filmed by the BBC – Corlett was able to examine it there in person. And from then on we decided that, given the extra few inches by which it was known to be possible in very special cases to raise the level of the water in the Floating Harbour by manipulating the controls at Cumberland Basin, the *Great Britain* would *just* go in. And as we now know, we proved in the end to be right.

In London itself there was much to be done at this time to build up the organization. Its purpose was to raise money. We had decided how to refloat the ship, we had a plan for bringing her home – or thought we had –

and we were clear about her immediate destination. So I set about trying to find the finance without which we were powerless to do anything at all. For this we had to have a fixed address. We had to have a clearly stated aim, which would commend itself as the purpose for which the money would be spent. We had to gather in more supporters to give credence to what we were doing, and if possible to help us to do it. And, by no means least if I was to survive, we had to employ someone as a continuing executive to deal with the growing volume of business and correspondence now coming in every day.

We solved the address problem for a few months with the help of the Falkland Islands Company, which let us print our first headed notepaper care of themselves at their address. The company thus acted as a post office for us.

The executive problem I solved by getting in touch with one of the people who had made contact with us after the September press conference. At an exiguous salary, paid out of our still exiguous funds, I appointed him acting 'General Secretary', working from his own home in Suffolk. He was a retired RAF Wing Commander, Dermot Fitzgerald Lombard, who also held – by some inscrutable means which I never did fully understand through all the time he was with us – the naval rank of Lieutenant Commander. He had in fact acquired it from a combined services activity covering air force use of naval establishments in the Indian Ocean during the war. And, although with us he would be dealing once again with a ship, he obviously continued in practice to use his more senior rank from the junior service. Inevitably he was known to all and sundry, as I think he had been all his life, simply as 'Fitz'. Besides working for us, Fitz rendered the Project two special services. He found us a rent-free office and our first informal, but highly experienced, fund-raising consultant.

The office was a room very conveniently placed just off Chancery Lane, which was given to us by a friend of his, Anthony Abrahams, and we moved the Project in there officially on 19 May 1969. This then appeared on our notepaper, and we remained there very gratefully indeed for nearly eighteen months. It was thus from this first base in Chancery Lane that the whole crucial period of the *Great Britain*'s actual salvage in 1970 was handled. Anthony Abrahams himself became a member of the Project committee or, later, 'Council'. Trained in law, his legal approach also provided precisely one of the elements among us which I was very conscious we had previously lacked.

Raising money for charities, or fund-raising to give it its more formal epithet, is a necessary evil. It is also an art, a matter of hard work, and a question of experience. Success can then be regarded either as a just reward or a stroke of luck, according to circumstances. And sometimes it never follows at all. I was thus particularly relieved one day when Fitz introduced me to an old acquaintance of his in this intricate game, Hereward Phillips. Phillips had been at it for a long time and by chance, now that he was half in retirement, his book was just coming out which he had called *Fund Raising Techniques – and Case Histories*. I read it at once. It was full of wise lessons about campaigns which had flopped, and others which by a touch of genius at the right moment had brilliantly succeeded.

This huge and elusive subject of fund raising was to remain with us for the rest of time. But the point about the early part of 1969 was that this was when we made our official start. With Hereward Phillips' active assistance we set about creating the first of four main brochures which we used during our first six years of existence.

It was also in this period that we took two quite separate steps which helped to put our whole effort into a higher gear. The first was to cash in on an extraordinarily well-timed coincidence – the *Great Britain* postage stamp. In September I had heard, correctly as it turned out, that the government was considering issuing a series of stamps depicting famous British ships from an Elizabethan galleon to the *Queen Elizabeth II*. And I had actually prepared a letter to the Postmaster General, John Stonehouse – none other – suggesting that the *Great Britain* should be included, when his Parliamentary Private Secretary, Andrew Faulds, rang me up with the news that they had already selected the *Great Britain* for the one-shilling denomination.

By January 1969 this was issued. And although this country's desperate inflation has since made the shilling of those days insufficient for even a second class letter today, my own delight was at the time tarnished by the thought that the denomination was too high for most people ever to use. Nevertheless, it gave our cause splendid publicity and even a shadowy, though unfortunately inaccurate, appearance of official approval. We applied successfully to the Post Office for permission to print a replica of the stamp 7 by $2\frac{3}{4}$ inches on the top right-hand corner of the front of our four-page brochure. And, as one does in any reproduction of the postage, we had to print a bar through one corner to invalidate it as a real stamp – in spite of its being several times the size of any genuine stamp which has ever so far seen the light of day!

The second and much more serious step was to underline the sense of responsibility with which we were trying to approach the whole task of saving the *Great Britain*. With this in mind I asked whether there might be any possibility of Prince Philip sending us some sort of 'Message' of encouragement – like the foreword to a book. And he did. It expressed vividly and summarily what we were at. We were extremely grateful. The Duke of Edinburgh's Message ran:

The transition from sailing ships to power-driven ships was the most profound in thousands of years in maritime history. Nothing quite like that revolution will ever be seen again.

The *Great Britain* represents a vital stage in that revolution and is therefore of immense interest to future generations.

I very much hope that the attempt to bring her home and to put her on display will be successful.

                                                                    Philip.

3. The Critics and Ourselves

It was now coming up to a year since I had first become involved with the *Great Britain*. During that time we had fully assessed the problem and established ourselves. And although no one could know it in January and February of 1969, there was in fact to be just another year before the salvage itself finally started – with the sailing for the Falklands of the salvage vessel on 4 February 1970. Meanwhile, our vital tasks for the coming months were quite clear. We had to raise money in earnest and, if successful, find and commission a thoroughly competent firm to conduct this most unusual and challenging salvage.

There was, however, just one other major aspect of our problem which had already begun to take shape, and which was to affect our fortunes very seriously all through our first few struggling years, in particular our ability to raise money. This was the question of Bristol. And, now that all has ended well, I hope that anything written here will be regarded only as an honest attempt to outline what happened and to account for it as the integral part – which it certainly was – of the genuine fight to save for posterity Brunel's unique and historic ship, the *Great Britain*.

So far as I personally was concerned, the feature of our contacts with Bristol during the first six to nine months of our operations had been that there were none. No one in Bristol had been approached for money. The City Council had not been asked for any special concessions, and we ourselves were far too heavily committed to want to rush any fences over long term decisions about the ship's ultimate destination for public display. As

I have shown, we had barely got past the point of being able to plan that restoration should at least start in a Bristol shipyard.

This was not, however, quite how matters actually stood on the spot. In the nature of things one of our most active and expressive members was frequently in Bristol as a parliamentary candidate for one of the city's constituencies. The Brunel Society and some of its individual Bristol supporters continued to take a lively interest in plans for the *Great Britain*, following the meeting at the City Museum in May 1968. And there was, of course, a precautionary concern on the part of some city councillors, as well as the docks and planning authorities, about the implications of having the ship in Charles Hill's shipyard at all. The whole legal process had already been begun to prepare a special bill in parliament for closing the outdated city docks to commercial traffic during the nineteen seventies, and the presence of the ship might affect the future use of this area.

Although I did not know it, the result of all this was that some people had already begun to take up positions in the matter. Most were not as yet strongly committed one way or the other. But their views about those who seemed to be concerned with the *Great Britain* encouraged them to be either profoundly sceptical or at least to desire not to become involved. In the main, perhaps, it was simply hoped that the whole idea of salvaging the ship would die a natural death.

During December 1968, nevertheless, and – again – unknown to me at the time, the City Council Docks Committee, which controlled the Port of Bristol Authority, had had on its agenda the question of the availability and disposal of 'Wapping Dock' after its existing long lease to Charles Hill and Sons expired in June of 1970; Wapping Dock or Jefferies Dock were alternative names for what we have now reverted to calling, as Brunel did, the Great Western Dock. The discussion, that is to say, was about the future of that very dock into which we proposed to bring the *Great Britain*. And this was being held partly because the dock was city property on lease to the shipyard, not the latter's freehold.

After the Docks Committee meeting, the Port of Bristol Authority replied to a question from Robert Adley with a letter, in which they said that they would be prepared to consider leasing the drydock for a period to be agreed, at a rental in accord with current commercial values. They added that planning permission would be needed because of problems of change of use, and that the entrance would need widening at the expense of the *Great Britain*'s promoters. The City Engineer and the Planning Officer had accordingly each been informed of the position.

What I did not hear until some few years later was that six months after these contacts, that is on 4 July 1969, the majority (Conservative) Citizen Party held a lengthy internal debate on the issue of whether or not the *Great Britain* should be admitted to Bristol Docks at all. And the motion in favour, put by Alderman Robert Wall, was carried by only 17 votes to 15. The dominant political personality of that period in Bristol was the leader of the Citizen Party, Alderman Gervas Walker. And while he accepted this policy decision in principle he was never himself in favour of it, so that he became in practice our severest critic. In this, nevertheless, he had the basic support of the two leaders of the then Labour opposition, Alderman Wally Jenkins and Councillor Bert Peglar, and they constituted a formidable bipartisan triumvirate. There were two fundamental fears. One, expressed through the Port Authority by its chairman, Sir Kenneth Brown, and by Councillor Edward Wright, was that, owing to the state of the hull the slightest accident with the *Great Britain* could lead to her sinking and blocking the port of Bristol for several weeks. The other was that her presence would sooner or later commit the ratepayer to a high and unpopular expenditure.

It was therefore a bit like Daniel walking into the lion's den, or perhaps sleepwalking would be a better term, that during the morning of that original January day on which I first met Richard Hill I also had another revealing conversation, though of a different kind. Through a mutual friend I had been introduced to one of Bristol's well-known business personalities and I asked him who was who in the city. He very kindly gave me a shrewd and valuable sketch of the political scene. But I vividly recall the sense of mild shock with which I listened to his more general observations.

'I'm afraid you won't find Bristol people falling over themselves to help you,' he warned me. 'You see most of them have never heard of the *Great Britain*, and those who have don't take it seriously. The ones who do inevitably regard you as an outsider and feel that all you want from them is their money. And people here don't like putting their hands in their pockets, unless they can see a good reason for it. It wasn't for nothing that Bristol long ago became known as the commercial traveller's grave.'

Then, after a slight pause, he added, 'I'm afraid you've got off to a bad start here, and that's the fact of it.'

His ominous words were as true as they seemed to me undeserved, since I felt that I myself had only just arrived in the city that morning.

There was no alternative, however, to proceeding as best one could, and I certainly hoped that, once the realities about us were better known and understood, all would be well. We had already sent a copy of Ewan Corlett's survey findings to the General Manager of the Bristol Port Authority, George Edney, and I now followed this up with a request to the Chairman of the Docks Committee, Sir Kenneth Brown, for some form of joint meeting between the authorities and ourselves, so that we could discuss our problems together. I added that, while nothing was finally settled about the *Great Britain*'s possible movements, I anticipated that she would in fact arrive in England within twelve to eighteen months – a prophecy which was to prove gratifyingly accurate.

In his reply, Sir Kenneth mentioned that from his own experience as a naval architect the crack in the *Great Britain* appeared to make salvage too hazardous to be worth backing, but that, if we did mean to go ahead, any appeal for funds would require an estimate of cost. As regards Wapping Dock, this was now in the hands of the Planning Committee. Having said that, he agreed to a meeting. I found this chilling but businesslike.

Accordingly, there took place on 14 February 1969 in the office of the City Engineer in the Council House an informal and, as I saw it, friendly meeting between five representatives of the authorities and myself. I had very greatly hoped that Corlett could be there, but at the last moment this was not possible. With Sir Kenneth Brown were Councillor W. Mather Bell, Mr J. B. Bennett, the City Engineer, Mr E. J. Steen, the Deputy Planning Officer, and, in the later stages, the Leader of the City Council, Gervas Walker, who I now met for the first time.

Though I could neither know nor have expected it that afternoon, there was not to be another informal and informatory discussion of this kind between the authorities and the Project for another five years. With rare individual exceptions we encountered each other only at larger more formal gatherings, where no personal discussion was really possible, or in fleeting, sometimes rather awkward, conversations at semi-official cocktail parties. Contact was indeed maintained through the Town Clerk, William Hutchinson, in his capacity as Chief Executive and therefore the mouthpiece of the Council; and he was excellent in conveying views back and forth. But this was not the same, and although I later specifically asked to meet Gervas Walker when our disagreements were acute, he always declined to do so, even in the private company of mutual friends. This lack of communication was one of the elements at the heart of many of our subsequent difficulties.

The meeting opened with my telling them as much as I could about our findings in Sparrow Cove and then of our general plans. Though sceptical, the atmosphere was all quite amicable. But I regretted that Walker only arrived after this initial outline was over. He then set the pace with a number of questions which I did my best to answer. They were mostly about our own prospects and intentions, but they ended with specific enquiries about the municipal services we expected to require, once the ship was in the drydock. To me this was a bit like designing the curtains before one had even built the house.

However, I tried to present the picture of the dock being open to the public as we had so far envisaged it. While local government was obviously concerned with such questions as public safety, car parking, access facilities, electricity and sewage, we were very far from being a large departmentalized institution. We were a tiny group of hard-pressed individuals whose hearts were out in the South Atlantic, and the time to become anything else seemed several light years away.

I mention these points because they were significant for two reasons. Above all, they reflected the very different approach of each side. I once heard us blamed later on for not taking the Bristol City Council in as a partner in our enterprise from the start. But who ever heard of a local authority in England taking part in a risky salvage operation on the other side of the world? They certainly would not have done so, and rightly. It seemed in any case clear to me from this preliminary meeting that, while the authorities naturally had to take various possibilities into account, they did not really think the *Great Britain* could be salvaged, whatever our survey said; and they did not seriously expect ever to see her come floating up the Avon into the City Docks.

The second reason is more specific. In response to Gervas Walker's request for more information about our municipal needs, I wrote to him shortly afterwards. As best I could at that time I set out our requirements in a two-page letter. He subsequently declared on more than one public occasion, however, that he had never received a satisfactory answer, and that therefore the Council could not have been expected to act more positively. We were already looking at things from altogether different angles.

For the next few months the Project's main energies had to be concentrated on trying to raise money. We could do nothing on any scale until we had our brochure printed, and its preparation took, as these things do, many weeks. One of the preliminary steps, for instance, was to clarify the role of the National Maritime Museum in our affairs. Working together as an editorial team, Fitz Lombard, Hereward Phillips and I wanted to indicate its support in some way. But this meant Basil Greenhill arranging for me to see the chairman of the museum's Board of Trustees, Lord Runciman, And it was a little while before I could go and have a talk with him in his office in the City. He agreed that we could say that the Project was being 'conducted with the technical co-operation of the National Maritime Museum'.

Then there were obvious personal contacts to be made with the shipping world, and if possible with the previous owners of the *Great Britain*. How far would any of them give us a fair wind, either by speaking up for the Project, or allowing their names to be quoted as supporters, or straightaway helping us financially?

The *Great Britain* had been registered under five successive owners during her service life. But a single strand had linked them all, the Gibbs family. When the ship was sold in 1851 by her builders, the Great Western Steamship Company, she was bought by Gibbs, Bright and Company, who were in due course absorbed by Antony Gibbs and Sons Ltd. But the original Robert Bright of Bristol, whose association with George Gibbs had started the company of Gibbs, Bright, had also been involved in the formation of the Great Western Steamship Company in 1835. Then at the end the last owner in the 1880s was Vicary Gibbs. When we came on the scene, a century later, therefore, it was exciting to find that Gibbs, Bright and Co. were still active in Melbourne, besides of course the fact that Antony Gibbs and Sons are part of the establishment in the City of London – though as bankers and no longer as ship owners.

In 1969, there was still a Mr Antony Gibbs in London in the bank that bore his name – though he was destined shortly to succeed on his father's death to the less interesting title of Lord Aldenham. I rang him up and we met in his family offices in Bishopsgate. He was extremely interested in all that we were attempting to do, but unfortunately the firm no longer possessed any records of any kind about the *Great Britain*. Later, when Ewan Corlett was in Melbourne and among other things doing his researches for *The Iron Ship*, his definitive book on the technical and service history of the *Great Britain*, he met David Gibbs of Gibbs, Bright and Co., and in various ways a good deal of valuable material came to light from the Australian end.

Just as I was about to leave, however, Antony Gibbs got up from his desk and said: 'Let me show you our picture. I don't expect you have seen it.'

'No', I felt bound to reply, not quite sure what he meant.

'Come and see.' And he led the way into their boardroom.

On the wall ahead of us was an old oil painting in excellent condition, clearly a treasured possession. It showed a well-balanced, six-masted ship with smoke coming out of her single funnel, steaming past a faintly allegorical, almost classic harbour water front, with the artist's hint of a great city behind. It was indeed the *Great Britain*. And I think the background represents Liverpool on the ship's return from her maiden voyage. It was a picture scarcely known outside the firm, and one of the best that any of us had seen anywhere. We used a print of it that year as our Project Christmas card.

While Antony Gibbs became one of our staunchest supporters and was later to help in financing restoration, I was less fortunate with the shipping world as such – though it was not for want of trying by the late Lord Geddes, that year's President of the United Kingdom Chamber of Shipping, with whom I had got in touch. Some time before, I had had a long session with the Chamber's public relations officer, Harry Bawden, and we had discussed together the glittering success that could follow from the implications of our survey in Sparrow Cove. The resurrection of the *Great Britain* would represent a most unusual tribute to the qualities of British maritime engineering and enterprise. Her physical recovery from the South Atlantic could highlight the long-term pioneering image of the national shipping industry. And this was a valiant theme which appealed to Lord Geddes.

When he found a suitable opportunity at one of the Chamber's Council sessions, therefore, he raised the question of whether and how the shipping industry might take an interest in the intended salvage of the *Great Britain*. But, in the words of one of those present, his initiative 'fell with a dull thud'. It could not have been worse received. He had stuck his neck out in vain, and we never recovered from this setback with the Chamber. It became in time more damaging that they had taken a decision against us than that they should have taken no decision at all.

A couple of weeks later when talking privately with someone else in the shipping world, who had not been present at the meeting, I felt I understood rather better how such a blow could have come about. He was at that time one of the household names in the business. And he has since been among the individual contributors to our funds

'I'm afraid you won't get help from the shipping industry,' he said in quite general terms. 'And there are really two reasons for this. The first is that they will be afraid of seeming to appear backward-looking if they have anything to do with the *Great Britain*. And you know we are very conscious of the need to keep our reputation in the forefront of world shipping.'

'But that's an argument stood on its head,' I expostulated.

'So you may say. But it's how people will see things.' Then he went on. 'Secondly, if you are hoping for any substantial financial help, I am sorry to have to tell you that the *Cutty Sark* has left such a nasty taste in our mouths, that people won't have anything to do with another ship restoration for quite some time. We were all persuaded to put up more money for her than we felt we could really afford, and, frankly, people just don't want to know.'

For many years great efforts had indeed been thrown into the ultimately successful campaign to restore the *Cutty Sark* in Greenwich, and undoubtedly we did suffer from its backwash. But I felt that this should be past history by now, and, although his words gave me much cause for thought, I knew that, once again, we ourselves had no alternative but to press ahead. Since those days, however, while there have been certain notable exceptions, the *Great Britain* never has had the kind of support from shipping interests which she has had, for instance, from the engineering world.

During this run-up period to our sending out our first appeal I sometimes used to wonder whether we could get any help from America. I had always hoped that in some way there could be some practical confirmation of the Anglo-American sponsorship which had emerged when we came on the scene. Not only had Swigert most generously promised us something personally – which he duly honoured – but just before Christmas one of the other trustees of the San Francisco Maritime Museum, Scott Newhall, who was visiting England, telephoned me from Newcastle and had lunch with me when he arrived in London.

Scott Newhall was at that time the Editor-in-Chief of the *San Francisco Chronicle*, a famous newspaper which his family controlled. And during our review of the whole American role in the story of the ship, as well as the progress we in Britain had made during the previous few months, he said he felt sure there must be lots of people in the States who would be willing to subscribe, 'particularly those with a British connection'. And he had gone away with the words:

'If you like, I'll have a look round when I get home.'

By May, however, any hopes I might have had were shattered by some extraordinary news which I was only gradually able to piece together. But it put paid for the time being to this particular group of Americans being likely to help us at that juncture, and it was a most vivid illustration of the ways in which our plans could be thrown completely off course by events entirely beyond our control.

The news was that two of our American friends, Scott Newhall and Karl Kortum, had nearly been arrested in the North of England at Newcastle upon Tyne. Along with a couple of British associates, they had been accused of trying to make off with a tug which did not belong to them. They were said to be going to take it to Holland and from there to America. And this had happened apparently – which did later prove to be the case – as a result of a strong disagreement with the National Maritime Museum authorities. Feelings had run so deep in fact that there was now a total rift between the two parties. As they were both good friends of ours, our only possible course was to keep well out of the way.

What had happened was that both the British and the American museum interests, Greenwich and San Francisco, had each decided that they wanted to acquire the last operational Tyneside steam paddle-wheel tug, the *Reliant*. She was the historic end of a long 140-year-old line of some of the most successful tugs ever built. Greenwich had obtained an option on her and planned to put the engines on show in the museum. When San Francisco, somewhat later in the day, heard of the *Reliant*'s approaching retirement, they found upon reconnaissance – Scott Newhall's trip in December – that there was in fact another similar tug still in existence, the *Eppleton Hall*, though it was by now disintegrating and not at all in as good order as the *Reliant*.

The Americans then offered to trade the *Eppleton Hall* for the *Reliant* on the grounds that, while they wanted to take what could not be less than a whole tug by sea to San Francisco, the British only really wanted the engines. And they claimed that those of the *Eppleton Hall* were quite as well preserved as the *Reliant*'s, even though the rest of the vessel was not. Upon this offer being declined, and incensed apparently by the way the proceedings had gone, they determined to achieve the exchange nevertheless. And this the British frustrated. Though force was not used at any point, there was a very present element of another Boston Tea Party which had gone a little wrong.

Today the whole of the *Reliant*, not just the engines, can be seen magnificently displayed as the centrepiece of the new Neptune Hall at Greenwich. And the little 'tugboat' *Eppleton Hall* rides safely off Fisherman's Wharf in San Francisco Bay, after one of the most astonishing and gallant voyages of modern times, begun in the autumn of 1969 and covering 8,000 miles all the way across the Atlantic, through the Panama Canal and up the Pacific Coast. And who was the skipper on the last great journey of this now famous, ocean-going little river tug? The man who was so angry with those who said it could not be done that he did it – the San Francisco editor, Scott Newhall. The epic had a touch of the *Great Britain* about it.

On our own front during this period our original group was slowly being expanded, while at the same time I was collecting a rather wider list of supporters who would be willing to have their names used. Two particular additions to the inner circle were Lord Strathcona and Maldwin Drummond. Euan Strathcona had the merit of living near to Bristol in Bath – he also owned a historic steam launch – and Maldwin Drummond the advantage of a good deal of experience of maritime charities as the chairman of the Sail Training Association, with its two well-known schooners for young people, the *Sir Winston Churchill* and *Malcolm Miller*. Strathcona was later to be the only Project representative present at the actual salvage of the *Great Britain*, and the man who received the formal release of the ship from the Governor of the Falkland Islands.

On the wider list, the names we were soon to print on our notepaper in a column running down the left-hand side, I was keen to include the support of people who had already had a good deal to do with the memory of Brunel. Thus, the late L. T. C. Rolt, Brunel's distinguished biographer, readily joined us. So did Grahame Farr, a Bristolian and the author of the outstanding booklet *The Steamship Great Britain*, written before ever we came on the scene. Then, among others, were Brunel's direct descendant, Sir Marc Noble, and the sailors and men of action, Commander Alan Villiers and Sir Peter Scott, whose wildfowl at Slimbridge are a stone's throw from Bristol. Rear Admiral Morgan Giles, whose fight for HMS *Belfast* was yet to be won, was loosely associated with our cause as well. We had a Falkland Islander, John Smith, as well as John Smith, the then MP for Westminster, who has since been one of the Project's leading benefactors. It quite soon became a long, but good, list; all part of the necessary authentication of our public image.

In putting the final touches to our brochure, Hereward Phillips was a firm taskmaster. It was not that there was any shortage of things to say, quite the reverse. They had to be brief and to the point, and one had to avoid saying them in ways that could be counter-productive. With this first effort we set out to be at once objective and yet persuasive, serious and yet arresting. It was to be a document that no one who was likely to be at all interested in helping us would throw away at sight. Then, having caught his attention, it must answer the genuine questions that sprang to his mind.

'Why was the SS *Great Britain* a turning point in shipbuilding?' was the leading headline. And the answer was followed by information about the state of the ship, the urgency and need for salvage, the prospects for restoration, and the estimated initial cost – which we put at £75,000 in those days, as a minimum to get the ship home. On the front page we printed, along with the large replica of the *Great Britain* stamp, our simple objective:

To bring back from the other side of the world, recondition, and put on display the most historic modern ship in the world.

We printed five thousand copies of this brochure, and just after Whitsun sent off our first mailing shot of two thousand. Although we had selected our addressees with care, we knew that this was not really a satisfactory method of approach unless perhaps for a long-established and well-known charity. But we needed to test reactions and we needed to make a start. Afterwards, individual approaches by personal contact could be made with more knowledge. In the weeks that followed money did begin to come in at last, and I was able to start looking round at the task of longer-term fund-raising with cautious confidence.

4. The Money is Found

Before we had got very much further an astounding turn of events created a new and totally unexpected crisis in our affairs. I suppose in retrospect that one might have foreseen something of the kind, but in the weeks leading up to it I certainly did not do so. The result was that we came within sight of losing control of our own operations.

There were three people concerned – Smith, Jones and Robinson. These are not their real names, but they will serve to outline what happened. After our first press conference, in September 1968, Smith had telephoned to me in London to ask if we could discuss together just how the *Great Britain* might be salvaged. As this was just before Corlett's own survey in Sparrow Cove, I put him off till it had been completed. When we published our findings in the new year, he rang again saying he had 'clients' who were 'interested', but declined to give their name.

As we still had no money to conduct any salvage ourselves, Corlett and I met Smith – together with Jones, as representing the clients – at Corlett's offices near Basingstoke on 24 April 1969. We were then given Robinson's name, though it did not ring any bell with us. All three, it turned out, were running a new salvage firm on the South coast. Jones, a stocky and vigorous figure in his thirties, told us of his salvage experience with small ships, and we were informed that Robinson was the financial expert in the background. Their aim, they said, was to build up a good reputation for exploring and raising some of the many dozens of sunken ships around Britain's coast, a business which had favourable prospects in view of the current trend towards marine archaeology, and could be made to pay handsomely out of valuable items sold.

Ewan Corlett and I agreed to keep in touch with them. We supplied them with some brochures, since they hoped to interest industrial firms in sponsoring equipment, and we felt this could be to our mutual advantage. But we emphasized that this represented no long-term commitment whatever, and let it become clear to them that we were not as yet in any position to ask anybody to undertake anything at all.

While they had expressed great enthusiasm for our cause, during the next few weeks I recognized that our relationship had no formal basis. At the same time this also led me to reflect that there was, of course, nothing exclusive in our own position. We had no legal standing in regard to the *Great Britain*. We did not own her. She was a Crown wreck and the Crown had not commissioned us to do anything about her. If anyone else could persuade the Crown to surrender the ship to them, they had just as much right as we, or anyone else, to try to salvage her.

On the other hand, we did by now have a strong moral as well as technical position. We were in unrivalled possession of the true facts about the *Great Britain*. The salvage, I knew, could only be carried out successfully with expert and up-to-date handling, and this we intended to deploy. If the ship was to be released to anyone, it seemed in her best interest that she should be released to us. In retrospect, I think one can also claim that our position was reinforced by the fact that, in view of the initial objections of the Falkland Islanders to letting her go at all, the authorities would not have released her to anyone without extremely careful consideration – not even, perhaps, to the Americans, when the politics of it had been fully assessed.

It was obvious, however, that our position could well go by default if we did not fight for it. And it was here that the ground suddenly seemed to be shifting under our feet. Jones gave a radio interview saying how he would conduct the salvage, making no mention of the Project. Smith kept coming back for far more brochures than he could possibly use within the terms of our understanding. And two major firms, with which we ourselves already had top level contact, queried with us what seemed to them to be a rival approach. I suddenly began to have a nasty feeling that we were being taken for a ride.

Corlett, Lombard and I insisted on meeting the third figure in the enterprise, Robinson. With Jones, he came to see us in London. It was a disagreeable, though not in itself decisive, meeting. We had no proof that they were working against us and we played it cool. As for the brochures, although they declined to tell us what firms they had approached, they pleaded that several possibilities looked promising and argued that negotiations were confidential.

I came away, however, quite clear that the whole thing had to be stopped at once. But the question was how. They had been positively unwilling to abandon their position. Yet if we continued with them our own position would become untenable, since we did not wish to be represented by them with third parties. On the other hand, the last thing we could afford was a public row just when we were beginning to raise money in earnest. We seemed to be in a trap which risked the future of the ship.

What I did not know as I left the actual meeting, were the full facts about Robinson's personal situation. And these were now to make a settlement suddenly possible. On our putting through a business enquiry about his credit rating, it emerged that he was an undischarged bankrupt. However much one might sympathize with his personal misfortune, therefore, it was out of the question for us to continue our association. And I guessed that he would be too much of a man of the world not to recognize that, once he knew how clear we were about it and its implications.

So I arranged with Fitz Lombard that he and I would go forthwith to their offices on the South coast and terminate everything, come what might. We drove down together the next morning. It was one of those absolutely idyllic English summer days, with a perfect green stillness over everything in the clear blue sunshine. We were both old enough, however, to have something of that sense of doom which I find these lovely conditions have always brought over me, since that glorious summer weather of 1940 when the German tanks were racing through France and the fate of the world was at stake. But this time we were going to a little Dunkirk of our own, and the sooner we got it over and done with the better.

The meeting with all three of them, which took place in a heavily charged and smoke-filled atmosphere, was not quite as tough as I had feared it might be. There could be only one outcome, since no other was possible in my own mind. But it took a little time before this could be understood, since I also wanted, if possible, to part on sufficiently good terms to follow up any worthwhile contacts they had made in industry about equipment for helping to save the *Great Britain*. And in the event we succeeded. Jones promised and later sent me a list showing what they had done. When Fitz and I stopped at a pub on our way home for what we felt was a well-earned drink, we toasted the future of the *Great Britain* with even more meaning than usual.

During this period Ewan Corlett first mentioned to me the name of a well-established company on the East Coast for which he had done professional design work, and which might possibly be interested in attempting the salvage, if and when we did have the money to approach them. This was the United Towing Company of Hull. At his suggestion I therefore met their managing director, Anthony Wilbraham, in London in May. He proved at once to be among those who were as drawn to the challenge as we were, and I had a very encouraging talk with him about the problems and possibilities presented by the *Great Britain*.

As part of our general need to make firmer plans, now that we were beginning to raise a little money and could seriously envisage the possible salvage of the ship, the question inevitably did arise of where she might eventually be put on display. I had been quite clear since the beginning of the year that, if and when she arrived, she would go at once to the Charles Hill drydock in Bristol, and this I knew was Ewan Corlett's view. But the factors which governed this decision about restoration were not the same as those affecting her final disposition. And while a whole series of trends and developments brought them all together in the end, this was not in the least how the realities of the problem looked at the beginning.

The most obvious aspect of the public visiting the ship after restoration was that one naturally wanted as many visitors as possible, mainly for financial reasons. And this was why the possibility of an eventual London site could not help but arise. Against the London idea, there was of course always the pull of sentiment. Within the Project, as well as outside it, we all felt that Bristol was the right place for the *Great Britain*, particularly if she could remain permanently in her original building dock, where she was going for restoration. But the London nettle had to be grasped at some point, and it was accordingly with great interest that I accepted a friend's suggestion one day, that we should meet for lunch and go down afterwards to St Katharine Dock, just below the Tower of London, to have a look round. His own concern was to try to preserve from demolition under the Greater London Council's existing proposals a famous and beautiful Victorian warehouse there which had been designed by Thomas Telford.

The significance of St Katharine Dock in terms of our own problem was in fact primarily its position so close to the Tower, which has over two million visitors a year. I did not ever feel, that is, that we should consider somewhere like Greenwich, since that seemed to miss the whole point which was to be very centrally situated. But there was a wider aspect as well. Our efforts to salvage the *Great Britain* happened to be taking place just at a moment in history when the rapid rise of container ships was causing revolutionary changes in ports all over the world. In London it was leading to the closing down of large areas of the docks, and these were now going to be scheduled for redevelopment on an unprecedented scale. Virtually the first would be St Katharine Dock. It was a curious chance and certainly one that would not recur.

My friend knew his way about, as he had already been studying the Telford warehouse for some time. So, although the Dock was officially closed, we obtained permission to go in. We climbed the old stairways of the great warehouse and walked endlessly through its low-beamed galleries, with their worn floors and doorways evoking an image of heavy tropical bales and the riches of nineteenth-century commerce. We looked out over the dark, still water wholly enclosed in the dock area, and then stepped through between other buildings to the river frontage of the murky, swirling Thames, with Tower Bridge rising grey, square and graceful to our right. It seemed to me that, if we could get the *Great Britain* into St Katharine Dock through the lock from the river, and if she could be placed in a specially drained concrete enclave in some section of that historic little piece of water, we would have a marvellous site. Not more than a few hundred yards from the Tower of London, there would inevitably be a considerable spin-off of visitors, and, if such things as the Telford warehouse and perhaps other aspects of the Dock were going to be preserved as well, then the whole could form the nucleus of a new and exciting maritime museum.

It was easy to get carried away. But during the next few weeks I took matters a few practical steps further. I spoke first to Lord Simon, the Chairman of the Port of London Authority. He was unable to be enthusiastic about the *Great Britain*, but he did very kindly open avenues for me in two directions. One was to get at the facts about St Katharine Dock itself and the other to see if there was, after all, any other potential site on that part of the Thames which might commend itself.

On his advice I next approached the Chairman of the Greater London Council, at that time Mr (later Sir) Desmond Plummer. He reacted with guarded enthusiasm and put me in direct touch with the man I really needed to deal with at that stage over St Katharine Dock. This was the head of the GLC Planning Department's Special Projects Section, Martin Hackett. I remained in touch with Hackett off and on for something like two years, since it emerged from the start that the idea of the *Great Britain* finding an eventual haven in St Katharine Dock fitted in quite well with the sort of amenity development which was already in mind for it.

At that particular moment the timing also looked quite good, as the development contract had not yet gone out to tender. By the time a developer had been appointed and had done his own homework on the project, the *Great Britain* might be a much more realistic possibility than she could be straightaway – lying, as she still did, on the far away beach of Sparrow Cove. But there was one point on which Hackett pulled me up quite sharply.

'I don't know,' he commented, 'whether you have really had a good look at that lock between the river and the dock or not. But it's the only way in and I'm not at all sure the *Great Britain* wouldn't be too big to get through.'

Shades of Brunel! This ship of his was always very nearly – if not quite – too big to get through lock gates. In this case I had had my own doubts, but short of some very accurate measuring I had felt that the idea must be explored further on the supposition that she would. Hackett, however, proved to be something of a pragmatic pessimist. And next time he spoke to me he said he had gone into the question, and the ship would not go through the lock in its present condition. 'What do you mean by "in its present condition?"' I asked.

'Well . . .' he replied. 'Obviously if the whole Dock is going to be up for development and a great deal of heavy structural work is done, this little lock could probably be widened temporarily at the top, possibly just enough to let the ship through on a once only basis.'

Again, the history of Brunel's achievement in getting his masterpiece into the Avon in 1844 might be repeating itself. Hackett was to prove a shrewd and accurate observer. Later on, much later on, Ewan Corlett was to come and cast his professional eye over the problem. And his verdict was very much in line with this early prognosis.

All that, however, was some way off. And my next call was on the Port of London River Manager, at that time Commander Parmiter. We met in his office in the great stone headquarters building near the Tower. On the wall we studied a magnificent chart of the River Thames showing every nook and cranny through the city and down to the sea, illustrated in various colours according to classification. It was one of those maps one felt like studying for hours just for the pleasure of it.

The *Great Britain* could not be got under any of the bridges above the Tower except possibly as a hull without any masts or funnel, and this was ruled out since any such plan did not accord with restoration elsewhere. She would have to have a dry berth, though this might be created out of something which had not hitherto been blocked in and drained – as was being proposed inside St Katharine Dock. As our attention moved along both banks of the river, shifting steadily away from the Pool of London itself, Parmiter's suggestions gradually boiled down to three. One I said that I had never favoured, though I could not say exactly what my colleagues' views might be. This was to join the *Cutty Sark* somewhere down at Greenwich. I felt that this might not be in the interest of either ship, and anyway that for us to come to the London area at all demanded a more central site to make it worthwhile.

Two remaining ideas therefore emerged from this conversation. One was to consider the old dry dock at Woolwich, which I was not too keen on either since it also raised questions of accessibility. The other, however, was full of potential interest and I kept it at the back of my mind for a long time. This was to go into what is called specifically London Dock. This is the one next to St Katharine Dock, down the river on the north bank.

There were three points in its favour. It was the next best thing to St Katharine, the nearest part of its enclosed water being almost as close to the Tower as the far side of St Katharine. Secondly, its outer lock from the river was larger and could almost certainly accommodate the *Great Britain*, though there was also an inner lock, which might present a problem. The only advantage of going through the second one would be to reach a site at the western end of the Dock, which would be more accessible for the public. The third point was that London Dock was scheduled for redevelopment only after St Katharine Dock had been dealt with, and this should give us much more time to get ready, several years in fact. That might be a great advantage, depending on our own rate of progress.

When I came away I thanked Parmiter warmly for his help, and I felt I knew a great deal more about the realities of what might be possible in London. But with that for the moment I let the matter drop.

Although at this time some money had started to come in as a result of our first so-called appeal, I was very much aware that we had still made no impact on the question of major donations. Every year in the Western industrialized and developed world millions of pounds are given to charity – or were in Britain until the national economic crisis of the early nineteen seventies began to bite. There were people who could and who wanted to give, and there are always a mass of good causes seeking finance. But our

Great Britain charity had not yet received any outstanding gift, and naturally this was something to which I had to devote more and more thought and time.

Consultants emphasize amongst others one very simple rule governing fund-raising. It is that, unless you can find some of your larger donations in the first part of your campaign, you probably never will. From wide experience it has been found essential to give priority to this aspect and to let the smaller sums come in later, however numerous they may end by being. The reason is partly that the administrative cost of raising small sums from a great many people is normally high, and you cannot risk it until you have something behind you. But perhaps even more important is the fact that sometimes people, who might well be glad to give more, are in practice only presented with a request for a trifling sum the first time round. This is known in the business as 'burning over the ground'. It should always be avoided, since the damage is usually difficult to make good later on. When it happens it is a pity from the point of view of both the charity and the giver.

To help eliminate one of the probable hesitations of a giver, a step we took at the same time as preparing our appeal literature was to secure our own independent charity number. Although from the start a year earlier we had had our money put into a separate account under the Society for Nautical Research, we now successfully took this a stage further. Eric Custance, as Honorary Treasurer, approached the Charity Commissioners and by July they had given us a separate status as a fund of our own. It was still specified that we should come under the wing of the SNR, since we had no legal identity. But henceforth we did have an independent financial position as Charity number 251474, a subsidiary fund within the SNR. Legal identity was to come later. I mention this here because we took such great care throughout to ensure that our charity status was watertight. Yet even so, as much as five years later, when we were the owners of the ship and had operated as a charity for a long time, I was still being asked whether and when we might be going to become one.

But what of the major donors themselves? Approaching them is certainly a matter of luck as well as judgement. The timing has to be right as well as the method. A consequent feature of active fund-raising is that one keeps one's eyes open and one's ears alert. It was therefore with perhaps not more than a passing interest – but interest all the same – that during this early summer of 1969 I noticed a press report that a Mr Jack Hayward had just given £150,000 for buying Lundy Island for the National Trust.

And I remember thinking that, having just given so much, he would surely not be willing to give any more.

Having accordingly put this out of my mind, it was nevertheless on to not altogether unprepared ground that a letter came dropping through my letterbox a few weeks later. It was from David Owen, the Minister for the Navy, who had helped us so much the previous autumn. He asked me whether I thought it worth his just mentioning the *Great Britain* to Jack Hayward, if the opportunity arose when he would probably be meeting Hayward privately during the latter's forthcoming visit from his home in the Bahamas. I naturally replied that he should certainly do so – though I had personal reservations about the likely effect.

The visit had been expected in early July. When the middle of the month had come and gone and I had heard nothing, I got in touch with Owen again at the Admiralty. He had by no means forgotten, but no suitable opportunity had arisen. Only a day or two later, however, he let me know that he had now broached the subject, and he suggested that I myself should get in touch with Hayward direct. I accordingly wrote on 24 July to the London address asking Jack Hayward if I might come and see him.

Nothing further happened for what seemed an agonizingly long time, so I rang and rang his London office; but all that anyone would tell me was that Hayward was still in England. By 13 August, on telephoning again, I elicited the news that he would be returning to the Bahamas the following week, and again I left my own telephone numbers, including my private London one where I had an answering service.

Late on the afternoon of Friday 15 August it told me that a Mr Hayward had rung. Nothing else. No private address. No telephone number. I rang his office. Too late. It had closed for the weekend.

By now I knew that his ringing meant something, but I also suspected that, unless we met before he returned to the Bahamas the whole thing would probably go cold. It was a worrying weekend.

On the Monday morning I managed at long, long last to cajole his office into giving me his private telephone number outside London – it ranked in achievement in my mind with persuading Barclays Bank, when I arrived in Cairo during the war among thousands of others in the army, to advance me cash to buy a radio set. I immediately rang the Hayward number and the phone was answered by the man I most wanted to talk to in the world.

Yes, he was interested in the *Great Britain*. But he was flying home on

Wednesday. So I asked him where I could come and meet him straight away. His reply was surprising.

'No,' he said, 'I don't think that's a very good idea. I will come and see you.'

Next morning, Tuesday, he was in my flat in London soon after ten. I had of course learned a little about him when the whole affair had started some weeks before. I knew that he was the son of (later Sir) Charles Hayward, who had built up a great business empire, the Firth Cleveland group, was still at that time its active chairman, and had given a great deal to charity. I knew that Jack, his son, had been settled in the Bahamas for several years, where a major family investment stake had gone into the highly enterprising development of Grand Bahama Island. What I did not know and was not wholly prepared for was that Jack Hayward should prove at once to be such a human, friendly and entertaining person, with no vestige of any sign of wealth, a man who had been flying RAF Dakotas on the Burma front during the war.

I had thought we might have half an hour together – and I felt it a shrewd move on his part to come and see me against my own background. Instead we had two and a half hours. Hayward asked me every conceivable question about ourselves and about the ship. He had clearly given the whole subject a good deal of thought beforehand. He seemed really interested. And he knew what he wanted to find out.

I answered him as best I could, giving him a complete account of how the Project had started, of our difficulties as well as our achievements so far, of our problems as well as our hopes. He then put into words some of the questions to which, as I was well aware, we ourselves had not yet obtained all the answers. In particular, I remember, we ranged over the question of ownership, and of the precise steps that would have to be taken for the Crown to release the *Great Britain* to us. He also wanted to know exactly how the ship had come to be in the formal possession of the Crown in the first place – passing out of the legal ownership of the Falkland Islands Company, when she was officially abandoned as a 'wreck'.

As we talked, I knew how the time was passing. But I would have talked all day and all night, if he had wanted to. It was nearing lunch-time, and just when I was beginning to feel that we might not after all be able to settle anything at this first meeting, I suddenly realized I had almost missed the crucial words.

'That's all right,' I heard him say in exactly the same tone as before and without the faintest degree of extra expression, 'I'll see the ship home.'

I did a kind of double-take, starting to say something else but coming back to what I could not believe I had heard.

'What did you say?' I asked rather quickly.

'That's all right,' Hayward repeated. 'I'll see the ship home. Obviously, we'll have to put a ceiling on the cost. But if it comes within the range of your present estimates I'll meet it.'

I looked at him. I felt a great sense of unreality. We had been talking of sums ranging from £75,000 to £150,000, varying according to the time that might have to be taken, and any extra problems that could arise – in those days formidable figures. And suddenly it had all been promised in one lump sum. At a single stroke this was the solution to our financial problems. It just seemed too good to be true.

Jack Hayward, however, was perfectly clear in what he was saying that morning. And as I thanked him to the utmost of my ability, I felt that we had entered a compact together from which nothing would turn us back. And nothing did. No signature was ever put on paper anywhere about his undertaking – later he was to assure me that he had asked his executors to honour the pledge in the event of his death. We were destined to go through a good many ups and downs between that moment and the ship's arrival at Avonmouth ten months later, and Hayward was usually 3,000 miles away on the other side of the Atlantic. The actual sum of money likely to be required was to fluctuate considerably and, as is always virtually inevitable, was to increase remorselessly to the top limit. But through all this he never appeared to falter and he never let us down. It was a noble undertaking nobly executed.

Once the die was cast that morning we parted fairly rapidly. He gave me his various telephone numbers and a forecast of his movements. I was to ring him at any time about anything – which I did quite frequently, whether it was on the transatlantic telephone or when we were both in this country, or either of us in the United States. I showed him out to the lift and he insisted on not being accompanied downstairs. As soon as he had gone, I phoned my wife and told her the news. She wisely replied:

'You must write it down at once. By tomorrow morning you simply won't believe it.'

I did. When I woke up the next morning, I realized she was almost right.

5. The End of the Beginning

Jack Hayward had given us his support without meeting Ewan Corlett. I knew his enthusiasm would be stimulated even further when he did so, and we all planned for this meeting at the earliest possible moment. It took place on 6 September 1969, when Hayward was already back in England again for another flying visit from the Bahamas. The three of us gathered at the offices of Burness, Corlett and Partners near Basingstoke. Ewan produced his authoritative and detailed technical drawings of the ship and spoke with confidence and knowledge arising out of his own reconnaissance in Sparrow Cove the previous year. Although I knew in general everything that he was saying, I found it myself both fascinating and confidence giving. And the effect on Jack Hayward was to make the common resolve between the three of us absolutely complete.

As Corlett had a long-standing business appointment for lunch, Hayward and I borrowed the two huge American scrap books from his office and took them away with us. Financed by William Swigert and put together with immense care and characteristically American sense of detail, I realized by now that they were in themselves a revelation of the amount of knowledge available about the ship. We took them just down the road to the Beach Arms Hotel at Clarken Green, and as they were so heavy I remember that in the car park we spread them out, first one and then the other, on the boot of the car and pored over them in the sunshine.

Jack Hayward's support had, of course, transformed the whole *Great Britain* operation. We were now in business. We had moved from the 'if' stage to one of practical reality. And there was a great deal to do. Above all we had to find and commission a thoroughly competent firm willing to undertake the salvage attempt. This was by no means something that could be done overnight, and, while Corlett now took up our negotiations with the United Towing Company on an active basis, I found myself deeply involved in the tortuous problems of the ownership and release of the ship. Without a proper solution to them nothing else would be possible at all.

Quite apart from the politics and procedures unavoidably attached to government action on the subject, the desirability of reaching a clear-cut agreement which could then be made public was soon highlighted in an unexpected way. Although we had decided to make no announcement about Hayward's crucial support until we could also say what actual steps were going to be taken over the salvage, knowledge about the existence and increasing activity of the SS *Great Britain* Project was by now becoming fairly widespread. And this provoked a claim, which secured some initial publicity in the West Country, that the *Great Britain* did not really exist.

Although we knew enough to laugh this out of court, denials never quite have the news value of original statements, and the last thing we wanted was to have doubts cast on what we were doing because of nonsense of this kind. What had started the rumour was someone writing to a local paper quoting, quite accurately, a book written by a retired naval architect shortly before the First World War in which he had stated that Brunel's *Great Britain* had been broken up for scrap around the turn of the century. Therefore, the writer presumed, the ship down in the Falklands was not the *Great Britain* at all – and how could we be so misled as to think that she was?

In the fight for the *Great Britain* it has often been difficult to be sure where folly ends and malice begins. Needless to say, those opposed to us for reasons of their own were quick to pick up the rumour, and it began to receive attention in shipping publications as well as in Bristol. The fact that the Edwardian naval architect was quite simply wrong – and he provided virtually no chapter and verse for what had been no more than a passing comment on his part – could be proved only by showing that *our* ship was indeed the *Great Britain*.

So we took two steps. Ewan Corlett wrote in reply, pointing out the precise way in which countless measurements on the ship that he had personally visited and inspected the previous year fitted the exact known plans of Brunel's original ship, many of which had survived in the Bristol City Museum, the Science Museum and elsewhere. And of course he was also able to quote the continuity of the records of the ship at Lloyd's, quite apart from the fact that the vessel's officially registered Lloyd's number was still stamped on the side of one of the hatches – of which he had a photograph. And we gave Corlett's letter what publicity we could in suitable quarters. This was all quite effective at the time. But later the whole *canard* arose afresh a year or so later, and we had to go through the exercise again.

Meanwhile, the other step was one I was taking in any case following Jack Hayward's original request, and this was that I secured a written statement from the Secretary of the Falkland Islands Company. This stated that the company had duly 'abandoned to the Crown' the remains of the old *Great Britain* on 13 April 1937, after she was beached in Sparrow Cove. Lloyd's records, as well as their own, authenticated their ownership up to that point, following the Falkland Islands Company's purchase of the ship from the Gibbs family in 1886. And we publicly emphasized the absolute continuity of this record of ownership, covering as it patently did the so-called date of being broken up around 1900, when the ship was in fact in continuous and visible use as a storage vessel in Stanley harbour.

When I renewed the contacts I had made earlier with the Commonwealth Office about securing the release of the ship, I was glad to find the same person in charge of the appropriate department, Mr A. S. Sugg. He now confirmed to me that, as a vessel in the charge of the Commissioner of Wrecks, the *Great Britain* came under the provisions of Section 523 of the Merchant Shipping Act of 1894. In a colony such as the Falkland Islands this meant that the power of release had not been delegated to the Governor alone. He could dispose of a wreck only if he were instructed to do so by the Secretary of State in London.

Under the workings of British constitutional procedure, however, this was by no means the full story. The Secretary of State would not in practice instruct the Governor in a matter of this kind, unless the Governor recommended that he should do so. And, even in a Crown Colony such as the Falklands, the Governor would not normally tender such advice unless his Executive Council favoured the recommendation. At the same time, the members of the Executive Council were themselves appointed by the Governor. But while these were the normal constitutional processes bearing on any eventual decision, it was also a fact that neither of the officials concerned was bound to accept the advice given to them. The Secretary of State, that is, could ignore the Governor's recommendation if he really wished to. And the Governor himself, having consulted his Executive Council, was not absolutely bound to act in accordance with their views.

It will be seen at once that this was a complicated constitutional situation. But what it boiled down to in practice was that, while the Governor certainly held the key to it, the whole characteristically British arrangement was designed to ensure that any decisions finally taken were broadly in line with what the local population favoured, or in the last resort would willingly accept. And here in our case came the stumbling block. However sympathetic Whitehall or even the Governor might become to our cause, Falkland Island opinion was already quite strongly set against the *Great Britain* being released to anybody. Having become a sentimental local landmark, for instance the ship had already appeared as such in a series of Falkland Island stamps issued in 1952.

Sugg, however, was fortunately able to make the very suggestion I hoped for. The Governor of the Falklands, Sir Cosmo Haskard, was just starting his leave and it would be a good idea if I had a talk with him myself while he was in London. At that moment he was at his home on Bantry Bay in Southern Ireland, and a meeting between us was arranged for 12 September.

Sir Cosmo expressed great interest in the ship and in what we were attempting to do. At the same time he was quite clear in his warning that it would take a good deal to persuade people in the Falklands that she should be raised from her lonely beach and taken away. Though intensely loyal to the United Kingdom, he indicated, more than one generation had now grown up to regard the old *Great Britain* as an object of affection and pride. He also repeated the fact that it was generally believed in the islands that re-floating her was quite impracticable, and that, even if this were successfully accomplished, the risk of her being subsequently lost at sea was too great to take.

It so happens that in the course of my own life I have had a certain rubbing acquaintance with imperial politics, having also studied the constitutional development of the Commonwealth as long ago as my days as a university student. As we discussed every aspect of the subject, therefore, I began to feel fairly sure that what we were really talking about was time – granted, that is, that one believed, as I certainly did, that one way or another the *Great Britain* could be refloated and would *not* be lost at sea. Time would be needed to move local opinion towards our point of view, or at least sufficiently so for the Governor to act. In the last resort he possessed full powers, even though he would never use them except, as he himself pointed out to me, for very special reasons – and the *Great Britain* could hardly be put in that category. But somewhere there would be a meeting

point between opinion and the exercise of his powers. The question was
not only where, but how long it might take to get there, and whether it was
within the range of what the momentum of our own Project could wait for.

'What would happen,' I therefore put it to him, 'if, just for the sake of
argument, you did feel absolutely convinced that the *Great Britain* could
be safely brought back to England, although Falkland Island opinion·
expressed through the Executive Council continued to take a contrary
view?'

It was rather a fast one. Haskard paused.

'That would depend,' he observed.

'On what?' I pressed him.

'Given time,' was his diplomatic reply, 'I have no doubt that the matter
could be satisfactorily resolved.'

We both left it at that. But the lesson was that, while success would
probably come in the end, the time might be more than we could afford.
And I became quite clear in my own mind that it was now crucial for us
somehow to win round Falklands opinion to what we were doing – not an
easy task, however, considering that the islands were over 7,000 miles away
and notoriously inaccessible.

At the Governor's suggestion I started the ball rolling at once by sending a formal application for the release of the *Great Britain* in a letter
addressed to the Colonial Secretary of the Falkland Islands in Stanley. He
would then take the first step of raising the matter on the agenda of the
Executive Council. I also sent him full information about ourselves and
our aims. Meanwhile in London at a second talk I had with the Governor
he was able to assure me that, when he got back, he would naturally be
discussing with leading members of the Community the points that I had
made. In this way the Governor himself set the pace in terms of familiariz-
ing Falklands opinion with the validity of our plans.

During this extremely active period I kept the other members of the
Project in the picture as best I could about what Corlett and I were doing.
But it had all been during the holiday period and we had had no opportunity of meeting. Now I myself was becoming extremely busy on my own
affairs and would be away a certain amount. Late in September of that
year I finally resigned over a policy question from the main board of the
group of companies with which I had been associated for seventeen years;
anyone who has been through that kind of trauma will know how much it
costs the spirit, not to mention the endless meetings and time. We were
also rebuilding part of our house, my wife's fifth book was just being

published, and I made trips to Holland and to America on other business. So things were pretty hectic.

On Monday 22 September, in a room kindly made available to us in the offices of the Falkland Islands Company in London, Ewan Corlett and I held a definitive meeting with Anthony Wilbraham, managing director of the United Towing Company Ltd of Hull, together with four of his colleagues. A chief salvage officer nominated by the Admiralty was also present. The meeting started in the morning, adjourned for a celebratory lunch, and reassembled in the afternoon. It had been called to thrash out the logistics of the proposed salvage and to settle the actual steps that would be taken. These would govern the terms of the salvage contract which we now proposed to sign with United Towing.

In reaching this point with United Towing we had also considered other firms, including a Dutch one, since the Dutch have an outstanding reputation in this field. But we excluded them in the end because we wanted to stay British if we could – and Hayward felt that strongly. The other main British possibility we found was likely to cost more.

The types of problem to which we addressed ourselves included labour availability, the probable time taken, and the materials required, some of which might be found on the spot, some from the mainland of South America, and some only in Britain. It was felt, for instance, that if some manpower help were available from the local detachment of Royal Marines, two dozen men would be enough for the salvage party itself, including the crew of the salvage vessel. And if, as seemed probable, for instance, use could be made of a suitable Admiralty salvage barge, towed down to the Falklands for the purpose, this would make the job both quicker and cheaper.

When we came to costs we tried to draw up a minimum and a maximum, so that the eventual figure would fall somewhere between them. But there were of course considerable unknowns. We did not immediately know, for example, what materials could be obtained in Montevideo, nor whether an Admiralty working barge would be available, nor what bonuses might be required – if any – for men to work in the Falklands. And of course above all we did not know what further technical salvage problems might arise – some would be almost unavoidable – as soon as the operation actually got going. But, taking everything we could into account, we arrived at a rock bottom figure of £96,000 (in 1969 terms) and a probable top one – though this was inevitably much more questionable – of £165,000. The calculations were made throughout on the generous basis that United Towing would charge no administrative overheads. In order to be safe, we took in certain further contingency calculations and made the upper limit come to £180,000. And these were the estimates which I reported to Hayward afterwards, the likelihood being that the result would fall somewhere between the round figures of £100,000 and £150,000. These were 1969 prices and would be the equivalent in mid-1975 to perhaps between a quarter and three quarters of a million pounds, allowing for the increased difficulty of organizing such a venture and the rise in the price of fuel, as well as pure inflation.

During our negotiations, however, one absolute condition had been laid down by Wilbraham. He would undertake no commitment of any kind, unless and until a recce party from his own firm had visited and reported on the ship.

This wise move on his part was nevertheless something of a check to the progress we had hoped for. For it not only called into question once again the basic viability of the salvage, but also meant delay in making a start, owing to the inherent difficulty of reaching the Falkland Islands and getting away again. And this introduced the additional slight doubt whether a salvage operation, lasting perhaps up to two months, could be undertaken at all within the current summer season which was soon to be upon us. No one felt that a winter salvage attempt should be envisaged.

In the event we were lucky. It transpired that at the end of October the SS *Darwin* was making a rather quicker turn-round at Stanley than usual. And what was more, the Falkland Islands Company, which owned and operated her, were able to book three berths for us on both the outward and return journey. Even they could not always manage this, owing to the seasonal nature of her traffic and the fact that she was often absolutely full.

I was therefore able to tell Wilbraham at the beginning of October that firm bookings had successfully been made for his three-man recce party to leave Montevideo on 23 October and to get back there on 11 November. All three had been among those present at our London meeting. They were Captain B. W. Garrod, Norman Spence, and Jack Grundy. And so the scene was set.

There remained the possibility of Admiralty help to be settled and our own domestic, but vital, question of when and how best to tell the world what was afoot. Through David Owen's continued support, the offer of a naval dumb lifting vessel was confirmed, though against suitable payment; and it was arranged that this would be gone into as soon as the recce party had been able to report back. The Admiralty also suggested our using the services of a retired officer, who had had salvage experience and who they recommended as someone suitable to take charge of the operation on the spot. But this in due course we all gratefully declined, since there were other ways of meeting the need.

Our press conference – our second, and just over a year since the first one – took place in the Park Lane Hotel on Thursday 2 October 1969. Adrian Ball felt that this time a straightforward and accessible milieu was best. And we had a rattling good story to tell. Jack Hayward's gift was announced. He himself was present, naturally besieged by reporters immediately afterwards. We reported on our arrangements with United Towing; Anthony Wilbraham was beside me on the platform. We mentioned the negotiations about release of the ship by the Crown. And as a *bonne bouche* we were able to say that, when she reached Bristol, the *Great Britain* would definitely go into Charles Hill's shipyard; and John Hill was there to prove it. Besides Corlett and myself, our own group consisted of Custance, Strathcona, Adley, and Naish, with Fitz Lombard as General Secretary.

The occasion was a great success, and a blaze of publicity followed. The Project had at last 'arrived'. The day was marred only by the very frustrating conundrum which is apt to arise nowadays in regard to television. In order to appear on the little box, the main person or persons concerned are apt to be required either to go into another room to be recorded at the height of the proceedings, or to vanish to a distant studio. In either case they are prevented from seeing their immediate meeting through to a proper conclusion. This may also mean missing valuable press publicity. The difficulty is to judge what is most worthwhile. A good television appearance is obviously worth a very great deal. But a scrappy, badly edited hash-up is almost useless and can be counter-productive, and it is likely to be impossible to tell at first sight which is being offered. There is also the problem that, if a TV offer is declined by the main people concerned, the media will either drop the whole thing, perhaps for ever, or get hold of someone else instead who really does not know or cannot present the essence of the facts. He will probably be chosen in any case mainly for his apparent glamour. It was a curious chance that no less than three of my colleagues grew beards during the development of the *Great Britain* Project and this stood them in good stead with the producers. Beards go well with the sea.

From this period on, it was clear that we ourselves needed to become still more formally organized, much though one dislikes getting bogged down in time-wasting committees as such. But, as Fitz sensibly pointed out, we were now embarking on the expenditure of considerable sums of other people's money. Suitable records should therefore be made of how decisions about it were arrived at, quite apart, of course, from the bare accounts which had been scrupulously kept by Eric Custance from the beginning. Thus it was that, after the jamboree of the press conference on 2 October, we had retired to another room and held our first formally minuted committee meeting, changing the name incidentally of our hitherto loosely styled Executive Committee to Steering Committee – which with tongue in cheek seemed more appropriate for a ship, however inappropriate in strictly nautical terms! It met fairly regularly every month from then on.

After the euphoria of the press conference the next three or four weeks were a slight anti-climax, since nothing further could be done about the actual salvage until the recce team had visited Sparrow Cove and made its report. But, although I was abroad for part of the time, I was constantly involved in various other aspects of our affairs. One in particular was that Graham Norton came to see me before writing about the ship in the *Illustrated London News* of 27 September 1969. His two-page feature article, called 'First of the Greats', was unusually welcome because it was the first serious analysis of our purpose since we had really got going, and it was curiously encouraging to find someone else putting our kind of thinking into their own words. The article also marked a renewal of the rather special connection which that long-established magazine had had with the *Great Britain* originally. In Brunel's day pages of text and line drawings had been published in the contemporary *Illustrated London News*, and these have remained valuable source material ever since. In 1971 the magazine republished some of them in a special booklet to celebrate the ship's salvage.

The three-man reconnaissance party caught the *Darwin* all right; and they duly arrived in Stanley on 28 October. They had two specific questions to answer. In their judgement was the refloating of the *Great Britain* feasible? If refloated, could she be towed in the open sea, after being fitted with reserve buoyancy? Telephone conversations with the Falklands, while perfectly possible – as I later found for myself – were conducted only by radio and confined to within one hour in the afternoon. Although difficult, it was obviously conceivable that the broad results of the survey could be known well before the three themselves returned to England.

It was thus with immense interest and a sense of anticipation that I heard Tony Wilbraham's voice, when he came through on the phone from his office on 7 November, having, I think, already spoken to Corlett. His message, however, was unexpectedly indecisive. He had had a telex that the team had completed their work and were embarking on the *Darwin* for their return to Montevideo. And that was all. At least that was all that was said at that moment. I was subsequently able to learn the flight number and the time they would be due at London Airport on 12 November. But a chill had already begun to seep through me. Why had more not been said? Corlett did not know either. We could only guess.

I met the party that autumn afternoon as they came out from the customs area at Heathrow. Their job was to report to their company and, as we warmly shook hands, this could only be a meeting between friends. But within these limits I could tell at once from their faces. The salvage was not on.

I drove all three of them to King's Cross. Without disclosing anything of their proposed report, they told me something of what they had observed about the ship herself. Weary from their journey, they reflected the complexity of the issues with which they had been faced. We talked also of the general impressions they had received in the Falkland Islands. From their assessment it seemed that the element in island opinion which was not in any case prepared to see the *Great Britain* leave was stronger than ever.

Although I had been prepared for adverse news, what I heard that afternoon was devastating. No doubt there were qualifications and reservations to be brought in. There would be some professional disagreement about deductions to be made from the known facts. There were decisions that could be taken to run certain risks. But the one, simple, solid fact remained – I felt sure – that this company was not going to salvage the ship. And because it would not, perhaps others would feel less inclined to try, quite apart from the delay and the cost. And this all raised the question – yet again. Was the task we had set ourselves impossible?

When I conveyed my impressions to Corlett and Hayward, we all agreed that we must of course await the full report. We discussed the situation backwards and forwards. Corlett had already indicated that he disagreed professionally with some of the findings which seemed to be emerging – for instance, about the state of the iron plating. And we left it that, whatever the report might say, for us this was not going to be the end of the road. We would go on. It was a crucial moment and a crucial decision.

Wilbraham came to my flat in London the following Wednesday, 19

November, to give his considered views, having sent a copy of his report to Corlett who could not be present. Hayward joined me and together we heard Tony Wilbraham confirm what I had supposed. He was just as disappointed as we were. This unique and adventurous operation had greatly appealed to him, and success would have been a feather in the cap of his company.

The reconnaissance party, however, had definitely advised against taking the job on. The reasoning, though complex, was unequivocal. They considered that the *Great Britain*'s ironwork was too far gone to make her seaworthy, whatever might be done to give her extra buoyancy. Their view was that the plates could be too readily penetrated with a chipping hammer, and that the vessel did not have enough longitudinal strength left to stand up to any proposed method for closing the famous crack in the starboard side. The masts they judged to be rotten – though this did not really matter since they would have to be taken out anyway for safety. This view of the masts, was, incidentally, to prove later to be inaccurate. In short, Wilbraham regretfully told us, the risk of towing the *Great Britain* in the open sea was 'unacceptable'. And so that was that.

There was an interesting and friendly postscript to our relations with the company. A couple of weeks later Ewan Corlett and I went up to Hull by arrangement with them, in order to go through their findings item by item and to gain what further knowledge we could about the state of the ship. It was a rather sad occasion, though a useful one. Ewan was able to check some of his own interpretations against theirs and to take full account of their thinking. For my part it was an absorbing exercise. In the thoroughly British tradition, when experts disagree the layman comes into his own, and I was naturally forming my own opinion about the realities of the situation.

I reached two private conclusions, which subsequent events and findings seem to me to have fortified. First, the *Great Britain* was in reality in rather better shape than the recce team had made out. This was partly because they attributed too much significance to their own attitude to the brittleness of the ironwork; modern engineers, accustomed to working with steel, usually do not have the appropriate experience on which to base judgements about iron. And it was partly because from the start their overall view of the decrepitude of the hull had been affected by Falkland Island opinion, a very understandable but inevitably negative factor. Secondly, nevertheless, I considered Wilbraham's decision from the point of view of his own company entirely correct. Towing Brunel's tremendous old ship in the open sea did involve such risks that they were indeed 'unacceptable'.

I felt it was characteristic of our own fortunes at that moment, as well perhaps as of the nation's gathering decline, that on our way back to London the British Rail locomotive simply ran out of diesel fuel at Grantham. And we had to wait quite a long time till more could be found. I wondered what Brunel would have made of it all.

6. A Fresh Start

It was obvious that a great deal depended on the real state of the *Great Britain*'s ironwork, particularly the plates. I felt that whatever had happened to this very old wrought iron had similar implications in modern terms to metal fatigue. Fortunately the reconnaissance team had brought back several samples, which they had given to us in Hull. We handled them delicately, almost reverently. Much had been said about the flaking of the iron and this was quite apparent. But there was also some very solid metal as well.

Corlett sent a specimen for examination to the British Iron and Steel Research Association (BISRA), and asked them to analyse the quality of the iron, letting us have a report on its present properties compared with those it could be assumed to have had when it was new. They sounded very interested in our request and promised an early reply. When their report came through a few days later, it did in effect validate his views. They had done an analysis and, while there was an evident tendency to flake, they observed, this was not in itself untypical of wrought iron when subjected to the stresses of time and oxidization. The iron which was visible beneath all the corrosion as white metal, BISRA stated, was just as good as it had ever been. In its way this report was extremely heartening. It meant, in spite of all that had so recently been said, that the truly remarkable old *Great Britain* was still a ship after all, not just a pile of rust.

What the BISRA report did not and could not do, however, was to alter the fact that a major British company, with the best will in the world, had declared that the risk of towing this ship in the open sea was unacceptable. How, then, to proceed? We were inexorably forced back into the line of thinking which I knew the Americans had pursued after the respective visits to the Falkland Islands in 1966 and 1967 of Karl Kortum and William Swigert. If the *Great Britain* was ever to leave the Falklands, she would have to do so either on or in another floating vessel. The Americans had considered removing her in some form of enormous barge. We began to think of a floating drydock. It seemed to us that this was the only realistic possibility, and Corlett turned the practical aspects of it over in his mind.

We started going into the question of costs, assuming for the moment that we would be able to overcome the physical problems of finding a suitable floating dock, of getting it out to the Falklands, of floating the ship, and then of towing the whole strange object back to Britain. The trouble was that, as soon as one went into such a question seriously, the costs rose to astronomic proportions. It did not seem that any salvage operation based on a floating dock could possibly be carried out within the range of money we had so far been talking about. And even that was putting the estimates at their lowest. Put at their highest, the figures began to go beyond what it seemed reasonable to spend on the operation, even to us. Thus, quite apart from the fact that we could not see how we could raise the kind of money needed, we began to feel that, if it was really going to cost several hundreds of thousands of pounds to get the *Great Britain* back, then perhaps she ought after all to remain in her desolate grave in Sparrow Cove for ever.

It was at this point that I felt the moment had arrived to make another attempt to see and assess the *Great Britain* for myself. The previous year my wife and I had booked a holiday on a little Chilean ship called the *Aquiles*, on charter to an American travel organization running summer tours for visitors to the Antarctic peninsula and calling at the Falkland Islands on the way. But we had cancelled the trip when Argentine pressure forced the Chileans to abandon the call. Now the Americans had a brand new vessel, the 2,300 ton *Lindblad Explorer*, doing the same thing, but sailing under the Norwegian flag. So we booked for her maiden voyage, leaving Buenos Aires in the first week of January 1970.

Whether the *Great Britain* was destined to be salvaged from Sparrow Cove or not, I felt that I would be extremely glad to have seen her there. For nearly two years I had thought and talked about her at the sacrifice of a good many other things. If she left, it would have been part of the story. If she stayed, to see her would have been to set eyes on the remains of one of the most important ships ever built before the winter storms coming up from Cape Horn and the Antarctic finally lashed her to destruction.

On 16 December, by arrangement, we drove down to Southampton Docks to put a heavy suitcase of warm clothing on board the *Lindblad Explorer*, when she called there on her acceptance voyage from Finland where she had been built. We would have less baggage going out by air to join her in South America. It was when we went up the gangway, however, that we felt that something inauspicious seemed to pervade her. Though gleaming in the sunshine like a new pin, her lines squat and businesslike and impressive, the rush from the shipyard had left a fairly general sense of confusion below decks, with loose electric cables and piles of unattached equipment everywhere. And we both felt a sense of foreboding in the apparent fact that, unless someone pulled things together fairly smartly, her ability to cope with the extremities of Antarctic conditions could be questionable. As we drove home, I felt we had committed ourselves to something of which we could not quite see the end.

A day or two before this, the third formally minuted committee meeting of the Project, and one of the most significant at any time, was held at my flat in London. Eight of us were there. In addition to Corlett and myself, they were Adley, Custance and Strathcona, together with a newly elected member, Adrian Swire, as well as Adrian Ball, and Fitz Lombard. Adrian and his elder brother, John Swire, the Hong Kong merchants, were later to help us greatly over office space, and with his background Adrian Swire added considerably to the expertise available within our committee.

The key business was our critically exhaustive and definitive review of the rather baffling situation we had reached over the true state of the ship and the possibilities before us. Corlett rebutted the reconnaissance party's report item by item, and he repeated his own professional faith in the qualities of Brunel's valiant iron hull still on the beach out in Sparrow Cove. We were unanimous in our determination to go on, if that was technically feasible. It was therefore resolved that Corlett should now make a confidential approach to one of the other British firms on our list, namely Risdon Beazley Ltd of Southampton.

By the end of the month, that is just after Christmas 1969, he rang me to say that, while requiring further information, they definitely seemed interested. And he confirmed what we had hoped, namely that, although these were still early days for such a new technique, they believed that in dealing with the *Great Britain* it might be possible to use a large submersible pontoon, which they were pioneering in British ship delivery and salvage operations. This technique had been developed only during the previous two years by the German firm of Ulrich Harms in Hamburg. And so began what was to prove the final and brilliantly successful stage of our own salvage story. Already the prospects of this possible fresh start were an enormously heartening development.

Four days before Christmas, however, I went down with flu, and it turned out to be one of the worst bouts I have ever had. Instead of lying low for two or three days and then feeling a bit superior through having had the bug that was sweeping the country and therefore now able to ignore it, I seemed to get steadily worse with a high temperature. When the days started slipping by without any apparent improvement, I began to feel alarmed that I might not be able to make the Falkland Islands trip after all. As the winds howled and the snow blew past my window that rather old-fashioned Christmas, the waters off Cape Horn seemed to get even steeper and higher – and more unreachable.

I had a special reason for being rather more worried about this than I might otherwise have been. It had emerged from Corlett's negotiations that both he and Risdon Beazley wanted to send one of their own people out on a reconnaissance of the ship before any final decision was taken. Only this time the survey would be made by the man who would be in charge of the subsequent salvage, if he advised in favour of taking it on. His name was Leslie O'Neil, and our initial plan was to try to get him a one-way outward passage to the Falklands on the *Lindblad Explorer*. We feared, however, that such a last-minute concession might be even more difficult to obtain from her American operators, if I had to cancel so late in the day and would not even be making the main trip. In the end as it turned out, we were to secure a passage for him in the *Darwin* on a fairly suitable date.

Meanwhile I did at last get better and my wife and I went up to London on 2 January resolved to fly as arranged to Buenos Aires on 4 January. It was on 3 January that a curious hand of fate intervened.

Towards the end of that Saturday morning the telephone rang and I was surprised to hear the voice of the lady from our travel agency.

'There's a bit of a panic on,' she said, 'and I'm afraid your trip's cancelled. The *Lindblad Explorer* caught fire off Rio last night!'

It took a moment or two for this shattering news to sink in, before I could ask: 'How badly?'

'We don't know yet,' she replied, 'but of course we will refund your money in full.'

A little later she came through again with the report that the fire had started in the galley and then been got under control, but that too much damage had been done, particularly to the electrical system, for her to continue her existing schedule. Recalling my fears in Southampton, my disappointment was tinged with a feeling of relief.

So there it was. I never did see the *Great Britain* in Sparrow Cove. But there was nothing more I could do about it since, although we were not in a position to be certain at that moment, the *Great Britain*'s thirty-three years there were destined to end in only a few more weeks.

As for the *Lindblad Explorer*, she was patched up enough to make her inaugural voyage late in the season. The following year, however, she ran heavily aground on the Antarctic Peninsula and was very nearly a total loss. All the passengers were got ashore to a permanent survey station and eventually picked up by a chartered Chilean vessel. Only by great good fortune were no lives lost. Refloated with much difficulty, the *Lindblad Explorer* was brought back to civilization and repaired. Then, like the *Great Britain* after the stranding in Dundrum Bay, the near-disaster brought a change in her ownership. With a controlling interest bought by the highly experienced Swedish-American Line, the *Lindblad* has since carried out a series of successful adventure cruises all over the world – including the Antarctic.

For my wife and myself at this point there arose the practical question of what we would do next. I had cleared myself of all commitments for a month, the expenses would be refunded to us in due course, and we had a great need of a holiday. I had also arranged with Ewan Corlett and Euan Strathcona about the following through of our plans while I was away. The next Tuesday morning, therefore, found us in a BOAC Boeing 707 at thirty thousand feet heading out across the Atlantic to Bermuda, from where we later went on to Mexico.

During a sort of welcome convalescence in Bermuda I was able to keep in touch by telephone with what was going on in regard to the *Great Britain*. I talked to Ewan Corlett in Hampshire, Euan Strathcona in Bath, and Jack Hayward in the Bahamas. And events were at last beginning to gather a certain momentum. Corlett told me that Leslie O'Neil would definitely be arriving in Stanley in mid-January by the *Darwin*, and that with Strathcona and Custance he himself was about to meet Allan Crothall, the manager and a director of Risdon Beazley, to discuss the outlines of a salvage contract.

The encouraging urgency about all this was that, if O'Neil could get a favourable decision back quickly, the company already had the advantage of having one of the Ulrich Harms pontoons and a tug out in West Africa just completing a mission. This meant that, if the same party could go straight on to the Falklands, they would already be one third of the way there from Europe and this would save us a good deal of money, as well as time. In addition, what none of us could know as yet was that, besides the question of cabling, O'Neil was to have exceptional good luck with his own much needed quick return to England. At the very moment he had completed his survey and when he was expecting to spend several days kicking his heels in Stanley, waiting for the *Darwin*, HMS *Endurance* came into port unexpectedly to land a member of the crew going into hospital. When she left immediately afterwards for Montevideo, O'Neil was on board – and once again Captain Buchanan had come to our aid.

Meanwhile, however, the rather confused and potentially intractable issue of the formal release of the *Great Britain* to us by the Crown was jogging along in the background. And I realized that, if the salvage really was going to take place during the next few months, we would somehow have to galvanize new life into this problem the moment I got back from North America. Shortly before leaving I had checked through the position with the Foreign and Commonwealth Office, and in agreement with them I had written direct to the Governor, Sir Cosmo Haskard, just in time to catch the *Darwin*'s mail at the end of December. I told him how we were placed and that Lord Strathcona would be in touch with him as soon as anything further might develop.

Thus it was that on the telephone Euan Strathcona had two additional items of information for me. He said that he had informed Sir Cosmo Haskard of the approaching arrival of O'Neil and that, provided the latter's report about the feasibility of salvage was favourable, we anticipated a fully fledged expedition arriving in the Falklands by 23 March. It would be bringing a large submersible pontoon on which the *Great Britain* would be placed, once she had been successfully re-floated.

Strathcona also told me that he had followed up my negotiations at the Commonwealth Office with a request that the Governor should, if possible, proceed further in his own consultations with his Falkland Islands Executive Council, taking them into his confidence about the steps we were embarking upon, but not seeking to make any general announcement, since we ourselves could not afford to publicize our plans until the contract had been signed and the salvage definitely launched. We hoped, Strathcona told Sugg, that by this means the discussions necessary for the ultimate release of the ship could be accelerated. Both the Commonwealth Office in London and the authorities in the Falklands greatly helped us by agreeing to proceed along these lines.

This, then, was the position when I rang Jack Hayward from Miami on my way back from Mexico and we arranged that the following day, 28 January 1970, I should fly over to Freeport on Grand Bahama Island to meet him and have a full exchange of views – which my wife and I accordingly did. It was an exhilarating turning point in our long adventure.

The flying time from Miami to Freeport is under an hour, and we went over beneath the great indigo dome of a limitless sky, with a vast stretch of dazzling blue water below us, so clear that we were able to see right up and down the American coast and then across to the low coral profile of the approaching Bahama Islands themselves. Jack greeted us cheerily at the airport and led us out to where the cars were parked. As we emerged, I suddenly noticed what was a relatively enormous Union Jack flying from a little metal post on the radiator of a Rolls Royce, and I felt surprised that I had not identified the VIP who must have been travelling on our aircraft. Then I looked again and saw that the Rolls, though spotless and gleaming, was far from new. And it dawned on me that this was of course the special Hayward transport. There was no VIP – except our host. Later in the day, when on our way back to the airport we all stopped at the American-style golf club, a group of Americans immediately clustered round this huge and rather spectacular old Rolls.

'Say,' one of them drawled to Hayward, 'that's a fine automobile you've got there.'

'Yes,' came Jack's immediate reply. 'It's a late 1948.' There was just a second or two before the impact of the word 'late' came through and then hearty laughter.

The Rolls was one of his ways of showing the flag, and in it he drove us rapidly to his house on the other side of the island. This was situated about 150 yards back from the edge of the sea, with a balcony and patio looking across a green lawn bordered by palms and leading to a beach of coral sand fringing the white Atlantic surf. The house itself was massively built of grey stone, spacious but practical, with high ceilings yet secluded in its own surroundings, a rare haven in the modern world. In this perfect setting Jack and Jean Hayward gave us lunch in the shade outside and the English winter seemed a million miles away.

By an extraordinary coincidence it was actually while Hayward and I were reviewing the position afterwards that the vital call came through from England. Corlett was on the line. He himself had only returned from a business trip to Chile the previous day and had been able to meet O'Neil that very morning as he too came in from South America.

'Richard is here,' Jack said, and then listened to Ewan's report, which we were thus both able to share.

O'Neil's verdict on the *Great Britain* was 'Yes', and he was advising Risdon Beazley to go ahead.

The news was a wonderful fillip to our own discussions. And at the end of our talk Hayward wrote out and handed me a cheque for £25,000. This was the first down payment in fulfilment of his gift, and we both saw it as marking a new stage in the story of the *Great Britain* – as indeed it did.

From the moment I landed at Heathrow on 31 January 1970, I was plunged into round after round of pressures, drama seeming to succeed drama continuously for the next eight months. For this was finally the crunch, the period in which the *Great Britain* was picked off the beach in the Falklands and put on show to the public in the same drydock in Bristol in which she had been built. I found that the news from O'Neil was every bit as good as it had sounded from the Bahamas. While he felt that no one could be certain, his view was the same as Ewan Corlett's, namely that by using a pontoon there was an eighty per cent chance of success. So this time there was no hesitation and there was certainly no going back.

The carefully prepared charter contract was signed at once by Custance and myself on behalf of the Project, and by Crothall for his firm which had just changed its name to Risdon Beazley Ulrich Harms Ltd. And on 4 February 1970, the two salvage vessels set out secretly from Port Kamsar near Boké in Guinea on the West coast of Africa. Their first destination was Montevideo in Uruguay, where they would collect stores and be joined by an additional party of six men, including Leslie O'Neil, flown out from England. In the end it had all been done with such a rush – because otherwise the two vessels would have had to begin their return to Europe – that we had had no suitable opportunity of clarifying the position in the Falklands. And while we would have to make some public statement before Montevideo was reached, there was fully a three-week voyage to get there during which we could sort things out. Meanwhile the expedition sailed on in secrecy.

What we had chartered were an ocean-going tug and one of the only three existing suitable pontoons in the world. This German pontoon was a considerable vessel in its own right, known as *Mulus III*, of 2,667 gross tons with 16 airtight chambers and a flat platform top 79 feet wide and

250 feet long – nearly, but not quite, as long as the *Great Britain*'s 289 feet. The tug which towed it was a 724-ton converted stern trawler, *Varius II*, a modern and seaworthy little ship with a variable pitch propeller. She acted as home and workshop for the 21-man team. Her base was Hamburg, her crew German, and her skipper Captain Hans Herzog from Heligoland. The expert in charge of the operation of the submersible pontoon was Horst Kaulen.

The planned stop at Montevideo was vital. Although the party had been able to refuel before leaving Africa, in other respects they were short of a good deal of essential equipment, since this extra and highly unusual mission had had to be taken on at a moment's notice. They ended by spending nearly two weeks there, buying lifting derricks to construct a 'sheerlegs' on the bow of the pontoon; acquiring rough baulks of timber to be laid across the deck of the *Great Britain* as a safe basis to work from; and welding upright steel tubes, or 'dolphins', to the pontoon itself as a kind of skeleton structure to hold the *Great Britain* in place, like the sides of a drydock. Pumps and other special salvage equipment were being hastily sent out from England by direct shipment on the Falkland Islands Company's supply ship, *Aes*. All this was the result of a quick shopping list drawn up by O'Neil in the light of his own survey. The work in Montevideo was completed as swiftly as possible because it was already getting rather late in the season, if the salvage was to be completed and the *Great Britain* got safely away from the Falklands before the full fury of the autumn and early winter gales broke upon her.

Meanwhile, the situation in the Falklands themselves had reached a particularly delicate stage. The charter was costing us £825 a day and even a few days extra delay would land us in serious trouble. Yet I felt that the Governor really had nothing much more tangible to go on than he had had before our own momentous commitment to the salvage. Indeed, he appeared to be in a potentially worse position, because local opinion might well harden on learning that we had dispatched an expedition on the assumption that they would give way and allow us to take the ship after all. And if events reached an impasse even temporarily on this question of release, I shuddered to think what our own critics and opponents at home might make of it all. Press and television, particularly in Bristol, would have a field day about our rushing into something we could not handle.

If the Falklands had been the Isle of Wight one could no doubt have gone over there, put the Governor fully in the picture, and thrashed out the facts with leading elements in the community. But they were on the other side of the world. And so on Monday, 9 February, I booked an appointment on the radio circuit to Stanley during the limited period for which it would be open that afternoon. When Sir Cosmo Haskard came on the line, we had a crucial conversation which set the scene for the next few weeks. Reception on the circuit was fortunately good. I was much relieved when Haskard told me that he personally knew all O'Neil's findings, having seen him just before his departure on board HMS *Endurance* and given him the letter which I had in fact just received. But the Governor emphasized to me most strongly 'how extremely important it is to the success of the operation' that Falkland Island opinion should be in favour of it.

On this basis we discussed the earliest date on which a statement about the Project's activities could satisfactorily be published simultaneously in the Falklands and in London. And we agreed that we might have to run till the full limit of the salvage party's expected arrival in Montevideo, namely 2 March. As luck would have it, nevertheless, one of the regular meetings of the Falkland Islands Executive Council was due the following day, 10 February, and the Governor would be able to bring them up to date on the whole position. To reinforce his hand I summarized the expected movements of the *Varius* party, underlining again the use of the pontoon. We then arranged that, as soon as the meeting of the Executive Council was over and its reactions were known, a cable would be sent to me via the Commonwealth Office and that we would continue to keep in touch by this means. We then rang off.

During the next three days two highly interesting telegrams passed between London and Stanley, which together carried matters forward more quickly and positively than I had originally dared to hope. The Commonwealth Office informed the Governor that it was looking forward to receiving his recommendation for the release of the *Great Britain* as soon as he felt able to make it. In reply, and heartened perhaps by this official encouragement, the Governor cabled back to the Commonwealth Office with the full text of what had been agreed in principle at the Executive Council. It was to be the charter of our release. Sir Cosmo Haskard's text began:

Advice of Governor-in-Council is that ship should be released on following conditions:
   (a) Release should be only for pontoon method and not some other method;
   (b) Any interference with shipping channel leading to Stanley Harbour which might result from salvage or towing would be remedied at expense of Committee.

And it went on to add what was in effect a third condition:

If at any point the pontoon method seemed 'unlikely to succeed', operations should be suspended before too much damage had been done to the old ship.

This last observation reflected in no uncertain terms the anxiety of the Falkland Islanders that the *Great Britain* should not be destroyed. If she was going to break her back during the salvage operations, they intended that she should remain in Sparrow Cove, whether or not she could be got on to the pontoon even though damaged.

I think that the Commonwealth Office was just as surprised as I was by the unexpectedly conditional nature of the release. But I felt at once that to get it at all so quickly was a big step forward and I could well see how each of the conditions had come to be made. After a brief consultation with my closest colleagues I therefore gladly accepted straightaway.

In order to carry out the terms of the telegram, however, Sugg at the Commonwealth Office told me that a contract would be required between the Governor, acting with the authority of the Secretary of State, and the Trustees of the SS *Great Britain* Project. My relief was therefore quickly followed by dismay at the prospect of time being taken at this juncture to draw up what I feared would be an involved legal document, instead of the straightforward unilateral release certificate which I had always pictured. I realized that this procedure would make it difficult, if not impossible, to obtain the Governor's signature to the final document before the *Varius II* actually arrived in Stanley – she might even take it with her. There was also the slight complication about drafting the document that the SS *Great Britain* Project had no trustees.

The Falkland Islands Legal Advisor was resident in London and he was immediately invited to draw up the proposed agreement. He was a retired former Chief Justice of Gibraltar, Sir Hubert Flaxman. After two long telephone conversations with me, he duly set about his task. The Office had eventually accepted the fact that we had no trustees, since we were in effect recognized by the Charity Commissioners as an affiliated body which was 'a subsidiary of the Society for Nautical Research'. Eric Custance sent a list of the SNR's 'office bearers' to the Commonwealth Office, and it was agreed that the two signatories for the Project should be myself as Chairman and him as Honorary Treasurer.

All this, however, took what seemed an infinity of time, and it was no less than a whole month later that on Tuesday 17 March Sir Hubert

Flaxman came to my flat with his completed draft of the proposed agreement. By then, *Varius II* with the pontoon in tow had actually completed her fortnight of final preparation in Montevideo and was two days out on the ten-day voyage to her destination, Stanley. And it was already some three weeks since, in concert with the Falklands authorities, we had made our public announcement that the salvage of the *Great Britain* was in fact taking place. This had been made on 23 February, thereby beating the deadline of 2 March arranged between the Governor and myself, by a definite margin.

Everything had continued according to the best of plans on the absolute assumption that the proposed agreement between the two parties would give no trouble – even though its final signature by the Governor before the *Great Britain* might be ready physically to leave the Falklands was now going to be a very fine run thing indeed. I had, of course, long ago had to abandon my original hope that we could obtain a release document before being deeply committed to the expedition itself.

It was therefore all the more dramatic that at this eleventh hour a most disconcerting hitch occurred. When I read Sir Hubert's draft, I had no alternative but to reject it out of hand. He had included in it a *personal* liability to be assumed by Eric Custance and myself, under which we would meet the full expenses ourselves of clearing any possible blockage 'of the shipping channel leading to Stanley Harbour'. This might run into very large figures and was out of the question. It was also, I felt quite certain, not what Sir Cosmo Haskard had intended in his telegram of 13 February. That had laid the responsibility on the Project as such, and it was only because of the confusion over our having no trustees that the form of wording had taken the wrong turning.

The fact was nevertheless that, whatever the reason, the draft would not do. If it was insisted upon, then someone else would have to accept this condition. I would not. Nor could Eric Custance. I did not really doubt that the misunderstanding – as I felt it almost certainly was – could be sorted out. The trouble was that time really was beginning to run out at last. Flaxman pointed out, quite rightly, that he would have to refer back to the Commonwealth Office and, if necessary, to the Governor of the Falkland Islands, for further instructions. And we both knew what this could mean.

I therefore addressed myself to Sir Hubert.

'Unless,' I said, 'your instructions can be altered and a new release document drawn up immediately, I will have to send a radio message to the *Varius* to turn round and put back to port. If that happens the salvage of the *Great Britain* may well have to be abandoned.'

Sir Hubert Flaxman had not had a distinguished career in the colonial civil service for nothing, and he fully appreciated the several implications. As soon as he had left me, I rang the Commonwealth Office, and told them what had happened, and that he was coming round to see them. They said they would check on the position.

Everyone was as helpful as they could be. Within the five precious days that remained before the monthly Falkland Islands mail closed, a fresh document was drafted and rushed round to me. I agreed to it and at once drove down to Greenwich to show it to Custance. We both signed it and I drove straight back to Downing Street and handed it in at the Commonwealth Office. It caught the mail to the Governor. But I could not help reflecting that this was not the ideal way of doing things. The negotiations, after all, had originally started half a year earlier.

To go back, however, to Leslie O'Neil's return and his vital report to Ewan Corlett at the end of January. On 11 February, the day after I had spoken by radio to Sir Cosmo Haskard, O'Neil came up from Southampton to my flat in London to meet Euan Strathcona and myself. All our dealings with him had so far been at one remove through Corlett, and I wanted other members of the Project Steering Committee, who were coming in for one of our sessions an hour or so later, to have an opportunity of meeting him as well. Corlett joined us too.

It was a fascinating afternoon. O'Neil, a man who I felt was more suited to doing than just talking, yet downright and confident when expressing his own professional views, succeeded in conveying an extraordinarily realistic impression of what had sometimes begun to seem to me to be an almost mythical ship. For the first time I could feel the winds af Sparrow Cove blowing through my own sitting-room. And I was left with the certainty that, even though he himself had a twenty per cent mental reservation about everything going entirely well, the *Great Britain* would in fact be back in England at some point during the coming summer.

Strathcona's special interest was that he had by now decided to go to the Falklands and be present throughout the salvage. This meeting therefore also put him in direct touch with the plans being made for the movements and operational role of the *Varius*. It was decided that he would fly out to Montevideo and travel on with the tug and pontoon from there, as would O'Neil and the other five who were coming with him from Risdon Beazley. What I did not personally know at that moment was that Euan would also be joined by his young brother-in-law, Viscount Chewton. This was an arrangement made between them nearer the time of departure, and it hinged on negotiations which Strathcona and Adrian Ball conducted to secure press coverage of the actual salvage in the *Daily Telegraph* and *The Times*. But it meant what must have seemed a really very odd set-up to people who did not know the background, with the Project appearing to have chosen to be represented by only two peers.

If the Falklands had not been so inaccessible and the exclusive time to be taken up so long, there would no doubt have been coverage by direct representatives of the international press and agencies. But, as things were, there was no press coverage. And Strathcona secured accreditation for himself as *Daily Telegraph* correspondent, with a similar position for Chewton from *The Times*. In the end this led to Euan Strathcona's nine graphic reports in the *Daily Telegraph* becoming the only immediate public record of the event as it took place. The arrangement with *The Times* unfortunately did not work so well, but they did print one superb first picture of the *Great Britain* on her pontoon, which appeared in the centre-top of the front page.

The other three people who visited the Falklands for the salvage – travelling on the *Darwin* – represented the BBC. One was Ray Sutcliffe, the producer from the BBC 2 industrial archaeology programme, *Chronicle*, who had been to the Falklands before and had built up a considerable footage of film about the *Great Britain*. Accompanying him were Tony and Marion Morrison. They constituted the camera team and amongst other things have covered a variety of South American subjects with great distinction. Besides film for the BBC they took some excellent colour photographs, which appeared with an article of their's in the *Observer* supplement the week-end before the *Great Britain* reached England.

During this period – February 1970 – while the *Varius* and pontoon, *Mulus*, were still ploughing their way southwards across the tropical seas of the Equator between Africa and South America, one or two other significant developments bearing on the future of the Project also arose in England. One was a further sign of the way serious misunderstandings were already beginning to circulate in Bristol. As a guest at a dinner of the Merchant Venturers there, I was succinctly warned not to expect the Society to take the lead in giving us money, nor to hope that people giving money would be satisfied 'just to subsidise Charles Hill'. So far as I was aware none of us on the Project had ever asked the Merchant Venturers for a penny; later on, when restoration of the ship had already begun to make substantial headway, they gave us a very useful donation. And, as for Charles Hill and Sons, the boot has always been very much on the other foot. After Jack Hayward they have been the *Great Britain*'s main benefactors.

A few seconds after this awkward exchange a further encounter took place on a rather wider front, which in itself was much more irritating at the time. Among those present was Lord Runciman, with whom I had discussed our *Great Britain* affairs the previous year, and he very kindly gave me some surprising information.

'I don't know whether you know,' he said, 'but the formation of the Maritime Trust will be announced in tomorrow's papers.'

This took me aback for two reasons. While I greatly welcomed the creation of the Trust, to do for Britain's maritime heritage something of what the National Trust has done on land – indeed I felt that it was basi-cally overdue – its actual emergence affected our own position in regard to future fund-raising. Some people would prefer to give to the wider Trust rather than to the *Great Britain*, and hence one hoped that our own support would come via the Trust if we were to maintain our position. But it was a complication which I had understood only shortly before would not arise for perhaps another year yet. Since I had carefully enquired originally about the early moves to form the Trust I was disappointed that I had not been kept in the picture. Apparently other ship preservation societies had been.

Secondly, however, of more immediate and tangible significance was the unfortunate actual timing of the Maritime Trust's announcement. This was going to appear on the last full working day, Friday 20 February, while our own rather historic statement would be coming out on the Monday, 23 February, namely that an expedition was now well on its way at last to salvage the *Great Britain*. It was absurd that these two announcements should not have been co-ordinated with at least some cross-reference between them. But all our *Great Britain* hand-outs had already been made up and put into envelopes and some had already been posted, with an embargo till Monday's publication deadline, and it was too late to stop them. I knew that coming on the later date we would be bound to be asked by the press and media what our relations with the Maritime Trust were, and indeed perhaps why we had not even referred to it in our own hand-outs. In the event I was embarrassed by being pressed on these points, though not as much as at first seemed likely. But it was a nonsense that should never have happened. A combined operation would have helped us both.

Meanwhile, of course, our own story was unfolding into an exciting reality. The *Varius* and *Mulus* had arrived in Montevideo on 4 March after an uneventful voyage from Africa. And, as I have said, they were joined by O'Neil and his party from England, as well as by Strathcona and Chewton. I have occasionally wondered since what this combined Anglo-German team may have thought about the two memorials to the Battle of the River Plate in the early months of the last war, which stand near the harbour administration building in the docks at Montevideo. One is the anchor of the German pocket battleship *Graf Spee*, which blew itself up after mooring in to the temporary shelter of this neutral Uruguayan port, following a losing action with the three British cruisers, *Ajax, Exeter* and *Achilles*. And while this massive anchor is set dramatically in modern sculptured concrete facing one side of the building, the other memorial, the bell of HMS *Ajax,* is mounted discreetly on a plinth round the corner on the other side.

After a short spell of shore leave for the crew of *Varius,* the little flotilla of tug and pontoon sailed for the Falklands on Sunday 15 March 1970. The voyage, which the *Darwin* used to do in four days, took them ten, and some of it was very rough – for these are among the stormiest waters in the world. They ran into a force 10 gale as soon as they left Montevideo. This lasted for three days, and was followed by only a brief lull before blowing up again to force 9. At times, Strathcona told us afterwards, the *Varius* was rolling through 60 degrees.

Captain Herzog decided to hug the Argentine coast for as long as he could, following it south about 30 miles off. At the last feasible moment he then struck out for the Falklands about 350 miles from the mainland. With a maximum cruising speed of 6 knots, wind and current were sometimes pushing him sideways so strongly that net progress was only one or two knots.

However, they arrived in Stanley in good order on 25 March and, as they dropped anchor among the rolling peat-covered hills beside the little red-roofed town, everyone profoundly hoped that the weather would be kinder to them when they set out again with the *Great Britain* up on the pontoon – and it was. Now, as the crew climbed back on the *Mulus,* they found in a cranny on the deck an empty wine bottle, left no doubt by a Uruguayan workman. And in spite of the storm it was still standing upright. With this good omen they set to work.

7. Salvage

The morning after arrival in Stanley, that is on 26 March 1970, the Thursday of Easter week, the expedition crossed the three and a half miles of water to the lonely shelving bay of Sparrow Cove. Although command was in effect split between three different men, they worked so well together that complete success lay ahead of them in just over two weeks' time – though none could know that, when they first sighted the formidable old *Great Britain* as she lay there in her gaunt silence.

Captain Herzog, in command of the *Varius* from which they all worked, had no salvage function except when his ship was involved – but when it was, this was vital as, for instance, in moving the pontoon and supplying it with power. Horst Kaulen was the expert responsible for the operation of the pontoon itself and had technical charge of all the German salvage equipment, including the cutting gear.

The third man was Leslie O'Neil from Southampton. As salvage officer, he was in control of everything to do with refloating the *Great Britain*. Quite apart from his reconnaissance some weeks earlier, O'Neil was no stranger to the Falklands. He himself had been serving in HMS *Exeter* at the outbreak of war; and before her brave share in the Battle of the River Plate, she had been in and out of Stanley several times. After the battle, badly damaged, she had limped back into Stanley, and the school there had been turned into a hospital to look after her scores of wounded. O'Neil had been among those of the ship's company who had helped to patch her up before her triumphant return to England. Now, with this Anglo-German team in partnership he was back again in Stanley – and, as we knew, he was solidly optimistic about their chances. Though nothing whatever could be taken for granted, and in spite of some hair-raising possibilities, their general plan worked well. As O'Neil was to say afterwards, the way things went always made him feel that:

'The old ship wanted to come home.'

In addition to the salvage party, Lord Strathcona was present both as the Project's representative and as a reporter and in practice he lent an able hand when required. Last but not least came the BBC trio, whose two main problems were that they had relatively little to do – since everything took a long time – and that they had only a somewhat anomalous position when on board the *Varius*, since they were not living there but were based in Stanley from where they came over by launch. Understandably, but rather absurdly, this came to a head over the question of who was to pay for their food.

A separate additional group consisted of the detachment of Royal Marines under the command of Captain Malcolm McCleod, likewise stationed in Stanley. They gave invaluable manpower assistance and help in other ways, particularly in the earlier stages with the unloading and movement of equipment, some of which had arrived in Stanley direct from England two days before the expedition. They also laid out eight tons of heavy timber as working walkways over the weatherdeck, most of which was rotten. And the detachment operated a hovercraft and a launch which gave lifts to and from Stanley. The generous support of these Royal Marines was one of the results of our long contact with the Admiralty in London.

The initial method of work was for the pontoon to be made fast end-on to the port side of the *Great Britain*, the 1968 survey of Sparrow Cove having established that there was just enough depth of water for this to be done. The *Varius* lay at anchor a few yards farther astern, lashed to the starboard side of the pontoon. A continuous operation could thus be mounted using the pontoon as a floating work base. The remains of the little deck house on the *Great Britain* was patched up and used as a combined office, store, and shelter from the icy winds. It became known as the Strathcona Arms.

The task ahead of the party was at once complex and yet clear. First, the three masts had to be taken down since they would be unsafe at sea. The holes in the hull, some known and some unknown, had to be made watertight. The starboard crack had to be closed by straightening the ship; initially this was to be attempted by the Corlett plan of 1968. The ship then had to be pumped out and refloated. Meanwhile, the pontoon would have been submerged in another part of the shelving cove at a sufficient depth of the water to enable the *Great Britain* to be floated over it with a few inches to spare. The final stage would be the pumping out of the pontoon, bow first and then the rest, so that lateral stability would be retained for as long as possible through its square stern still resting on the sea-bed. Eventually, with all the airtight chambers of the pontoon pumped out in the right sequence, it would rise to the surface and the *Great Britain* would be lifted clear of the water.

Operations were begun the moment the tug and pontoon arrived in Sparrow Cove on 26 March. Divers started the long task of patching the holes, beginning with those deliberately made in the stern in 1937 to prevent the ship floating off the beach. The baulks of timber were laid out on the deck as the walkways. And by the following morning the specially acquired steel sheerlegs was being erected on the bow of the pontoon, in order to tackle the lifting out of the masts.

One of the most immediate jobs was as tricky and dangerous as any in the whole mission. This was to lower the 4-ton, 106-foot iron yard arm from 70 feet up on the mainmast, where it had been since 1886. No one really knew how strong or rotten the mast itself was, and in order to get the first rope up someone had to scale it. Staff Sergeant 'Yorkie' Stott of the Royal Marines volunteered – and made the climb successfully. Burning equipment was hauled up and, not without a struggle, Horst Kaulen cut through the heavy rusted attachment, so that the great yard was in due course lowered to the deck. During the operation the woodwork of the mast itself had caught fire, but this was swiftly put out.

The first mast to be tackled was the smallest, the mizzen, and for this the pontoon was moved farther aft along the *Great Britain*'s side. One difficulty was that the equipment available was not really tall enough to enable the whole mast to be pulled out complete. So a section was cut off the bottom. But even so, when the sheerlegs was used to try to lift the mast clear, it pulled at too much of an angle and the mast broke near the main deck level. It then toppled over and fell on the little deck house, though fortunately rather slowly. Luckily no one was inside and, although the work of making the Strathcona Arms weatherproof had to be done all over again, no permanent damage was caused. But the lesson had been learnt, and when it came to dealing with the mainmast and foremast, each of which weighed nearly 20 tons and had a diameter of about 4 feet, the decision was taken to cut them at the weatherdeck level. The stubs were only hauled out later on when the *Great Britain* was back in Avonmouth. All the masts were safely out by 1 April, the seventh day of the salvage.

Meanwhile, work had gone steadily forward plugging the holes underwater. This was done by fitting light wooden patches with soft rubber edging to the outside of the holes and hooking them to pieces of angle-iron across the inside. A seal was then created with quick-setting hydraulic cement. As the three divers – one of whom was a local Falklander – worked their way under every part of the ship it became certain that rumours of large gashes in the hull, made by touching a rock at the moment of beaching in 1937, were without foundation. As has happened time and again in the fight to save the *Great Britain*, events alone were able to make the ardent pessimists, some of whom were to be found among the island population, eat their words.

The divers were also engaged in exploring the full extent of the starboard crack, and in assessing the amount of underwater wastage in the engine-room bulkhead, on which the Corlett plan for straightening the ship depended. To get a view of the crack, mud and seaweed were forced away from underneath by a portable air compressor. So far as could be seen, the crack went rather farther towards the keel than had been expected, but was reduced to hairline proportions some way before it got there. The whole of the port side seemed sound. When the ship was finally raised, this assessment proved correct, and the net result was that, serious though the crack was, it presented the expedition with no insurmountable problem.

The fact was, however, that the crack had been getting worse at a compound rate over the previous year, and the salvage was taking place only just in time. Since Ewan Corlett's survey sixteen months earlier the width of the crack and the relative twist of the hull had doubled. He had then given the ship five years before she would almost certainly have broken in two. In the event he was optimistic rather than pessimistic. Another winter's storms in July and August of 1970 might have damaged the *Great Britain* beyond salvation. If they had not and the salvage had still been feasible in 1971, the chances were that yet another winter would have seen the end. But to have any certainty of success 1970 was indeed the last possible year, and it is extraordinary in its way that after a century and a quarter the hull of the *Great Britain* was saved for posterity at this very final moment.

What proved to be much more of an operational obstacle in the actual salvage was the state of the engine-room bulkhead. As can be seen in the ship today, this was so wasted that any plan to make use of it in refloating the *Great Britain* had to be abandoned. This meant giving up Corlett's concept of straightening the hull before putting it on the pontoon. This had involved making the stern section watertight first and then pumping it out, so that its buoyancy would provide a controlled lifting movement sufficient to force the crack to close. Instead, the ship would now have to be floated off the beach in her existing hogged condition, and the final straightening would have to take place as she settled on the pontoon. Although at first sight a tougher experience for the rest of the old ironwork in the hull, there was no alternative. And so this was the method which O'Neil actually adopted – with such success that once again the evil-wishers were routed.

By the end of the first week's work a steady swing had begun to be evident in Falkland Island opinion. This was due to the obviously business-like approach of the salvage team and their no-nonsense ability to make rapid progress with each step they undertook. Lord Strathcona and Ray Sutcliffe were able to make sure that everyone knew about the progress, as they were given a few minutes on the local radio station every morning to report and comment on developments as these arose. And this became a regular feature which the community listened to with a mounting sense of anticipation. In addition, the two or three available motorboats in Stanley Harbour were in constant demand by sightseers, who made their way across the sound to see for themselves what was going on.

The revised plan for refloating the ship involved two preparatory courses of action. One had been necessary in any case and carefully prepared. This was to bolt steel straps across the crack along the stringers at each of the three deck levels. These strips of steel were 30 feet long, 3 feet wide, and seven-eighths of an inch thick; drilling the appropriate bolt holes in the old iron girders of the ship proved just as laborious as drilling the modern steel. So much for the *Great Britain* being just a pile of rust.

The other line of action was to block the crack itself by a method as old as Nelson's day. A call therefore went out on the Falkland Islands radio for any old mattresses that could be spared for stuffing into the crack, as a first step. About a dozen were produced, mostly of rubber and including a number condemned by the Royal Marines as well as four sold to the expedition at the Falkland Islands Company store. The divers then had quite a job pushing and pulling these down into the crack, owing to their buoyancy. Once this had been achieved they were fastened into place with plywood and hooks and, after flotation, they would start being squeezed tight by the lift of the water on the long hull.

By Sunday 5 April, the eleventh day of operations, preparations had been completed and the pumps were started – slightly ahead of the original schedule. To reach this point had been no mean achievement in the time, particularly when it is remembered that the whole operation was taking place in a basic temperature of 40°F and constantly swept by icy gale-force winds at the tail end of summer down near the Antarctic. It was in fact found better to do some of the work at night, since conditions were usually calmer then – and there was not much else for anyone to do anyway!

For hour after hour the pumping went on. As the water level inside the ship gradually went down, fresh holes which were revealed were sealed off. All through the day of Monday 6 April, this slow drama continued. Then in the early hours of Tuesday morning, at 5.30 am on 7 April, the historic moment came with disconcerting suddenness. With a quick and unexpected heave the *Great Britain* came afloat. It was the thirteenth day of the salvage.

This exciting and long-awaited success was disconcerting, because on this particular morning the usual dawn wind was already rising to gale force and a critical situation immediately developed. Inadequate lines had been attached to the shore, so that the bow began to swing away to port. For a moment it looked as if the ship might get out of control and tragic damage be done. The position was saved by two little boats which arrived on the scene at that moment by chance. One was the launch *Lively*, which had just got back from Stanley with a repaired generator, and the other was the *Malvenas* which, in spite of the very early hour, had also just come from Stanley with sightseers who had heard that something special was afoot. Together they helped to hold the *Great Britain* while fresh lines were hastily rowed ashore, and the situation was saved.

The wind, however, continued to rise until it was blowing at full force 10. Leslie O'Neil and Horst Kaulen had to make a hard decision. Ready though they were to take risks, they reluctantly concluded that, since there was no possibility of even attempting to manoeuvre the *Great Britain* over the pontoon in such conditions, the best course was to let the ship settle back on the beach until the storm had blown itself out. So the pumps were stopped and after only a few dramatic hours afloat the *Great Britain* was gently grounded again.

The weather remained bad for three days and there was nothing for it but to wait. *Varius* went over to Stanley on 8 April for fresh water and returned to Sparrow Cove the same evening. The team's frustration can be imagined. Not only were they being thwarted of the real moment of truth which would be the actual lifting of the ship by the pontoon; but they had all set their hearts on bringing the *Great Britain* triumphantly into Stanley harbour on 12 April, the precise anniversary of the day she had been taken out to Sparrow Cove thirty-three years before, on what no one had dreamt for a moment would not be her last voyage.

By the night of 9 April the weather had moderated enough to restart the pumps. And on the morning of Friday 10 April the *Great Britain* came afloat again, this time slowly and rather grudgingly. Meanwhile, the pontoon had been sunk at what was thought to be a suitable spot several hundred yards away. The old ship was finally towed away from her beach, and the manoeuvring began in order to bring her up between the steel dolphins sticking out of the water above the submerged pontoon.

It was at this point, however, that another agonizing hitch occurred. The *Great Britain* had no sooner begun to be edged forward over the pontoon than she seemed to stick. Her bow was only thirty feet in, and nothing the party could do would move her farther. With something approaching consternation it was realized that, unless she could quickly be either got all the way in or completely withdrawn again into deeper water, she would probably break her back on the end of the pontoon as the tide fell. With some difficulty they backed her off and abandoned the immediate attempt to dock her on the pontoon.

What had happened was that insufficient allowance had been made for several special factors, which combined to make her draw a deeper draught than had been calculated. And the pontoon was in too shallow water. The draught forward should have been 9 feet 9 inches, and aft 11 feet 9 inches. Instead it was found to be 12 feet and 14 feet respectively, or over two feet deeper than planned. The three main causes were the fact that the ship had had to be refloated strapped in a hogged condition, so that bow and stern were slightly lower than the centre section; omission from the calculations of the seventeen-inch wooden keel that had been added in 1852 and was not in Brunel's original drawings on which the calculations were based; and, by no means least, the existence of between 200 and 300 tons of mud, old iron and other accumulated junk, which it had been decided on second thoughts not to remove from the hold before refloating, in order not to risk unnecessary disturbance and possible damage to the hull.

When all this had been worked out, it was simple enough to refloat the pontoon and to move it to rather deeper water. And this was done by the middle of the afternoon (10 April). Then they waited for the tide to rise, so that the ship could settle gently on to the deck of the pontoon as the tide began to ebb. During the early evening, however, the wind steadily increased, until soon after nightfall it had reached storm force 11, even higher than in the previous three days' gales. The barometer dropped to what was reputed to be its lowest point for two years. Obviously operations had once again to be abandoned.

This time, although Horst Kaulen was only persuaded with difficulty to agree that the pumps could handle the situation, the *Great Britain* was kept afloat rather than being put back on the beach. They lashed her to the pontoon and there she rode out the storm. She was even steered to some extent by her rudder, which had been successfully freed from its rusted-in position of 30 degrees to port. It was a thrilling performance – but by no means what anyone would have chosen to go through on the *Great Britain*'s first full day afloat after thirty-three years.

Next day, Saturday 11 April, the wind dropped and they moved the ship up between the dolphins, though not without difficulty and only after pumping out more water and removing a little more of the junk in the hold. By evening when the tide was at its height the *Great Britain* was at last precisely poised in position over the pontoon. During the night, as the tide fell, the main keel made exact contact with the carefully prepared blocks. The two docking keels, nine foot out on each side, also came to rest on their respective blocks, so that the ship settled successfully on to the deck of the submerged pontoon, standing upright on her own.

At about 1.30 am, however, members of the salvage party in the *Varius* alongside were startled for a moment to hear two loud bangs inside the *Great Britain*. Inspection showed that these had been caused by the sheering of two of the bolts holding the steel straps to the iron stringers – and there could hardly have been a more promising development. For the straps themselves were buckling, as it had been hoped they would under the tremendous pressure exerted by the closing of the crack. As the tide fell, the weight was being taken by the pontoon and the great ship was straightening herself.

Now came the crucial task of bringing the pontoon itself to the surface and thus lifting the *Great Britain* clear of the water. O'Neil and Kaulen had at first disagreed about any need to tie the ship down to the pontoon for this process, which involved pumping out the forward end of the pontoon before its stern left the bottom, where it had to remain till the last possible moment to maximize lateral stability. This was even more necessary than usual, since one of the airtight chambers was out of action as it contained the reserve oil fuel of the *Varius*.

The result was, however, to incline the pontoon so sharply upwards at the bow that there was some risk of the *Great Britain* simply slipping off backwards before the stern could be raised. Although the pontoon was being operated near its maximum depth, Kaulen felt sufficiently confident to persuade O'Neil that the friction of the keels would be adequate to hold the ship in position. In the event he fortunately proved correct – but only just. The ship stayed on all right, but a fractional sideways movement at the bow did slightly dent two of the port forward plates against the pontoon's winch-housing.

Shortly before dawn – it was now Sunday 12 April – the pumps at the forward end of the pontoon were started up. And as the bow of the pontoon began to rise, carefully and slowly at first, the process of settling was steadily taken further. Finally, when by noon the full weight of the ship was on the pontoon and the *Great Britain*'s bow itself was out of the water, they all knew they had won.

After this dramatic start, pumping went on all day, till during the afternoon the whole of the *Great Britain* slowly began to emerge above the sea to tower over the *Varius*. And her hull was straight and true. Even the twist had gone. The crack had closed. There was no damage on the port side. She was all in one glorious piece. Everyone was a little awed by what they had done, and on seeing the beautiful lines of the ship for the first time one of the weary and hardened divers could not help exclaiming:

'She looks like a yacht.'

Pumping was completed on Monday 13 April, and on that day the ship was finally lifted completely clear of the water. It was one of the several extraordinary coincidences in the life of this vessel that this was the anniversary to the very day of the date on which the scuttling holes had been knocked in her stern 33 years before, to prevent her floating off the beach in Sparrow Cove for ever.

O'Neil and his party still had some work to do before they could move out of Sparrow Cove, and they spent the rest of the day doing it. Between some of the blocks they drove large, specially prepared steel wedges to hold the ship more firmly in position, and they pumped out some more of the water still inside. In particular, they made a start in burning off the buckled steel straps across the inside of the crack, in order to straighten them and lap weld them back into place. They were also able to take full stock of the state of the crack itself. Surprisingly little water had seeped through the mattresses, now pinched and crushed by the closing of the ship's side, which had taken place to an astonishing degree of accuracy. As for the underwater plates, when the ship had emerged from the water whole slabs of scale and marine growth had fallen away, so that in a number of places the entire plate was clean, leaving a curious effect. But it did enable them to see how very good the condition of the underwater ironwork basically was.

Then, on the morning of Tuesday, 14 April 1970, they lashed the *Varius* to the side of the pontoon and sailed in triumph across the sound, through the narrows and into Stanley harbour. It was a journey that most people had never expected would take place. As the *Great Britain* came in, riding high on her pontoon, surrounded by a bevy of little boats, almost the entire population turned out to greet her. Every car sounded its horn and the church bells rang. No one who was present will ever forget it.

On the way over, the eternal wind of the Falkland Islands had been rising again. And as soon as the pontoon and tug had dropped anchor a fierce mixture of hail and snow drove down with the force of a full gale. If there had been a moment of euphoria before, it now had to be put behind them. The two vessels began swinging about through 180 degrees and it seemed for a while as if they must be driven ashore. The high wind continued all that night, and an anxious night it was. Captain Herzog remained on watch till dawn and was on duty when the anchors started dragging. As daylight broke he had just concluded that he ought to up anchor and move to the outer harbour of Port William, when the wind moderated. By the afternoon the decision had been taken, however, to take the *Mulus* alongside the Falkland Islands Company's jetty and to tie up there, even though it meant paying the daily rate of £50. And so it was here that for the next ten days they all remained, while vital further work was done to prepare the *Great Britain* and the pontoon for their long ocean tow to England.

In order to secure the ship more tightly to the pontoon more upright steel supports, the dolphins, were welded to the deck, more big metal wedges were driven in between the deck and the hull and, finally, a number of massive chains were used to tie her down. Several special holes unfortunately had to be cut in the old iron platework of the *Great Britain* to allow these to be fastened at the top and inside the ship to the upper 'tween deck stringers; at the bottom they were shackled to lugs on the pontoon. Their purpose was to prevent the hull rocking between its supports – and they were very effective.

During this period the ceremony of formally handing the *Great Britain* over to the Project was performed by the Governor. Standing on the deck of the pontoon in the shadow of the ship, Sir Cosmo Haskard made a short speech congratulating everyone on all that had been accomplished and then gave to Lord Strathcona, as the Project's representative, the famous release document, on which the Governor had now been able to add his own signature to those of Eric Custance and myself, and for which I had worked so hard. A number of objects which had been on the *Great Britain* when she originally arrived in Stanley in 1886 were also presented to the Project, among them the ship's barometer given by Mrs Madge Biggs – a most treasured gift, which is now on show in Bristol.

By 24 April the days of wedging, fastening, and generally cleaning up were over. All was ready. At nine o'clock that morning the lines were cast off and the *Varius* began to tow the *Mulus* out of harbour through the narrows and down towards the sea. Watched by a fascinated crowd the long tow home had at last begun.

Escorts were provided by the Royal Marines' hovercraft and a Beaver aircraft which circled overhead. The launches *Lively* and *Cleo* and two of the tugs which had fussed round the ship when she came in now did their best to see her out. And it all seemed a lifetime since the tug and empty pontoon had first arrived only just over a month before to tackle the unknowns of the great salvage adventure. And, brilliantly successful though the whole rescue expedition had proved to be, this departure held a touch of sadness too. Something of the Falklands' own most intimate background was passing slowly into history.

As the speed of the *Varius* and the *Mulus* in tow was only between 5 and 6 knots, it took them a couple of hours to get all the way down the sound to the open Atlantic.

'The wind was quite fresh and cold,' Strathcona later noted, 'and we cleared the lighthouse at about eleven o'clock.'

By nightfall, as they ploughed on with the north coast of East Falkland dropping astern, the wind increased, but not dramatically, rising eventually to force 8. Everyone had been very relieved to get away and to make a start on what was a fairly unknown prospect, even though there was a good deal of well-founded optimism about it. How well would the pontoon, with the high bulk of the *Great Britain* on top of it, ride a really rough sea? The ship was not in herself too heavy for the design of the pontoon. But she was so large that she overhung each end by several feet and so high that she presented a large aerodynamic surface to the wind. She was also – intentionally – not on the pontoon straight; because of the fixed winch housing on the pontoon's port bow she had had to be placed at a slight angle, rather like the flying off deck of a modern aircraft carrier. As it turned out, by pure chance this angling was a great help in reducing sideways roll, since the pontoon tended to dip a corner in a cross-sea and this gave the *Great Britain* herself more of a fore and aft movement.

By nature one has to be fairly phlegmatic in the salvage business, and when he got back to England Leslie O'Neil summed up the position that first night for me with the words:

'As darkness fell we hoped for the best. There was quite a sea running and it was a fair test to get straight into. If anything had gone wrong at that point, there was not much we could have done about it anyway. When dawn came and I looked back and saw that she was still there, I knew we would be all right.'

As events turned out, the *Great Britain* had indeed slipped out between storms. It was already late in the season to be covering this first thousand miles of dangerous water with the best chances of success. Nor had there been much scope for postponing the little flotilla's departure by more than a day or so, if the immediate forecast had looked particularly bad, since everyone was extremely keen to get going and every delay made the season later. But the fact was that we were lucky. That first wind was the strongest they met.

After four days it had died away to an almost complete calm. So the *Varius* was stopped and a little motorboat was launched and a party went across to the pontoon to have a good look round. They checked on everything and found that nothing had moved. It was clear that the pontoon would get the *Great Britain* home. Four days later, after a much better trip than on the way down, they reached Montevideo. Their average speed had been 5·3 knots. It was 2 May 1970.

By now the world's press was alerted to what was going on and a flock of journalists descended on the quayside. They were surprised not only by what had been achieved already, but by the businesslike confidence about the rest of the 6,000-mile voyage. It so happened that the *Darwin* got in a day before the *Varius*, and Kaulen and Sutcliffe had travelled on her. Thus, it was here in Montevideo that the party as a whole split up. They, like Strathcona, O'Neil and the British salvage team, flew on to Europe. This left Captain Herzog and his own original crew in sole charge of their unique prize for the rest of the journey.

Before they set out again on 6 May, however, several things were done to the ship and pontoon. And by a remarkable combination of luck and skilful planning it was possible during the four days in port for Ewan Corlett himself to oversee them. He had been able to time a business trip of his own to Chile, so that he flew in from Santiago just as the flotilla arrived. It can be imagined what a moving moment this was for him – on whose professional interest, judgement and assessment of risks the whole great enterprise had been based. As he put it, however, in as matter of fact a way as possible:

'During the time in Montevideo some further cleaning was carried out and more cradles and lashings applied to hold the ship in position.'

Corlett's own visit nevertheless came near to ending in tragedy. Naturally determined in the circumstances to carry on, he ignored a fever which he already had on his arrival from Santiago. When he was flying back to resume his affairs there, he was taken ill at Buenos Aires with a very high temperature and was rushed to hospital, where he was lucky and in due course recovered completely.

When Captain Herzog sailed from Montevideo on 6 May, he made good progress up the South American coast. The weather was fine and all went well. By 14 May they were passing Rio de Janeiro and on 21 May were off Recife in north-east Brazil, the take-off point for the northward crossing of the Atlantic. What passing vessels thought of this strange sight, the classic outline of a 3,000-ton ship without masts or funnel, moving slowly along above the level of the water, has not been recorded. From a certain distance she looked quite alone.

As for those of us at home in England, it was still hard to take in the full drama of this critical voyage, bringing, as it was doing, not only the reality of Brunel's historic hull closer and closer, but also a kind of Nemesis which day by day was bearing down on one's whole future. For once the *Great Britain* had arrived, it was no use thinking that that would be the end of the matter. In many ways it would prove to be only the beginning.

I received regular reports of the little flotilla's position from Crothall at Risdon Beazley in Southampton, and he usually had something also to say about the weather and the speed the *Varius* was making. I then plotted her course on a map and watched the line draw steadily closer to the United Kingdom. Romantically, we called this the completion of 'Voyage 47', the official description given in the *Great Britain*'s log of the voyage she originally started from Penarth in South Wales on 6 February 1886 and never finished. Much later on, in fact several years afterwards, Ewan Corlett was to publish his calculation that on that first leg of the voyage in 1886 the ship only averaged 4·5 knots down to the Falklands, whereas coming back on the pontoon, slow though it was, the overall average speed ended by being 5·3 knots.

The *Varius* crossed the Equator at noon on 26 May not far from St Paul's Rocks. By 1 June she was nearing the Cape Verde Islands and making 5·85 knots with a favourable current. The weather, however, then deteriorated and Captain Herzog told me afterwards that the worst of the whole trip was off the Canary Islands, when for four days they made little headway at all. It was depressing and uncomfortable. But no damage was done, and by 14 June they were forging ahead again past Madeira. On 18 June – the day of the general election in Britain – they were level with Cape Finisterre on the coast of Spain and were truly in European waters at last. An epic voyage was nearing its end.

A normal activity of the Royal Air Force is to use vessels approaching the British Isles as practice missions for training crews to find small objectives in the wide expanse of the ocean, and particularly small or unusual ones. It was as the *Varius* and *Great Britain* were entering the Bay of Biscay, therefore, that they were first picked up and circled by an RAF Nimrod aircraft. On board was a press photographer, and one of the pictures he took appeared across a half page of the *Daily Express* the following day. It was at once a splendid welcome and a curtain raiser to the scenes of arrival. But quite as striking was the characteristically pithy caption. It caught in four words the whole significance of the tremendous technical breakthrough which Brunel achieved with the *Great Britain*, as being the first vessel ever built with the basic characteristics of subsequent modern shipping. It ran:

'Grandmother of them all.'

1 Restoration was well under way by October 1973 when Terence Cuneo painted the *Great Britain* in drydock

2 This famous print by Fox Talbot, believed to be the first ever photograph of a ship, shows her being fitted out in 1844

3 Ready for sea – from a contemporary painting by J. Walter

4 A historically accurate impression of the original Brunel ship at sea – from a modern painting by Keith Griffin

5 As she looked later on during the Australian period

6 Beached in Sparrow Cove, the Falkland Islands, since 1937 – the photograph which inspired the author

7 Half way up, as the pontoon is refloated bow first

8 At sea on the pontoon during the 7000-mile ocean tow

9 Afloat on the Avon and coming up river under Brunel's Clifton Suspension Bridge

10 *(above)* Brunel's original drydock is ready. The side wall on the right shows the curve, designed to accommodate the rounded hull of the *Great Britain*

11 *(below)* Entering drydock at last – 9 pm, 19 July 1970

12 *(opposite page)* Some months after arrival

13 (above) Prince Philip, accompanied by the author, examines the state of the after hold on the ship's arrival. The sea came up to the cross beams

14 (opposite page above) By Prince Philip's third visit to the ship almost all the internal ironwork had been descaled, cleaned and painted

15 (opposite page below) The lower forecastle deck interior, cleaned and with new steel support. These were the crew's quarters

16 A contemporary impression of Brunel's original upper 'tween deck promenade (*Illustrated London News* of 15 February 1845)

17 The same deck today, seen from the opposite end. Full restoration is planned here

18 The author and Jack Hayward who put up the money for the ship's return. In the background the ship waits to be towed out of the ocean lock, Avonmouth

19 Talking to Prince Charles are the author, Dr Corlett, Lord Strathcona and Commander Blake – four leading members of the *Great Britain* Project

20 The state of the forecastle deck on arrival

21 The forecastle decked and the new bowsprit fitted

22 The massive stub of the 1857 mainmast being lowered onto the exhibition blocks in the dock. Note the four tree-trunks, squared off and bound together

23 Stern windows and decoration restored

24 *(above)* The Prince of Wales at the restored bow, October 1973

25 *(right)* An exact replica of the original six-bladed propeller

26 *(opposite page)* The beautifully rounded hull

27 The *Great Britain* as she is now with her upper sides painted and her funnel up, 1975/6

8. Run-up to Arrival

While the great events in Sparrow Cove had been taking place on the other side of the world, the three months between mid-March and mid-June of 1970 had been hectic ones in England. Anyone who has had experience of running anything, from a public company to a village fete, will know why. Anyone who has not will probably find this hard to understand. But the facts are that nothing can be arranged or done unless someone arranges or does it. Apart from accidents, nothing happens unless it is made to happen. And in our case almost every step had to be unusual, which on the whole makes people resist it more.

From my own point of view, my leading colleagues were away for a good part of the time (Corlett in South America, Strathcona in the Falklands) and I was still committed to business activities of my own which had nothing to do with the ship. In spite of Jack Hayward's generosity, we were still in practice operating a fairly major undertaking on a shoestring with no reserves, and in the certainty that from the moment the ship arrived we would have to start spending money which we did not yet have. Behind the dramatic image of Brunel's returning ship, therefore, lay some bottomless anxieties.

To get the 3,000-ton *Great Britain* from sailing the seas, high on her pontoon, to being safely ensconced in her drydock six miles up the River Avon in Bristol City Docks involved a number of very tricky developments. And I was determined that, so far as was humanly possible, nothing should go wrong. The first problem was to decide on the precise steps to be taken on arrival at Avonmouth, both for floating the *Great Britain* off the pontoon and then for towing her up the river afloat on her own bottom. The pontoon itself was too big to go up the Avon, quite apart from the difficulty of de-pontooning within the shallow and limited confines of the old City Docks area. And the nature of this problem was at once political as well as purely technical, since obviously everything now had to be done with the concurrence of the Bristol authorities.

Accordingly, I opened the bowling on 18 March with a long letter to the Leader of the Bristol City Council, giving him the latest news about our position and what we hoped to do. The contents included an outline of the programme envisaged in the Falklands, an estimate of the probable period of arrival at Avonmouth, an assessment of the likely requirements at the drydock, such as car parking facilities, and an enquiry as to whether anything further had arisen which would influence the long-term, but by now increasingly tangible, question of a permanent site for the *Great Britain* in Bristol. I also said that I hoped we might have an opportunity of meeting at an early date to go into these and any other points which might arise. Unfortunately, no reply was ever received, so that we had to proceed without the sort of clarification which could have been valuable.

At the same time, however, we had approached the Port of Bristol Authority (PBA) direct, since they were responsible for the disposition of shipping in Avonmouth and the City Docks, as well as movement on the six miles of the River Avon which connected the two. It was soon clear not only that they were glad to hear from us, but that they themselves had already done a certain amount of thinking about the several special problems inevitably presented by the *Great Britain*'s potential arrival. The result was a meeting at the Authority's offices in Queen Square on 3 April 1970, at which Councillor Edward Wright, who was then chairman, presided.

We on our side were at first dismayed by the Authority's initial reactions. Nevertheless, this was a pleasant meeting and one of the most productive we ever had with any part of the city administration. With me were Ewan Corlett and Robert Adley. Across and around the table were a considerable number of people, including members of the PBA Board, port officials, and representatives of the Bristol pilots and tug companies. Perhaps the leading expert witness, as it were, was the Havenmaster at Avonmouth, Captain R. A. Gibbons.

Although the authorities had more or less made up their minds on several points, they listened to our account of current developments in the Falklands with pin-dropping interest. At this moment, it will be recalled, work on the *Great Britain* had been proceeding in Sparrow Cove for over a week with heartening success, and the expedition was within four days of the vessel's first flotation. As Corlett completed his account of these operations, and outlined the technical procedure for getting the ship off the pontoon on arrival, however, Ted Wright indicated that the authorities had three stipulations to make.

'First of all,' they said, 'we must have a really thorough survey made of the hull of the *Great Britain* before we can agree to letting her be towed up the Avon. It would probably take about a week. And the pontoon must stay in Avonmouth until the survey has been completed.'

While one appreciated their concern, the assumptions on which this demand appeared to be made came as a shock. It reflected an entire lack of confidence in our own existing surveys, which were not even referred to. It suggested that, if the result of the new survey was unsatisfactory (though by what standard?) the ship might have to abandon the idea of coming up to Bristol altogether. For us it presented at the very least the prospect of extending our charter of the tug and pontoon, which meant an extra bill of over £800 a day. And, of course, to have to remove the *Great Britain* from Avonmouth altogether and find another port at short notice could prove nothing short of a total financial disaster.

So we fought this stipulation in its original form tooth and nail. Ewan Corlett suggested that, if an exhaustive survey of this kind had to be made, it would be perfectly practicable for surveyors to be taken out to meet the little flotilla while still at sea, and to begin their work on the pontoon before reaching port.

'In any event,' he added, 'two or three days at most should be quite enough for such a survey.'

After some further discussion we gained most of our point, not that surveyors should fly out to meet the ship, but that more expeditious survey arrangements could be made in Avonmouth, and that they would be completed before the pontoon was released under our basic programme. We then came to the second stipulation.

'You must,' they said, 'take out an insurance policy for a million pounds to cover any damage or blockage to the ocean lock at Avonmouth or any part of the inner port.'

Back in 1970 a million pounds was a very large sum and we genuinely felt that it was higher than seemed reasonable. Even if the *Great Britain* had sunk in the ocean lock, it was difficult to see how her removal could cost more than, say, £100,000 – granted, that is, that she could be destroyed in the process. The Authority's view, however, was that there might be considerable claims against them for any period of time in which the lock was unserviceable to other shipping. We suggested that, if they felt as strongly as this, they might themselves take out some additional insurance policy or perhaps contribute towards the premium. The fact of their participation could well lower the premium itself. But they only replied that it was our problem and that we must face it.

'Thirdly,' they added, going on to their last stipulation, 'the *Great Britain* can only come up the Avon on a full spring tide – that is, either on 20 June or, if she can't catch that one, not until the next one on 19 July, or a month later.'

Although this raised the fairly nightmare hazard of what to do with the *Great Britain* for perhaps a month if she just missed the tide, it was so much more disputable that we took it more easily. Clearly the pilots had started by being extremely cautious, and we felt at once that nearer the time we could persuade them to relax a bit. Corlett successfully began the process straightaway.

The problem of where to hold the *Great Britain*, if she had to wait for even a few days once she was off the pontoon, was a real one. She would have to be kept afloat and at moorings where the least inconvenience and cost would be incurred if anything did go wrong and she were to sink. In view of the firm, if realistic, attitude adopted by the Port of Bristol Authority, this problem of a waiting period brought up in any case the whole question of where the *Great Britain* would best be taken off the pontoon. We were discussing doing it at Avonmouth, but there was no overriding reason why it should not take place at some quiet spot out in the Bristol Channel, once a suitable depth of water had been selected. Alternatively, we could use some other near-by harbour, for instance, in South Wales. The ship could then be towed to the mouth of the River Avon (which lies beside, not in, the port of Avonmouth) and up the river at the appropriate moment.

All this was for the future, however, and I did indeed spend a good deal of time going into it during the next few weeks. That afternoon at Queen Square, as we all left the meeting, I knew that we had established a viable working relationship with the authorities immediately concerned. And Ted Wright and I shook hands on a basis of mutual confidence, which I felt remained unshaken all through the hard times that followed in later years.

As to the three stipulations themselves, we ended by getting over them all successfully. When it came to the point, the survey of the ship was carried out in Avonmouth, while she was still on the pontoon, by the local Lloyd's surveyor, Jim Goodier, and he proved to be as sympathetic as he was effective. There was no hold-up at all, and he became one of the firmest friends the Project ever had, joining with Ewan Corlett and myself in due course as the triumvirate who constituted our so-called 'Ship Committee', which in effect decided each step of the restoration from 1970 to 1975.

Although the question of insurance ended well, it at first took an even worse turn than originally expected. I went to the market and secured a very reasonable quotation for the million pounds cover. But when I reported back to the PBA, they immediately said that a second insurance for another separate million pounds would have to be taken out to cover the passage up the river. The way this was done made me suspect that they were surprised at our success and accordingly had raised their price. But the ship proved to have good friends at Lloyd's, and insurance cover for two million pounds was duly secured for a few hundred pounds.

The pilots, too, soon ranged themselves among our warmest supporters. Once they had become more familiar with the actual issues involved, they relented to the extent that they brought the ship up the Avon on a half spring tide. And they gave their services free.

A week after the Queen Square meeting our Project Steering Committee held one of its own most significant sessions. This took place at Robert Adley's home in Sunningdale and it was the moment when we laid all our main plans for the ship's arrival two months later. We were elated to have heard, after all, that the *Great Britain* had been successfully floated a couple of days before. The key questions were where to get the ship off the pontoon, the timing and towing arrangements for the passage of the Avon, and the preparation of Charles Hill's drydock to receive not only the *Great Britain* but the flow of public visitors afterwards. I was always determined that we should admit them at the earliest possible moment, both because that was part of what we were in business to do, and because there would not be much of the summer season left anyway in which to begin earning some much-needed money.

If the *Great Britain* was to be floated off her pontoon at Avonmouth, the best place to do it was in the graving dock there, since this would allow precise control of the water levels. So we decided on three courses of action, which I was to implement. I would check with the harbour authorities whether a provisional booking could be made for the middle of June;

although Charles Hill's associate company, Jefferies, actually operated the large Avonmouth drydock, we had been told that in the unusual circumstances we would need to book a place in the queue through official channels. With the authorities I would at the same time go into the various possibilities of a site within the docks, where the ship could wait for a suitable tide. And meanwhile, we were all agreed, we would examine the pros and cons of using a Welsh port for de-pontooning up to as far west as Milford Haven. During the next three weeks I took action in all these respects, including an interesting visit to the Harbourmaster at Newport, Captain Boyd.

The difficulty for the authorities in Avonmouth was that, understandably enough, they could not really make up their minds whether they were going to be dealing with a floating sieve or a normal ship. And nor, to be absolutely honest, could I. We all veered from one concept to the other. And when it came to discussing a suitable place to park the *Great Britain* in this busy commercial docks where she might, by definition, sink at her moorings, I could sense them blanch at the very idea.

The booking of the graving dock was accepted in principle, though it had to be understood that, even if the *Great Britain*'s pontoon arrived approximately on schedule – and it was still far too early to be at all certain about that – she would have to stand aside if any emergency use of the dry dock were required. That being agreed to, I discussed with the Dock Master, Captain L. V. Seymour, the question of a site, where the ship could float and so far as possible be both out of the way of other shipping and least liable to damage from other vessels. After a good deal of thought he offered me a position at the farthest, or eastern, end of the basin known as Avonmouth Dock proper, on the north side of the two dolphins in the centre of the waterway, with the stern of the *Great Britain* tied up alongside the short jetty. We went along together to have a look at it and I accepted his offer, if the requirement should arise – which also was by no means certain.

Although there was now a provisional programme covering Avonmouth, the possible costs, delays, risks and need for insurance cover meant that it was by no means ideal. This was not anybody's fault, but was inherent in the fact that Avonmouth is an active and thriving commercial gateway to the West of England and the Midlands. We therefore felt it only wise to continue with our search for a possibly cheaper and quieter arrangement on the Welsh coast. As we suspected, however, the moment we started our enquiries this fact rapidly got back to Bristol. And there it had a somewhat double-edged effect. On the one hand, there was mild relief that Avon-mouth might not after all have to cope with this very questionable vessel. But on the other, owing to traditional rivalries, a sense of indignation also emerged at the thought that – once again – the Welsh might be out to steal some of Bristol's thunder. The net result was perhaps more helpful to the *Great Britain* than otherwise.

Before leaving for South America, Ewan Corlett had briefed us about the minimal technical requirements for depontooning, and, while Maldwin Drummond looked into certain possibilities farther along the Welsh coast, it was the end of April before I could get over to Newport in Monmouth-shire. As the nearest potential Welsh port, I took the enquiry there very seriously. When I met the Harbourmaster, he was not keen on our pro-position, but consented nevertheless to go into it with care and in detail. The upshot was that we agreed that there was no reason why the *Great Britain* should not be got off her pontoon in Newport South Dock. The water levels seemed right and there was room. It was also a quiet enough spot for her subsequently to ride at anchor. But what put me off was the problem of the tides for the return journey. It soon emerged that the *Great Britain* could not clear Newport, cross the open water of the Bristol Channel, and proceed up the Avon, without waiting in the Channel from one high tide to the next. This immediately raised additional hazards, not least the weather, and the more I thought about them, the less I liked them. Thus, the die was in fact cast for Avonmouth.

There was not much we could do ahead of time about the passage up the Avon, except – as we did – to get the pilots to agree that a full spring tide was not necessary. The *Great Britain* is as large as any ship which has normally used the river, but her length does not exceed the regulations. The problem was that she could not steer herself, and the job would have to be done by a special tug at her stern. With the bends in the narrow river, even at high tide this was bound to leave no room for error. When I went and saw Richard Hill to discuss the mutual arrangements for our use of his drydock once the ship was there, we began by talking about the passage up the river.

'There have always seemed to me,' he said, 'three stages in the recovery of the *Great Britain*, each with its own special risks – the salvage, the ocean tow, and the passage up the river. And I'm not sure that the third isn't the greatest.'

Then, as I let this ominous view sink in, he added, 'Come.' And he led the way up to the boardroom, where a large framed photograph on the wall showed a German ship, the *Kron Prinz*, which had struck the bank at the Horseshoe Bend in 1874 and turned over on her side as the tide ran out. She was refloated and repaired by Charles Hill and Sons. I learned later what an extraordinary number of vessels have been stranded in the Avon mud over the past hundred years – and when you look at this treacherous little river at low tide you can see why. In the photograph one of the group seen standing on the ship's side was William Patterson's son, and it is an interesting coincidence that Charles Hill and Sons was formed as a company, changing the name from that of their predecessors, Hillhouse and Hill, in 1845, the very year of the *Great Britain*'s maiden voyage. William Patterson, building Brunel's ship on their doorstep, was Charles Hill's great rival.

The man with whom lay the final decision about whether or not the *Great Britain* could enter the river at any given time was the Avonmouth Havenmaster, Captain Gibbons. And when it did finally come to the point in July a very tricky time of it he had. But in these preliminary days I also saw him a good deal about our other problems too. He was always very interested in our whole enterprise. However, I realized that a turning point had been reached one day when I came into his office down on the south pier of the ocean lock and he produced a map, on which he, like me, had been marking the course and progress of the *Varius* and pontoon as the news of their Atlantic voyage came in. Thereafter, I knew that he was on our side.

Amid all these absorbing preparations for the physical reception of the *Great Britain*, I could never afford to forget the other side of our own particular coin. Here some of the Project's other problems were in their way equally pressing and urgent. First, we simply had to raise more money. Secondly, after the near fiasco of the release contract and with our approaching obligations in Bristol, I saw that we must also become either a trust or an incorporated charity company at the earliest possible moment, in order to have a legal identity. Thirdly, to run the drydock and the ship once she had arrived at Charles Hill's yard, we would have to find, recruit and employ a permanent staff, headed by a responsible and suitable person; he would also have to be capable of overseeing the executive side of the restoration. The drydock itself would have to be equipped to deal with the entry of the public, and in such a way that it complied with all the local bye-laws and regulations, in particular about safety, sanitation and fire – quite a performance. In addition, at the crucial moment shortly after the actual arrival in Avonmouth I and my colleagues hoped that Prince Philip might be able to visit us and see the ship while she was still on the pontoon – an honour which I knew would require very detailed arrangements to be made.

During this busy period in Bristol, I was also active in London. Besides starting negotiations with our solicitors about forming a charity company, I was at that time in contact with Anthony Wedgwood Benn's Ministry of Technology in Millbank Tower about a scheme they had for starting an engineering exhibition centre on the *Great Britain*, once restoration had made a little progress. The advantage for us would be that the Ministry would finance restoration of that part of the ship which was involved with the exhibition. The scheme came to nothing, however, when the Labour government lost office in June.

In this general situation of heavy pressure on one's time something of a breakthrough suddenly came about from an unexpected direction. Before Euan Strathcona had left for the Falklands in March he had suggested that his wife might temporarily take his place on the Project committee, and we had all agreed. Known to everyone as Jinny, Lady Strathcona simply put a bomb under us – so that I came to understand something of what it must have been like working with Florence Nightingale. She took a direct hand in three of our problems and none of them ever looked the same again. With her insistent help, Drummond and I managed to put our fund-raising on to an entirely new basis. She revolutionized the position at the drydock itself and made it possible to open the gates to the public on time. And together with Euan she subsequently found and indoctrinated the man who was to take charge of the *Great Britain* during restoration – Commander Joe Blake. It was a formidable achievement.

What we did about fund-raising was to put ourselves at last into the hands of a fund-raising organization; Hereward Phillips was by this time committed to a new venture of his own. When Jinny Strathcona and Maldwin Drummond came to my home in Hampshire and, together with my wife, we all thrashed out the problem, it became evident that we had no alternative but to give this method a trial. Its supreme disadvantage is its cost, since the pattern is that these firms charge a fee which is not linked to any sum of money raised. But when we went the next day in London to see the one with which I had already opened discussions a year earlier, we felt that, unless we did break into new ground, we would never be able to launch the restoration programme successfully. And that was now a reality which was almost upon us. The exercise was for a trial period, as is usually the case, and, although we never achieved any long-term solution, we made critical progress that would not have been made otherwise. Above all, we learned some invaluable lessons.

The problem at the Great Western Dock, where the *Great Britain* was to be opened to the public, was that it had to be converted from a working part of Charles Hill's shipyard into a self-contained tourist and educational centre, while at the same time continuing to remain part of the shipyard for the purpose of work on the ship herself. Charles Hill were extremely generous in handing over to us office and warehouse space, but the lavatory facilities, for instance, were naturally inadequate to meet the official requirements for premises open to the public. The only pedestrian access, which lay along the harbour towpath, had no workable entrance. Considerable safety precautions in the form of chain-link fencing would need to be put up to prevent the danger of children falling into the dock, not to mention breaking their necks crossing the caisson. Telephones had to be installed in order to operate the office, including an internal link with the pay kiosk. There were of course no desks, chairs, filing cabinets, or safe for cash. Additional fire precautions to those for the ordinary shipyard had to be taken. And by no means least, some form of car park had to be found in what was a peculiarly intractable dockland area.

It is the fashion nowadays to see that everyone is more equal than everyone else, and no doubt that is all as it should be. But one of the factors that Jinny Strathcona brought to bear, when battering her way through the fearful problems which all this presented, was the confidence born of being the daughter of a twelfth earl. Allied with her own know-how and the consciousness which pervaded us all at that time that, although no proper start could be made until early May when the *Great Britain* had actually been salvaged, everything simply had to be ready by the expected docking in July, she achieved the impossible. Whatever some people may have thought afterwards, they found themselves doing things which they never expected to do in the time. By the skin of our teeth the essentials were just completed when the moment came.

On Friday 29 May at 11 o'clock there took place in the Council House the second of our formal meetings with the Bristol authorities. It was strictly a nuts and bolts affair, with Gervas Walker in the chair, in order to reach a number of decisions about such questions as public admission – or non-admission – to the docks when the ship came in, and traffic control when she came up the Avon. Although it might have been an opportunity to bring into better focus some of the wider long-term aspects of our presence, which had by now to be assumed to be inevitable, nothing of this kind was discussed at all. Our side consisted of Euan and Jinny Strathcona, Fitz Lombard and myself. And while everything within the limitations went off well, I was sorry that the high spot could only be the helpfulness of the police, once they had learned from us what the probable course of events would be.

There were also, of course, a multitude of more technical problems to be taken care of, and, although everything worked out all right, most of them had to be dealt with without Ewan Corlett's help, since it was several weeks before he got back from South America, owing to the severity of his illness and the need to recuperate afterwards. This he did in the Canaries, where his wife flew out to meet him, and they were both in Las Palmas when the *Great Britain* was passing somewhere beyond the horizon. Leslie O'Neil was able to visit Bristol on one occasion and liaison was established between Risdon Beazley and Charles Hill. Fitz Lombard was in Bristol a good deal, though this had to be somewhat limited owing to the cost; for a period the Strathconas lent him a flat in the house they had at that time in Bath. I was able to drive over from Hampshire.

Among the questions I reviewed with Alec Foulds, the managing director at Charles Hill, and his number two, Alastair Peck, who was in charge of the actual drydocking, were such aspects as the state of the tides, the depths required, the personnel needed, the control of the access to the drydock from the rest of the yard, the methods of accounting for what would be done, the channels of communication and instruction, and the appointment of our own staff. To cover the detailed administration of the arrival at Avonmouth – including port dues for both ship and pontoon, and so on – I was advised that we would need the normal services of a shipping agent, and so I appointed the Bristol City Line, an associate in the Charles Hill group, whose relevant executive was Mr C. R. F. (Chris) Verity. It seemed symbolic of the reincarnation of the old ship that her arrival in port should once again be handled professionally.

As to the *Great Britain*'s physical ability to get into the drydock at all – which for some months now we had decided to take as settled – the approach of the moment of truth naturally heightened one's sensibilities. After all, everything depended on it. And in view of subsequent events I have never quite been able to forget a conversation I had on 1 May with Alastair Peck. By that time, with the *Great Britain* safely on the pontoon and nearing Montevideo, final figures of presumed flotation depth and other data were becoming available to check with the earlier estimates.

'I am quite certain we can do it,' Alastair reiterated. 'But it will be a very tight fit indeed.' Then he added: 'But, of course, the last thing one wants is to have any press or television people present while we do it.'

In the event it was watched by eight million people partly on a live outside television broadcast, and the Duke of Edinburgh was actually on board for the entire operation!

It was during the early run-up period that I had begun to discuss, by letter and telephone, with Prince Philip's office the real possibility of His Royal Highness coming to see the ship soon after she arrived. Back in February I had been told that there was just a chance that he might be able to. But, of course, no one knew at that time when the moment of arrival would be, so a visit could not be planned and inserted into his extremely heavy programme, even if everyone had settled that it should be. It had therefore had to be left that, if he came, it would be a private occasion and would probably have to be on a Sunday when there might be a little more room for manoeuvre. One of the particular difficulties was that during part of July Prince Philip would be away in Canada with the Queen, and this was in any case one of the busiest periods in the year for him.

So we waited and kept in touch. I informed Buckingham Palace of the successful salvage when it had taken place, and as the *Great Britain* moved steadily north up the Atlantic I kept Rear Admiral Sir Christopher Bonham-Carter, Prince Philip's Treasurer, up to date with the news. On 5 June I was at last able to be specific about the expected time of arrival, as the tug and pontoon were by that time 'between the Cape Verde and Canary Islands'. I said that they should reach Avonmouth on 20 June, that the *Great Britain* should be towed up the Avon on 4 July, and that she should be drydocked in Charles Hill's yard on 19 July. And I suggested that Prince Philip might be most interested of all to see the ship before we had got her off the pontoon. In which case, Sunday 28 June, would appear to be the most suitable day, the visit taking place at Avonmouth.

Soon after this there was the delay due to the storm off the Canaries. But a few days later, on 19 June – the morning after the general election that put Edward Heath into Downing Street – just as I was preparing a fresh note with the now fairly definite estimated time of arrival (ETA) at Avonmouth as dawn on 23 June, my telephone rang. It was Major Randle Cooke, Prince Philip's Equerry. His news was splendid. The Duke of Edinburgh did expect to be able to come. And I was to make preliminary plans for his visit to Avonmouth during the late afternoon of 28 June. For the moment this was still confidential and I should speak only to the one or two people who at this stage 'need to know' – a regular expression on such occasions, with which I later came to be quite familiar. Apart from notifying any essential colleagues, I was instructed to make immediate contact with the Chief Constable of Bristol. I found him ready for me.

From there on in, we had a royal visit on our hands. It was an immensely exciting and gratifying development – even though it involved an enormous amount of extra work at a moment when there was no time for anything anyway.

Meanwhile, Nemesis on her pontoon was bowling across the Bay of Biscay, speeded by a following wind. By now there had been a good deal of publicity and many people all over the country were watching our progress. Both the *Daily Telegraph* and the *Daily Mirror* each put their final cachet on our adventure by using the *Great Britain* as the basis for their political cartoon just after the general election. In the *Daily Telegraph*, Keith Garland had shown ship and pontoon inexorably bearing down on a little Ted Heath figure in a rowing boat, desperately starting to ply his oars, loaded to the gunwales with awkward packages marked 'Tax cuts', 'Europe' and 'East of Suez' – words that already sound terribly dated. As Prime Minister, he later autographed the original for us.

The ploy of the moment, of course, was to go out and meet the *Great Britain* and to see this historic mission before it actually made landfall. At first this could only be done effectively by air, but then as the *Varius* neared Bishop Rock she was within range by sea. The Strathconas made what sounded like a hazardous flight in a friend's aeroplane from a French airfield to take pictures for the *Sunday Times*, but poor weather lost them the early edition. Risdon Beazley sent their little ship, the *Queen Mother*, to make contact with Captain Herzog and escort him up the north coast of Cornwall and Devon. Naval minesweepers on stand-by training and rescue patrol found themselves by guided chance in the path of the little flotilla at the right moment. And of course press, television, and others made various arrangements of their own.

For my part, I knew the critical moment was approaching when, having had a certain hand in creating all this fuss, I would actually set eyes on the *Great Britain* for the very first time myself. I had wondered not only where and when this would be, but what in the world I would really think of her when I saw her. No blind date has ever been more fascinating. Would it all be a ghastly disappointment? An acute embarrassment? Or a sense of elation? Or just a rather dead-pan feeling that perhaps we had made a bit of a mountain out of a molehill after all?

The time and place had in fact been resolved for my wife and myself when I had received a telephone call from the Bahamas on 16 June.

'Richard', Jack Hayward's cheery voice had come over the transatlantic cable, after I had given him the latest news of how things were going, 'could you charter an aircraft for me? We'll all be over in England by tomorrow night, and Jean and the children would like to fly out and see the *Great Britain* come in. Would you and Deenagh care to join us?'

So that was most happily agreed. He had, however, added a rider which was to complicate the arrangements considerably. He would – understandably enough, as he had put up the money for both – greatly like to try to get a photograph of the *Great Britain* passing Lundy Island. Unfortunately, this involved timing it all so that the ship and pontoon would be at the appropriate point in daylight. And with the following wind in the Bay of Biscay and beyond, Captain Herzog was beginning to get ahead of schedule, so that he looked like going by during the night of Sunday 21 June.

I kept in constant touch with Crothall at Risdon Beazley in Southampton and we passed instructions on to Herzog to slow down. For reasons best known to the gods of the sea, however, we received the impression that this was not altogether possible. We gathered that the ship was acting like a sail and the towline had to be kept taut. But I think Herzog's heart was not really in it. And, naturally his German crew were already counting the hours till they could get back to Hamburg. They had been away from home for several months longer than they had expected.

This question also rather confused the charter of the plane. When I rang round to try to arrange it, I could not at first be certain whether I wanted the aircraft for Sunday afternoon or Monday morning. And it was not until I spoke to a firm in Kent, which had a suitable twin-engined Dove, that I could find someone willing to do either at the last moment. Herzog was by now going so fast that he might even make Lundy by the Sunday evening.

In the event, we made the flight on the Monday morning – though some two hours later than planned. This was because the pilot had put down for fuel at Biggin Hill while on his way to us, and then, owing to the local air show, ground control had maddeningly not allowed him to leave again when he was ready. However Jack and Jean Hayward, together with two of their offspring, were eventually picked up at Hurn, near Bournemouth, and my wife and I at Lulsgate, the Bristol municipal airport, along with Derek Milward, a photographer for the Press Association. And we knew as we took off that the *Great Britain* had passed Lundy during the hours of darkness. The weather was in any case not propitious for good photography, with visibility gradually deteriorating and, as we flew out into the Bristol Channel, with a thin misty cloud cover coming down almost to the water. It became so poor in fact that, although I had received the latest position from Southampton while waiting for the plane, it looked for a few minutes as if we might have real difficulty in locating the convoy at all. We headed for Ilfracombe.

Then suddenly the mist thinned and someone shouted:

'There they are!'

We all looked down to port and I saw three specks through the haze. They were still too far away to be recognizable, but there was something about the relative positions of the second and third which suggested a towline. And so it was. The pilot swung the aircraft to the left and I watched over his shoulder as we dived towards them. As we got lower we shot over the little *Queen Mother*, which was dead ahead of the *Varius*. And then we were on them, first the tug and then the pontoon, *Mulus III*, with the *Great Britain* on top. We flew straight down at about two hundred feet, did a tight turn and came back from behind just off the water, passing them about a couple of hundred yards to our right. It was one of the most thrilling moments of my life.

Hardly more than a glance was required to dispel every doubt. As we came round again and again, I knew that everything had been worthwhile. The *Great Britain*, truncated though she was, looked every inch a ship. Brunel's lines were as splendid as one had always supposed them to be, with a peculiar blend of dignity and beauty that had only gained from the ravages of a century and a quarter. Nor was that all. What struck one instantly as well was the colouring. I had expected the ship to look rusty and old. But there was also a fresh light brown on the bow and on the upright dolphins of the pontoon from the waves and the wind during the long ocean tow. This created a kind of patina which enhanced the appearance of the ship in an extraordinary way. If this was the hull of the world's first propeller-driven ocean liner, it was also something which had a simple grandeur of its own.

As we twisted and climbed and roared up and down, Derek Milward was not alone in taking photographs and I suddenly realized that, if the process went on much longer, more than one of us was going to be sick. So a final picture was taken of Jack Hayward at the window of the plane; Milward pressed the button just as the ship flashed by. Then we turned for a last flight directly above the convoy and a little higher than we had been before. I remember looking down on the beaten old weatherdeck of the *Great Britain*, noticing again the remains of the little deck housing, the three hatches, the chains holding the ship to the pontoon, the windlass up forward, and the Uruguayan timber used as walkways in the Falklands by the salvage party. Now, too, for the last time, we were over the *Varius*, giving the impression of a more considerable vessel in her own right than I had expected, with her surprisingly light green foredeck vivid against the darkened sea. Then we were gone.

As we landed back at Lulsgate and said goodbye gratefully to the Haywards before their aircraft took off again for Hurn, there seemed – and was – nothing adequate to say. It was enough that I had seen the *Great Britain* at last. And all was well.

9. Home and Dry

From Lulsgate, after leaving my wife at the hotel, I drove down to Avonmouth where two of the divers, who had worked on the ship in Sparrow Cove, were waiting to get a lift with me round to Barry in South Wales. There we were all to meet O'Neil and go out with the pilots to greet the *Varius* as she came into Barry Roads, which is the arrival point from overseas owing to the bends in the coastline of the Bristol Channel. On the way across the Severn Bridge and down the M4 the divers gave me their own graphic version of the salvage. Nothing could have been more telling after the adventures of the morning.

By late afternoon it had become sunny and warm, with black clouds only in the distance. As the pilot cutter ploughed its way out to the distant rendezvous, all was calm and beautiful. After several miles we came up with the little convoy, went alongside the *Varius*, and climbed aboard. As I had observed from the air, this smart 700-ton ship was higher and bigger and altogether more of an ocean-going vessel than I had somehow imagined. When we stepped on deck we were welcomed by Captain Herzog, who I had never of course previously met, and most of his crew. Conversations were in a mixture of broken English and broken German, but as we shook hands all round everyone was obviously glad and happy to be where they were. Herzog himself I saw at once was more of a deep-sea trawler skipper than a man who would lose any sleep over shore signals about photography! All the same, I think he was quite relieved to see us and to know that he would soon be handing over his awkward load.

Up in the captain's chartroom behind the bridge, a vigorous discussion immediately began about the detailed plans for the night and the following morning between Herzog, the two pilots, O'Neil and myself. It had already been arranged that the *Varius* would drop the tow and hand over to Bristol tugs that very evening, and set course for Hamburg the moment she had done so. Meanwhile, as we all waited for the tugs to arrive, the *Varius* continued to keep the pontoon moving at slow speed and had pulled the tow line up fairly short so that the *Great Britain*'s bow, though by no means towering over us, was very close astern. No anchor would be dropped as it was felt safer to keep moving, like an aircraft stacked over an airport.

After some drinks and a good deal of Teutonic toasting, a quick tour of the ship and some busy photographing of the *Great Britain* and pontoon in the evening sunlight, we had to take our leave, since the pilot boat was required elsewhere. On behalf of the Project I thanked Captain Herzog as warmly as I knew how and followed one of the pilots down the rope ladder over the side. By that time two other little boats were circling the *Varius* and the pontoon, and, as we joined in to have a good look at the *Great Britain* from the pilot cutter, I saw to my astonishment that in one of them was Ewan Corlett. He had of course witnessed all this before, in Montevideo, but from that moment to this he had been abroad and we had none of us known the exact hour of his return. We waved and shouted mutual greetings, and then the cutter had to go back to Barry. I was extremely grateful to fate that I had just been able to have this quick visit to the *Varius*, which had played such a great part in our fortunes, as she did indeed hand over that night and sail for Germany, so that none of us saw her again.

The next morning, Tuesday 23 June 1970, the *Great Britain* came into Avonmouth. Although the decision had been taken to close the docks officially to the public, the surroundings of the ocean lock, through which every vessel has to enter and leave the docks, were swamped with sightseers by soon after breakfast. Press, television cameramen, radio reporters, Bristol officials, and most of our own Project group mingled with port workers, men from the crews of ships in the harbour, and what must have been quite an army of unauthorized visitors.

With Ewan Corlett and Jack Hayward I walked down past the meteorological and signal station on the south pier of the ocean lock. It was a gentle morning with a light wind and high overcast sky. Some way out still, the *Great Britain* and her pontoon were edging their way towards us between a number of small boats. And it was through field glasses that we suddenly made out the name of the little Bristol tug which, with the departure of the *Varius*, had been chosen to bring her in. It was the *Sea Challenge*.

There was immense interest among everyone present as tug and pontoon nudged the north pier of the lock entrance. As they touched, we felt that the *Great Britain* had completed at last the voyage she had begun in 1886, 'Voyage 47'. Then they came on forward into the lock, the gates were closed, and as the water levels were adjusted we all studied intently the state of the old plates, wondering at the massive wooden cladding bolted on to her sides in 1882, now perhaps the most dominant feature of the hull when seen from close to. Huge incrustations of mussels still clung to her lower sides and on parts of the cladding were traces of the muntz metal, a mixture of copper and zinc, with which this pitch pine timbering had originally been sheathed.

It was all an extraordinary sensation. And as the cameras whirred and the television reporters asked me their stock interview question, with the ship behind us, I found it as impossible to give a satisfactory answer as I have always noticed other people do, whether after a sporting event, a train crash, or winning the pools.

'Well, Mr Goold-Adams, how do you feel now?'

For us at that moment it was a mixture of thankfulness and triumph, but at the same time an abyss-like anxiety for the future which it was better not to face – as yet. And it was really better not to say so, too.

By this time the inner gates had been opened and the pontoon was almost through into the main Royal Edward Dock. Then suddenly I, and I think quite a few others, nearly jumped out of our skins. With a shattering roar every ship in the harbour let off its hooter and kept it up for an incredible minute or two. A tremendous, cascading jumble of noise, I never knew whether it was as premeditated as it seemed. But it gave the *Great Britain* the welcome she deserved, the miraculous home-coming of one of the greatest ships that ever sailed the seas. There were tears in a good many eyes.

My negotiations over the booking of the graving dock had ended by working out quite well. Although a ship was still in it, the pontoon could go in two days later. So for the first forty eight hours we tied up the pontoon at the North Wall of the oil jetty, and, when I came back in the afternoon, it was there that I first clambered aboard the *Great Britain* herself. To get there I had first had to pass the notice now pinned on the main gates of Avonmouth Docks, which ran:

SS GREAT BRITAIN
NO VISITORS

She might be an old ship, I reflected, but not quite the invalid that this implied. However, the police intention was legitimate enough and, although we wanted publicity for the sake of our funds, I knew we would get it as time went by – as we certainly did.

When Corlett arrived soon after I did, he warned me about the dangerous state of the deck. What I had not quite expected was the giddy sensation of height, as I climbed the immensely long ladder which had been lashed from the deck of the pontoon to the top of the ship's side throughout the voyage. Once on board I moved little and only with great circumspection.

I sat up there for a long time that afternoon in the hazy sunshine, and, as I drank it all in, three main thoughts came into my mind. The first was the quite extraordinary boldness and confidence of Brunel in putting untried screw propulsion into this huge new ship of his. For the *Great Britain*, the size of many a modern cross-channel steamer, was far larger than any vessel man had ever built before. And, as she was also of iron, not wood, no one at that time had had anything like the experience to know just how she would behave at sea. I marvelled at his decision, as I sensed the scale of his ship under my feet.

The second reflection was how in its own way the recent salvage itself had been an achievement of remarkable skill and courage. We had also had our full measure of luck in that no one had been seriously injured, or indeed killed. The men who pulled it off down there in Sparrow Cove near the Antarctic had inevitably taken risks, and in applying their modern technique had made it all sound like routine. But I knew that afternoon that it was no such thing. Their deeds would live for ever in the annals of the sea.

Lastly, in view of all this, I could not help but ponder on the folly of those who still did not want us to succeed. At first I had found their attitude quite simply unbelievable. But now I realized that, whatever their reasons, they really were genuine. Yet I also saw that in the end they could not win – though I was not to know at that moment what a long and stubborn fight was still to be fought.

Although at this time I was living at a hotel in Bristol, the day after the ship's arrival I had to go up to London on my own business. I also spent some time with our fund-raising consultants and part of the morning with Major Cooke at Buckingham Palace. Inevitably Prince Philip's visit on the coming Sunday was having to involve people such as the Lord Lieutenant and the Lord Mayor; but Major Cooke reassured me that the object of the exercise really was for Prince Philip simply to see the *Great Britain*. That night I caught the newspaper train back to Bristol, but the signal wires had been cut by vandals and I was even later than I might have been in the early hours of the morning.

Meanwhile, the pontoon had been put into the graving dock and settled on the special blocks prepared for it, most of the water in the dock having been drained out. Everyone was hard at work dismantling the fastenings which had held the *Great Britain* to the pontoon. This was a considerable task, for which O'Neil remained at hand and Horst Kaulen was flown over from Germany to assist. And, while Prince Philip would certainly be able to see the ship still on the pontoon, I began to feel happier that the job ought now to be successfully completed in time to catch the planned half-spring tide up the Avon on 4 July. It began to look as if in any case the *Great Britain* would not now need to hang about in Avonmouth for long, afloat – or not afloat – at her moorings.

Thus we came to the great day of the Duke of Edinburgh's visit. As it dawned, I little guessed how it was to end. He was to arrive at Filton by air and be met by the Lord Lieutenant, the Duke of Beaufort, at 6.45 p.m. With a police escort he was to arrive at the Havenmaster's office in Avon-mouth at 7.05 pm. After a certain amount of negotiation with the Bristol authorities, conducted through Jack Purchase, the Lord Mayor's Secretary, this little building, standing beside the ocean lock and near the graving dock, had been made available. There the Lord Mayor of Bristol, Alder-man Geoffrey Palmer, was to meet him, introduce about a dozen leading Council members and officials, and then hand over to me. I would intro-duce my colleagues, about half a dozen of us, including those closely associated with us, notably Jack Hayward and Richard Hill. Precisely a quarter of an hour was allowed for drinks upstairs, during which Ewan Corlett would point out on a plan of the ship some of the main features of interest. Then we would all walk over to the graving dock, Prince Philip would tour the ship – for which I had had special walkways constructed to be used later by the public – and leave by 8.40 pm for the royal train at Temple Meads station, to depart at once for Glasgow.

Although nothing was admitted, or indeed hardly said, about the long term future, the atmosphere in which this and other functions took place in the immediate period of the ship's arrival was pleasant enough all round. As one Bristol official put it to me some years later:

'We had no option. So we sank a quick gin and put on a grin . . . and that was it.'

When the City Council members and others had therefore assembled in the Havenmaster's outer office at 6.30 pm, there was an agreeable sense of anticipation on all sides. And it was only after a moment or two that I saw Captain Gibbons come in from his own office, catch my eye, and come straight over.

'I've just had a phone call,' he said in a low voice. 'Someone on the line who said he was the Duke of Beaufort rang through to say that Prince Philip has had an accident and will not be able to come.'

Gibbons and I looked at one another. The same thought appeared to be in both our minds.

'It may be a hoax,' I said.

'That's what I felt,' he replied. 'But I am not sure. What shall we do?'

'Ring back to Filton at once and check with the Duke of Beaufort personally.' And we both moved towards the door.

The Duke came on the line immediately. And, alas, it was all too true. Prince Philip had indeed been thrown from his horse that afternoon and, though not seriously injured, was receiving medical attention. It was out of the question that he could come to Bristol. The Duke then indicated that, in view of all the preparations that had been made, he felt it best if he himself carried through with the proceedings in place of Prince Philip. I gratefully agreed.

After Gibbons and I had gone back to the main room, I had a quick word with the Lord Mayor, then banged on a table with an ashtray and announced the sad news. People were stunned for a moment; then in the instant buzz of conversation which followed everyone agreed that we carry on as suggested. The Duke and Duchess of Beaufort were, of course, quite well known to most of those present and we all welcomed his gesture warmly.

After the Duke had been round the ship and we were walking back to his car, he told me that, when he had first heard that Prince Philip would spend an hour visiting the *Great Britain*, he had wondered how that amount of time could be filled in. Now, he said, he would report to him on the telephone and tell him that an hour was not enough. Our gallant ship had won another distinguished convert.

It was a sickening blow, nevertheless. And, in view of the immense trouble that had been taken to fit the visit into the Duke of Edinburgh's busy timetable, it naturally seemed that that inevitably was that.

'My heart bleeds for you,' one of the Prince's staff said to me on the telephone the following day. And we all slipped back into our stride, confronting, as we did, the challenge of getting the *Great Britain* off her pontoon and up the Avon without disaster.

Wednesday, 1 July, was the day for de-pontooning. After this had been done, Risdon Beazley would hand over technically to Charles Hill. Meanwhile the two men whose word was law were Leslie O'Neil and Jim Goodier, the Lloyd's Registry of Shipping surveyor. Goodier had already given the ship a clean bill of health, provided a large vertical steel plate was welded to the modern steel straps across the starboard crack, and this had now been done. It meant considerable additional strength for the river tow. Meanwhile, everything had been removed from the pontoon – dolphins, wedges, chains, plus the two masts which had lain on the deck – and the *Great Britain* simply rested on the blocks, waiting for enough water to float off. The great question was at what draught she would do so, in view of the tight fit anticipated at the sill of the drydock in Charles Hill's yard.

Around midday the water started to be let into the graving dock. It was a slow process, but one that we watched with a gradually mounting sense of tension and anticipation. New draught marks had been painted on the ship near the crack, as well as at the bow and stern. Besides the question of draught, I tended to feel irreverently, it would be amazing to see her float at all. Although she had done so twice on the other side of the world, this time our whole future depended on it. If there were any major mistake or delay, we would be in deep trouble – not least financially.

The water rose rather ominously higher and higher up the draught marks. It was just creeping past the figure of 11 feet, which had been the most optimistic guess, and we were all keyed up for a first almost imperceptible movement as the ship freed herself from the blocks, when I suddenly heard a rending sound and saw men running for cover. I was standing with one foot on the dock gate near the stern, and I could see a little way round to the port side as well as clear up the starboard side. The sound increased. There was a sort of groaning noise and a spurt of water to port. And the *Great Britain* began, not to rise from the pontoon, but to tip slowly over several degrees to starboard. As she did so, I saw a mooring cable on the port side sheer off – it was this danger which had sent the men running – and the steel strands of another were beginning to go one by one. What on earth had happened?

After another second or two it was obvious that it was not the ship but the pontoon which was tipping. I moved quickly across the top of the dock gate and saw a huge frothing of air, as it burst up from under the water on the port side of the pontoon, most of it being near the bow, but some beginning to be towards the stern as well. There was some shouting, the press photographers hurled themselves about with furious clicking, and then in an instant the whole proceeding seemed to come to a deathly halt, with the *Great Britain* leaning horribly over to her right and cascading bubbles continuing to pour from the by now uplifted port side of the pontoon. While it lasted, it was a terrifying experience. To have come so far and then to damage the ship unnecessarily – as it seemed might have happened – was appalling.

Unknown to O'Neil and Kaulen, what had happened was that air had been trapped in one of the compartments of the pontoon through the release valve sticking. Then, as the water rose, the pressure was such that it partially opened. Before it could do so, however, the excessive buoyancy of the air had lifted the port bow of the pontoon. As soon as the nature of the trouble became clear, we knew that nothing further would occur. But with others I immediately went round to the area of the ship's crack on the starboard side, and we shouted across to Goodier who had remained on board for the floating to see how the ship fared.

'Is she all right?'

'Yes,' he shouted, and added with British understatement: 'though it can't have done her any good!'

A diver went down to check the faulty air vent, and it took several hours to sort the whole thing out. But by nightfall the *Great Britain* was safely floating free and had been moved forward to the inner end of the big graving dock, with the pontoon afloat behind her. Goodier himself had naturally had a bit of a fright when the ship began to tilt, as he could not know what was happening and the groans from the old iron hull were considerable. Before I left Bristol for a two-night stay at home that evening, it was confirmed that, as the proposed tow up the river was now only just over two days off, the ship could stay afloat in the graving dock, till she began her momentous journey. I was relieved that no other moorings should be needed after all.

The first suitable tide was late on the Saturday afternoon, 4 July, a date and time we had had in mind for a month or more. Consequently it had received a certain amount of publicity and people began pouring in from far and wide. British Rail had even advertised a special train from Paddington which, so I understood, would be parked on the single track line on the south side of Avon Gorge.

For ourselves, this very exciting event had become complicated by what had developed into the tiresome timing of a celebration party, wished on the Project by some of my more exuberant colleagues. Originally planned to take place on a boat accompanying the *Great Britain* up the river – for which the port authorities had most kindly offered the use of their port tug, the *Cabot* – this had finally devolved into a large general party at the Grand Spa Hotel overlooking the gorge as the ship came through. (Excellent use was made of the *Cabot* in the end for entertaining the press and TV.) It was unthinkable that our ship's triumphant return should not be celebrated in some way, but, as I would really have to be there, and Corlett was determined to be on board the *Great Britain* herself, this was not the moment for it. At best, I might just be able to see the historic passage of the *Great Britain* out through the ocean lock, afloat now on her own bottom, before scrambling back to the hotel. The same applied to others. We also needed to be taking photographs for our records and for future fund-raising.

Fate, however, was yet to take a hand. The key question was the strength and direction of the wind. From the direction it was blowing that afternoon, if it exceeded Force 4 the tow up the river would have to be postponed. The decision lay with Captain Gibbons; and Corlett was down at Avonmouth with him. The wind in fact was marginal, basically not more than Force 4, but gusting at times to 5 and 6. The decision was a very difficult one, as the forecast suggested that it might drop towards evening. And of course a cancellation, besides being a great disappointment to the crowds collecting along the banks of the Avon, would involve the considerable extra expense of reassembling everyone for this unique job on the Sunday morning, particularly the special crew for the ship. A final decision was held back to the last possible moment. But then, dramatically, the word came through. It had to be – No. The gusts were too strong. Another attempt would be made the following morning.

Our party, though superficially a great success, was in fact somewhat ill-starred from the start – quite apart from people not seeing the ship go by. We had invited all the Bristol dignitaries that we could and some of them came. None, I think, of the city's leading business people accepted. But a wide range of our own friends, helpers and supporters from all over the country made incredible efforts to get there. The fact was that the complexities of local politics were already overshadowing our freedom of action. And in these ticklish circumstances, although I felt that something really had to be said on an occasion like this by way of thanks to those who had made the Project possible, and I leant over backwards to avoid contention, I was told later – by one of those whom it suited to say so – that my speech was a disaster. It seemed that, in spite of being well applauded at the time, my attempt to beat the Project's drum inevitably bore the possible interpretation of being a slight to Bristol. I can well believe that we would have done better not to hold this particular party at all – even though no costs fell on our charity funds and a good many people had wanted it to happen.

The one bright spot was that my wife and I had hired buses to take anybody to Avonmouth who wanted to go down after the party to see the ship. We had arranged this as a long-stop, in case the river tow was cancelled – as it was. So, when everyone had eaten, we piled in and drove to the graving dock. When we got there a few of the bolder spirits climbed the long steep ladder up to the weatherdeck, only to be followed after a brief hesitation by most of the rest. I think that one of my own worst moments in the whole *Great Britain* saga was when I suddenly realized that it was so late that everyone would have to climb down again in semi-darkness, including the ladies in long dresses, one at least of whom was nearly seventy. Fortunately their euphoria carried them through.

There remained the realities of the hazardous tow the next morning. All that night the wind blew, and I listened to it sighing in the partly bricked-up chimney of my hotel bedroom. But towards dawn conditions seemed a bit better, and at about 6 am I had a telephone message that the ship would probably go. I rang through to Jack and Jean Hayward who were also in the hotel, dressed hastily, and in two cars we drove straight to the Havenmaster's office. Ewan Corlett was already there in consultation with the pilots and Captain Gibbons. It was only gradually that a few more people turned up. The wind was still worrying; but, as Gibbons said afterwards, he saw only too clearly that with every hour of extra delay the disadvantages of hanging on were increasing. For one thing, the *Great Britain* could not stay on any longer in the graving dock, since this was wanted for another ship. For another, the special crew signed up to handle the ropes and man the ship during the tow would have to stand down and another be produced. And since the two tug companies, King's tugs and Rea's tugs, as well as the Bristol Channel Pilots Company, had given their services free, it would also be a question for them how they would allocate their duties on a later occasion. Moreover, compared with the previous evening, the wind was gusting less.

So we went.

There was one moment of drama, and from the shore we could not quite see what had happened, though it was obvious that something had gone wrong. This took place when the *Great Britain* was out in the open water at the entrance to the mouth of the river. Very slowly and carefully, accompanied by three tugs, she had made the passage of the critical ocean lock, afloat now on her own bottom and a ship once more in her own element, compared with the strange, though moving, ride high on the pontoon twelve long days before. Our one million pounds of insurance was in operation, but was never at risk. Then, to the further whirring of TV cameras and the clicks of umpteen photographers' shutters, she had been towed – almost incredibly, as it seemed – smartly out to sea.

While I wanted to get my own photographic coverage from the shore, Corlett had always intended to travel on the ship, the last voyage, as he felt, of Brunel's *Great Britain*. And the incident, as he later reported it, gave immediate, though fortunately brief, cause for anxiety on board. A fair wind was blowing. And just after they were committed in their approach to the narrow tidal entrance to the Avon, one of the tugs had to manoeuvre across the bow of the ship to pull her head clear of the 'rip-rap at the foot of the jetty'. As it did so the main hawser snapped, caught, it seems, on the sharp stem of the ship herself. If another had similarly gone, they would have been in serious trouble. But it held. And after a minute or two the situation was brought back under control.

After that, the whole journey right up to Y wharf in the City Docks, lasting about four hours, went without a hitch. Although it was still at first quite early on a Sunday morning, and in spite of a slight sense of anti-climax after the false start of the night before, thousands of sightseers began lining the banks of the river. Some had slept in their cars. Traffic was brought to a halt on the busy Portway along the north side of the Avon, and the press estimated that in the end 100,000 people turned out to see the *Great Britain* make the historic six-mile trip.

After the ship had disappeared round the lower reaches of the river, I leapt into my car and drove to the high bluff overlooking the famous Horseshoe Bend, followed by the Haywards. There, several hundred people had already collected, and when the first boat appeared in the straight leading up to it, a hush fell on them. It was the *Cabot*, with all the press and TV on board, followed by a naval launch doing the honours, and then the official civic 'barge' with the Lord Mayor prominently on deck accompanied by various city dignitaries. We had a wonderful view looking down on the whole proceedings, the river snaking below, the flat green fields beyond, and the group of little boats that followed behind the ship. Away from the sea the wind now seemed to have dropped. At last, slowly and somewhat majestically, the *Great Britain* was eased round the Horse-shoe Bend below us, steered by the tug tied to her stern.

'A piece of cake', I heard someone murmur. Then I quickly left to drive by back roads to the hotel overlooking the gorge, where I managed to snatch a cup of coffee as a much delayed breakfast, before going out to see the convoy come up between the sheer rock faces of this famous narrows and under the Clifton suspension bridge. It seemed now that nothing could stop the stately progress of our phantom ship. She had made the passage only once before, on 12 December 1844, and at that time the suspension bridge had not been built. Also a Brunel design, it was only constructed after Brunel's death, and the *Great Britain* had never returned to Bristol City Docks after her launch – until now. History indeed.

As the ship approached the part of the gorge just below the terrace of the hotel, I had to jump into the car again, drive it as near to Cumberland Basin as I could, and then take to my heels and run. Geoffrey Palmer, the Lord Mayor had boldly and generously decided to present us with a little mounted crest of the city arms, the presentation to be made on the quayside at the Cumberland Basin, the entrance to the City Docks. And I had to be there to receive it.

A number of my colleagues had already assembled, and I found a reception going on that was really worthy of the ship. A mass of flags were out. A band was playing. Tens of thousands of people had somehow collected to fill not only the immediate surround of the Basin itself, but also the overhead by-pass roads and bridges, and even the windows and gardens of the houses on the hill sides above us.

At one time earlier in the year there had been a sharp correspondence and editorials in the local paper, the *Bristol Evening Post*, most strongly urging that, if and when the *Great Britain* did arrive, she should be received with full honours. And to-day, whatever the political storm clouds in the background, the city had decided at all levels to welcome the incredible return of its greatest ship with open arms.

I arrived in time to see the convoy slowly enter the lock – and to get my breath back, amazed meanwhile at everything around me. Then, while the

Great Britain waited, as she had to for an adjustment of the water levels, the presentation was made. It was the high spot of her welcome home. Afterwards, several of us were invited to travel the rest of the way on the Lord Mayor's barge. And we followed the *Great Britain* as she was towed up the length of the Floating Harbour, past the old *Flying Fox* and past the drydock where she now lies, to be swung round in the wider water at the entrance to St Augustine's Reach and finally tied up at Y Wharf by Canons Marsh, with her bow pointing downstream – to wait. It would be Sunday exactly two whole weeks away before the spring tide would be high enough to warrant our trying to get her into drydock at last.

That evening the leading members of the Project were guests of the Lord Mayor at an informal cocktail party at the Mansion House, an event which we greatly appreciated. Naturally there was some talk about the future. But in spite of this pleasant social contact I am afraid that, again, less than nothing came of it.

The unique period at Y Wharf presented its own special problems. The key fact was, of course, that it was here in Bristol City Docks and not down at Avonmouth that the *Great Britain* was destined to spend her longest time afloat since before the Second World War. For the river tow and to cover this period, we had installed on the ship an oil-driven pumping capacity of 700 tons of water an hour, not to mention a mobile generator and an emergency lighting system. And although no more than a tiny fraction of this capacity was ever used, there was the risk that it might have to be. In the event, the pumps only had to deal with between five and seven tons an hour, which is no worse than a modern ship in certain conditions.

There were also such questions as a twenty-four-hour watch on the pumps – for which two of the original salvage team who had been in the Falklands came forward as volunteers – a police guard, the activities of the public, and possible bumps from other vessels in the harbour. I had fully accepted Y Wharf as a site which the authorities believed would be quiet and relatively out of the way, and we were quite as surprised as they were by the extent to which this was proved wrong – at least as far as the public were concerned.

By this time there had been a good deal of press and television coverage of our activities, and it very soon became evident that the general interest was far greater than had been anticipated. In itself this was immensely gratifying and indeed exceeded our wildest hopes. But it meant that extra steps soon had to be taken to control the crowds, together with the ice cream vans, hot dog stands, and dozens of parked cars. Nor could we possibly allow any unauthorized visitors on board at this delicate stage, and so this meant additional ropes and notices to keep matters in hand. And it was only after a day or two, for instance, that I woke up to the fact that people wanted to give us money. So a collecting box was arranged, chained to a dock pillar, and its contents helpfully and painstakingly banked every day by a supporter, Geoffrey Hughes. In small change the final total came to over £800. It was a tremendously encouraging start to this side of our enterprise.

There were two rather special visitors who on separate occasions I took round the ship during this period – though neither in a sense was really a 'visitor' at all, since each had had close associations with the Project from the very beginning. One was Bill Swigert from America. It was just over two years since I had last seen him at the meeting in the City Museum in May of 1968. And now that the Project had so successfully accomplished the salvage and the return of the *Great Britain*, our relationship had subtly altered. My mind was inevitably packed with current problems, all of them only too real and needing continual solutions. For him, it was rather a journey of might-have-beens, and I sensed his sombre mood.

The other visitor was Eric Gadd. Here again there was an element of joining two ends of a circle, of setting the record straight. A well-known figure in Bristol and much loved by many who knew him, with a local printing business, he had originally been one of those who had spoken out most strongly in favour of the salvage of the *Great Britain*. Unfortunately, in the early days of our own sometimes desperate struggle to be taken seriously ourselves, we had felt that to be associated with what we regarded as the eccentricity of his methods – such as not cutting his hair till the ship came in – was counter-productive. It was hard for the general public to recognize or understand the realities on this point – either way. Very regrettably the issue had therefore become part of the complex web of our Bristol difficulties. But now that the ship had been saved I felt that Eric's visit set a certain seal upon it.

Meanwhile, on the afternoon of the day the *Great Britain* came up the river, we had held a long Project meeting at the Strathconas' house in Bath, and I had been able to make two announcements before we considered other business. The first was that the Duke of Westminster, as chairman of the recently formed Maritime Trust, had just given us a cheque for £5,000 – which was not only a most welcome and timely donation, but also established a solid public relationship of mutual interest between the Trust and ourselves. Secondly, I was empowered to reveal that a visit by Prince Philip, so sadly cancelled the previous week, might now after all take place in two weeks' time, that is on 19 July when we proposed to drydock the ship. This was an electrifying development, though still subject to final confirmation.

What had happened was that, by arrangement with Prince Philip's office two days after the cancellation, I had sent in a long and detailed outline of the *Great Britain*'s anticipated programme, ending with the expectation that, if all the conditions were favourable, our first attempt at docking would probably be made on the Sunday 19 July. And I had invited His Royal Highness to visit the ship on any day that could be managed, either at Y Wharf or during the docking afterwards.

I had, however, also made three particular points about 19 July. Since we could not be sure at that stage which tide would be used, the arrangements for any visit might have to be rather flexible. I had urged nevertheless that to be present during the actual docking would be the most interesting, since it would be a tricky business in any case. And lastly I had drawn attention to the quite extraordinary magic of the coincidence of the date. While 19 July was the precise anniversary of the very date on which the *Great Britain* had been launched from that very same dock by the Prince Consort in 1843, we had now settled on it in 1970 simply and solely through the accidents of the timing of the salvage and the timetable of the tides. By the merest chance the 19 July happened to be the first date on which the technical conditions for drydocking the ship could be met. And just before the weekend I had been told on the telephone that plans were being made to enable Prince Philip to be there on the day.

So we had another royal visit on our hands. Only this time it would be an integral part of the most intimate planning which we would be doing to clear the final hurdle in the homecoming of the ship – her drydocking. This was an intriguing and challenging situation.

It meant of course, a redoubling of effort. I was again involved in detailed timetables, lists of people, and security arrangements with the Lord Mayor's Secretary, Buckingham Palace and the police, in which I had the assistance of Jinny Strathcona and Fitz Lombard. I was in constant touch with Foulds and Peck at Charles Hill and Sons, and sometimes with Commander Ainslie, the Docks Liaison Officer, both about the docking problems and requirements, and about how they could be squared with the flawless planning needed for the Duke of Edinburgh's visit.

In conjunction with the Palace and the Central Office of Information, Adrian Ball and I also had to get the news coverage right. This became a saga of its own, since it ended by including a major outside television broadcast on the BBC at a peak hour on the Sunday evening. And lastly, what I thankfully did not know at the beginning of the final fortnight, we were destined to be counting absolutely on moving the ship across the harbour at the height of a rational dock strike, when everything was supposed to be at a standstill.

As in the earlier stages of the ship's progress, wind and tides were again crucial. It had finally been decided that the first feasible tide would be on the evening of 19 July, but if there was too much wind the docking attempt would have to be postponed till the next day. And this meant drawing up an alternative scheme at each stage for Prince Philip. Equally, while we could practically count for certain on the tide reaching its projected high point, we might just be foiled at the last moment by the chances of nature – mainly if a strong enough wind arose from the wrong direction. Alternatively, as I subsequently discovered, the lock arrangements for holding the very highest water at its top level in the Floating Harbour might just conceivably prove inadequate at the first attempt, since they had not been put to the test for some time. Yet if they were sustained for too long, I gathered they risked flooding quite a few cellars in Bristol. Obviously, it was going to be a close-run thing.

As finally worked out, there would be twenty crucial minutes from 8.40 pm to 9 o'clock, during which it was essential that the whole hull of the ship should get clear across the sill of the drydock. If she could not be got in, she would have to be rapidly withdrawn, in order not to stick in the narrow entrance and risk serious damage. We would then have two more days of spring tides to make further attempts. But if we did not succeed, nothing more could be done for a month. The mind boggled at the problems which would ensue. In fact, it sometimes boggled anyway.

This, then, was the setting for yet another great day in our story. And I was much relieved that Sunday evening of 19 July, when the Duke of Edinburgh's car, flanked by its outriders and followed by the other supporting vehicles, arrived from the airfield at Filton (kindly kept specially open for us by the British Aircraft Corporation) and drove on to Y Wharf dead on time. Followed by the Duke of Beaufort, Prince Philip stepped out at 7.25 precisely.

Although this was our party and the visit was officially 'purely informal', protocol demanded that we should not be the people to greet His Royal

Highness on arrival. So Geoffrey Palmer stepped forward as Lord Mayor and 'presented', as the word is, the fifteen people in his mayoral group and then myself at the end of the row. The group represented the city establishment and included Gervas Walker, Sir Kenneth Brown, Councillor Bert Peglar (who was Lord Mayor three years later) Councillor Ted Wright, Alderman F. A. Parish, and John Hill as the current Master of the Merchant Venturers.

I had met Prince Philip twice before in two other capacities. So when he came to me, it was not difficult to present in turn those of my colleagues who it had been arranged should be with us on the wharf (the others would be at the buffet reception later), namely the Corletts, the Haywards, the Strathconas, Leslie O'Neil and my wife. Although time was very short, I think I was not alone in feeling that this was a rather special moment to savour after all that had happened.

The cardinal requirement at that point was that in a few minutes, that is at 7.45 pm, the *Great Britain* must at all costs cast off, in order to enter the drydock on time. Though cold for the time of the year, the weather was excellent for our purposes, with no rain and virtually no wind. And by a spontaneous and unanimous gesture all the trade unions concerned had decided to help move the ship in spite of the prevailing strike, a measure of their sympathy with our enterprise which I deeply appreciated. Without it we would have been in considerable difficulty.

So we were quickly on the move. Prince Philip studied the stern, which was near us, and then walked forward along the quay to level with the bow, the thronging crowd behind the rope barriers falling back to let him pass. There was a round of clapping, some little union jacks appeared from nowhere and were waved, and, smartly on the dot of 7.40 pm, we mounted the gangway and went on board the *Great Britain* – for the very last journey she now seems destined ever to make.

The plan was for Prince Philip to see the inside of the ship while she was being towed down the harbour. We therefore immediately descended a ladder to a platform which had been constructed on the lower 'tween deck level beside the vertical steel plate behind the crack. And it was here that a nasty incident occurred. Although protective helmets and other clothing had been prepared, we had decided at the last moment not to use them. So it was particularly unfortunate that, just when our little party were all assembled on the platform, that is Prince Philip, Corlett and myself, Hayward, Strathcona, Sir Christopher Bonham-Carter and two security men, one of the volunteers hauling in the gangway immediately above us put his foot through a bit of the rotten deck, instead of treading on the lines of the beams and dowels. We were showered with debris from the broken timber. Mercifully, only one piece was of any substance and this hit Corlett rather than Prince Philip. But, though not more than a glancing blow on the side of the head, it left him feeling rather woozy for the rest of the trip – and I vowed we would never move important visitors without safety helmets again.

Undeterred, and accompanied by a number of press photographers, limited by special royal rota, the party made its way to the bottom of the ship, along the still filthy tank top through the area of the former engine room to the rusty stern, returning to go forward up on to the broken floor of the original Brunel cargo hold. We stopped many times, examining the old flaked ironwork or the mussel shells left from the Falkland Island tides, or simply to gaze in fascination at the still heavily encrusted structure. The occasion was at once so vivid, strange, and evocative that it seemed entirely unreal. And it was only when I happened to glance up and, through the after doorway on the upper 'tween deck, saw the roofs, lamp standards, and lattice girders of the gas works gliding by in total silence that I re-awoke to the realities of our strict and inexorable programme.

So we climbed the two ladders by which we had come down, went aft along the walkway at the upper 'tween deck level and then on into the remains of the stern gallery, with its spare tiller still lashed to the deck as it had been left in 1886. After looking at the top of the Victorian lifting trunk for the propeller – later than Brunel – we emerged on to the weather-deck above by the old companionway. The ship was still moving slowly down the harbour just off the towpath entrance to the dock, and this was the first time that the Duke of Edinburgh could be seen on board by the many thousands of people lining the banks. We paused in the little deck housing, where Corlett ran through some of the plans and details about the ship, and then went forward by the walkways to a special upper level of scaffolding which had been erected over the forecastle to help navigation during the tow up the river. And it was from here that we watched the first manoeuvres for the docking. By now it was 8.35 pm, the *Great Britain* was lined up right across the harbour, ready to go stern first into the dry-dock, and, for us high up over the bow, there was a curious sensation of being practically in among the vast crowd on Hotwell Road and on the terraces above. There was a cheer. Prince Philip waved. And the moment of truth had arrived.

Ropes were being passed to two heavy tractors, one on each side of the drydock. Then at 8.40 pm sharp they started slowly moving forward, foot by critical foot. As we now proceeded down towards a special working platform at the stern, however, I thought I detected beneath the rather studied calm of the Charles Hill staff who were running the operation a faint but growing sense of urgency.

There was some rapid to-ing and fro-ing and looking over the side, and a moment later to my dismay I noticed that the tractors had ceased moving. We had stopped – with the bottom of the rudder post almost at the very sill of the drydock. Had we grounded after all? The stern, I knew, drew fractionally the deepest draught, even though we had trimmed the ship by bringing the bow down with fifty vital tons of water in a special rubber tank in the forecastle, a dracone lent to us by Dunlop.

Precious seconds and then minutes slipped by. No – it was a rope that had fouled the rudder post. But could it be cleared in time? Dramatic efforts were made to do so, and after some fairly frantic hauling they succeeded. Thankfully, I saw the tractors start moving again. Nearly ten long minutes out of the crucial twenty had already passed. But, if nothing else went wrong, we could still make it.

The movement into the dock went inexorably, but it seemed so slowly, on. As when the *Great Britain* had gone out of this same drydock in 1843, it was undoubtedly an exceedingly tight fit. Indeed, with the timber cladding it was even tighter, and we were virtually scraping the dock wall at the full beam amidships on both sides at the same time – though from up above, with the famous rounded shape and tumblehome of the Brunel hull bulging out over the stonework, we could not quite see how many of the mussels and barnacles were being removed. At the tightest point the VIP observers on the port side surged forward, led by the Lord Mayor and the Duchess of Beaufort, and leant their weight against the hull in an effort more psychological than physically effective to fend the ship off.

Then, as the arc lights for the television cameras were switched on in the gathering dusk, it was suddenly clear that we would make it. With the hull rapidly narrowing towards the clipper bow, where the draught was also marginally less, it was obvious that the critical point had been passed. In another few minutes we were in.

No one on board could disembark for a quarter of an hour, while the entrance caisson was being inserted and the ship positioned exactly over the blocks awaiting her on the dock floor – a highly technical and precise operation. Only then, of course, could the water start being drained out. During this pause I waited with Prince Philip at the end of the narrow walkway on the upper 'tween deck where the gangway would come on board, and we reviewed the problems of the *Great Britain* along with those of the Maritime Trust. During the years that have followed he has frequently spoken of the ship, both in conversation and in speeches, and this has helped us significantly to be better known and understood.

At the foot of the gangway Richard Hill met us, and at the start of the buffet reception, which took place in what is now our chart room at the Project Office, I presented the remainder of my colleagues, with their wives – Custance, Adley, Naish, and Drummond, Fitz Lombard, and, now with us for the first time, Commander Joe Blake, just out of the navy and soon to be our resident Project Officer. Similarly presented were the others, too, who had come this far with us – Crothall from Risdon Beazley, Foulds, Peck, Michael Hill and Verity from Charles Hill, and Goodier from Lloyd's. I mention them all because this in its way was really our definitive celebration at last. It was only now for the first time that we could all say to each other:

'Well, we've done it.'

With the civic party there was of course convivial talk. On such a night, how could there not be? But behind the banter ran as always the serious vein of the future and all its unknown, and there was inevitably a little serious argument too. As we threw the issues back and forth, in the centre of it all Prince Philip stayed with us until his appointed departure at 10.15.

Then, with his small staff and the handful of us who were specifically his hosts, he moved down the stairs and out into what was by now the full darkness of night. After a pause to look at the *Great Britain*, her sides still flooded with light from the arc lamps, we walked swiftly along the dock to his car. I thanked him deeply. We shook hands. And he was gone. It had been a unique and utterly memorable occasion.

For myself, however, it was not quite the end of a momentous evening. All through the last few minutes, I had been a little on special tenterhooks as well, because at 10.40 precisely I was to be interviewed live at the harbour end of the dock by Magnus Magnusson as the closing episode in the television spectacular about the docking. And fortunately everything worked out all right to the minute.

I had been desperately keen that something at least should be said about our plans for the future, and that the impression should not be left with the viewers as I felt it had been in a previous BBC broadcast about the salvage on 13 June that this was the end of the road, a romantic and fanciful story, but one with no underlying sense of direction, management or objective. Magnusson asked me the questions and this time I felt it had been possible to give the answers.

'If it was a miracle,' I concluded, 'for this great ship to come slipping up the Avon out of the mists of history, it was also one that we, who are concerned in it, are determined to carry through to its full completion.'

The *Great Britain* was home and dry at last. We had now to turn our minds to her restoration.

10. The Tasks Ahead

A great deal has happened since 1970 both to the ship and to the country. And it would be wrong to pretend that in the middle of that now very distant summer one could foresee at all accurately what would in fact happen to either. The country has plunged into its fundamentally longterm political and economic crises even more rapidly and deeply than seemed certain at the time, and, partly in consequence, the restoration of the ship has been a good deal slower than it was legitimate to hope. But substantial progress has been made even so, and I believe that in terms of history the saving of the *Great Britain* came in the nick of time.

Not only would she have broken up in Sparrow Cove in another year or two, but by then it would also have begun to be impossible for a private group such as ours to operate as we did. Quite apart from the mountainous rise in costs, our aims and ideas would have been subjected to public and political criticism to a degree which would have made it extremely difficult to make headway. On top of everything else, the national situation would have prevented the money coming in. As it is, while we have had our full measure of denigration, we have won through just enough to come out on the other side. We have already produced, that is to say, something which in the trends and ethos of the times is accepted as socially desirable. And the *Great Britain* will, I firmly believe, therefore receive increasing public support as being a national treasure in the modern mould.

If it was impossible, however, to foresee the way our affairs would go in the immediate aftermath of the ship's dramatic homecoming, the problems themselves were only too obvious, pressing and numerous. As

I drove home from Bristol on the morning after the drydocking, I reviewed in my mind the outline of what I would have to tackle in the next few weeks and months. It would all need a very great deal of time and attention.

The first requirement was finance. I had been tempted to put a really large advertisement in the national press with an appeal for funds to appear the day after the drydocking. But I had been warned that we would not even get back the very considerable cost of such an advertisement. And we never tried it. On balance, later experience has made me think the advice was probably correct, though there is always the exception which breaks the general rule – namely that this is not in practice how people respond. Certainly we have often been criticized since, for not in fact doing something of this kind in the first flush of popular success after the home-coming. The trouble was that we had very little cash in hand and no room for mistakes.

As events have turned out – apart from substantial gifts in kind, such as the propeller and funnel – the restoration of the *Great Britain* over the first five years has been largely financed by some half dozen major well-wishers, in addition to the money we have earned for ourselves at the dock. These are Charles Hill and Sons, the British Steel Corporation, John Smith (the former MP), the Maritime Trust, the Imperial Tobacco Group, and a fraternity of consulting engineers under the inspiration of Sir Ralph Freeman.

Each, as will be seen, felt some link with the ship as well as being generously disposed to help us. Thus, with the ship in what was their own yard, Richard Hill, his family and board have led the field. The long survival of the *Great Britain* is one of the finest tributes that could be paid to the British iron and steel industry. John Smith, himself one of the leading supporters of the Maritime Trust of which he is a Vice-President, has given widely to help preserve the nation's heritage. Imperial Tobacco came to our aid partly as a Bristol-based firm. And almost every engineer is proud of Brunel's immense contribution to the development of his profession.

In the fight to secure finance, which we now had to take up from 1970 onwards, I knew that one of the main problems would be to identify the sources at all likely to help us. And this lesson was to be more succinctly defined by our fund-raising consultants, as the autumn and winter came and went. The difficulty was that the net could be so wide as to be almost meaningless, since, although there has always been plenty of goodwill towards the *Great Britain* and frequent admiration for what has been accomplished already, there is no built-in group of people to whom to appeal, as with, say, a cathedral or a school.

If income was the main question, expenditure also presented many challenges of its own. The restoration of the ship demanded that expenditure be related to a whole series of policy decisions, and it was esential that we should get the answers right. The *Great Britain* had undergone many radical changes during her lifetime. In military language the ship now in our hands was perhaps about Mark 20, the remains in fact of the closing stages of her life as a cargo-carrying sailing ship. Clearly, we wanted to restore her as nearly as possible to her great days as a screw-driven passenger liner. But which version even then? And how completely? What was practicable? What materials should be used? What would it all cost? And how quickly – or slowly – would it, or could it, be done in terms both of the level of expenditure and of the physical resources available? These, I knew, were some of the restoration problems we would have to face, even before we got down to priorities of work and the planning of details.

There would also be the very serious question of the proportion of our expenditure to go essentially on restoration as such, both short and long term, compared with the amounts we could – and should – devote to the best possible public presentation of the ship meanwhile, in order to earn immediate revenue. This was in fact to become one of the only two questions, on which opinion within our own ranks was at all seriously divided during the first five years of our work at the dock. The other – which came later – was whether we really ought to get ourselves taken over by the Maritime Trust or not.

Both partly hinged on yet another of the leading issues, which I knew that morning as I drove home from Bristol would take up a good deal of time and effort during the coming months. This was the relationship with Bristol itself. Even if the ultimate question of a site for the ship could not yet be settled – and we always kept up our hopes that it might – there were negotiations to be conducted meanwhile about the current terms and costs of keeping her where she was.

The tasks ahead certainly included, too, the development of a practical relationship with Charles Hill and Sons. There was no certainty, for instance, about how they would fit the *Great Britain* into their own schedules, or what our mutual financial arrangements would be. Much would obviously depend on how busy they were with normal commercial contracts, and how far the *Great Britain* would be something to fall back on when jobs were scarce elsewhere. This would naturally also be affected by the financial terms, and with Richard Hill and Alec Foulds I quickly reached an appropriate ship repair agreement covering our special case. They generously wrote into it the quotation of work on non-profit terms and the granting of extensive interest-free credit. This enabled us to get started, first with cleaning up the ship and then with positive restoration. The Project has a very great deal to be grateful for to Charles Hill and Sons.

Relations with the trade unions would, I knew, be another problem in our everyday working. As I had suspected from the start, one of our inherent difficulties proved to be that, because of our position in the shipyard, we were virtually never able to be in direct contact with them ourselves. But as far as they were concerned this meant that all the normal rules about demarcation and manning automatically applied. Moreover, work on the ship came to be relatively unpopular, since from very early on we felt bound to take a decision that as a charity we could not afford to pay overtime. This contributed to a lack of continuity of labour on particular jobs, which slowed things down considerably.

Up at the London end there were also several important questions awaiting attention. Perhaps the most complex was the completion of the official aims and rules of our charity company in its Memorandum and Articles of Association. Stephen Beharrell, our solicitor, was to draw up a whole sheaf of valuable suggestions, but he and I went through them with a tooth comb together before we could be satisfied that they would cover every contingency.

Finally, as far as the immediate opening of the dock to the public was concerned – I reassured myself – everything seemed to be in hand. Commander Joe Blake, just recruited to take charge, had been at the dock all the week. He and Lady Strathcona had been over the ground innumerable times together, and for the opening to the public careful plans had been laid, to which we had all agreed, to meet the deadline of Wednesday, 22 July 1970, three days after the drydocking. Unfortunately I could not have been more wrong about what was actually about to happen – though it was through no personal fault of either of them.

I should say here that over the years Joe Blake was destined to bear the brunt of all our problems at the dock. I had first met him five weeks earlier on 15 June, when he had come to the Strathconas' house for a final interview before we agreed to ask him to join us in the capacity of what we called 'Project Officer'. In effect, he has worn two hats, one as the man in charge of the dock and its personnel, the other as a technical liaison officer and executive between the naval architect and the shipyard or the outside contractors. Richard Hill wanted someone in this role from the beginning. I wanted it because the Project obviously had to have a man permanently in charge on the spot. And Ewan Corlett naturally needed a man he could trust not only to see that our agreed restoration plans were properly carried out, but to report back when they were not. The end result has been that Joe has had a very good shot at turning himself into a sort of poor man's Archangel Gabriel and has emerged with something of a halo.

22 July 1970 was one of the most shattering days of my life, however, when our run of luck with the *Great Britain* was for the time being cruelly reversed. It was two days and three nights since the tremendous euphoria of the ship's drydocking. If ever there had been a moment to relish the sweet triumphs of success, this had been it. I had had to be in London on my own business all the Tuesday. And, though still extremely weary, my wife and I were in a pleasantly reflective mood, as we prepared to leave again for Bristol at a fairly early hour that Wednesday morning to see how things were going on – when the telephone rang. It was Pam Blake, Joe's wife.

'I hardly know how to tell you,' was her message, 'and I hate to ring you at this early hour. But my husband has been struck down by a virus which is going the rounds, and he can't even get out of bed. As with others who have had it, it seems to have affected the middle ear so that he can't keep his balance. The doctor is on his way. But I'm terribly afraid he simply won't be able to get to the dock today and it may be some time before he can.'

As is sometimes the case with bad news, it took a moment or two for the full horror to sink in. At that instant Joe was the lynch pin of our entire operation. He alone knew all the details of the arrangements for opening the dock, including who the staff were who had been recruited, where they were coming from, what each person's job was, where all the keys were – a pantomime in itself, as it turned out – and a mass of other vital information. Jinny Strathcona could have helped us, but she, Euan and their six children had already taken off for Colonsay, their island on the west coast of Scotland. And, above all, what I fortunately did not know at that first moment of impact, we were about to be besieged by the public. There is no other word for it. People had been crawling about on neighbouring walls trying to see the ship before we opened the dock. And, after we did so, where we had thought in hundreds, thousands came pouring in. We were about to be swamped by 100,000 visitors in the first seven weeks.

Now, to deal with all this, there was no one but my wife and myself; and, at that time, before the completion of the M4 motorway, we lived two and a half hours' drive from Bristol, an aggregate of five hours' driving a day. Public transport to cover the journey is effectively non-existent. Instead of going in, therefore, that first Wednesday morning to help support an organization on the spot, however new and struggling, we suddenly found instead that we ourselves were the organization. There was nothing else. None of my colleagues lived in the Bristol area and they had mostly departed on postponed holidays anyway, and in those days we had still not been able to establish satisfactory relations with any responsible Bristolians either, who would be free and willing to give time to the Project.

I put the phone down and we raced off to Bristol, since I would now have to arrive in time to get the keys, open the dock, and sort out our staff before 10 o'clock. They consisted of one or two older people who had already been to the dock previously and knew roughly what they had to do, but most of our first staff were students who, though on the whole enthusiastic, knew nothing at all. And what was so absolutely baffling was that neither did we. My wife and I tried to rationalize what we could, but it was terrible to be operating without knowing of all sorts of arrangements that Blake had already made, and always with more and more visitors pressing to come in.

The publicized schedule was that the dock would be open every day from 10 am to 8 pm – and we were heavily criticized by a few people for not staying open till 9 pm or even 10 pm. But we got through that first day somehow, seeing that no one fell into unsuitable places, answering endless telephone calls, meeting innumerable special callers at the embryonic and disorganized Project Office, and putting up signboards. We also realized that dogs would have to be excluded. There were so many, and their behaviour was less than perfect. Closing to the public at 8 pm meant that we got away finally ourselves by 9.30 pm, but had a full two-hour drive still ahead of us. Arriving home at 11.30 pm we knew we had to leave again the following morning by 7 am at the latest.

By the time we had done all this for the second day running, the Thursday, and reached home that night absolutely dead beat, I knew that it simply could not go on. Yet until we could find time and opportunity to recruit one or two more senior staff and actually have them arrive, the basic problem seemed to stretch ahead inexorably.

So that night we dragged ourselves round the house and made our arrangements to close it down. We tried to sort out all the greenhouse plants which my wife grows for her considerable amount of horticultural writing. We wrote putting off other engagements and left messages. We selected clothes and packed our suitcases. And the following morning soon after the summer dawn of Friday, 24 July, we set out for Bristol for, as one used to say in the war, 'the duration', adding if one wished to be quite clear, 'of the emergency'. We would simply have to live in Bristol, not knowing how long it might be before we could become normal human beings again and have some say in what would happen to us from one hour to the next. It was a sombre drive. The ship's homecoming seemed to be part of another world and to have happened about twenty years ago.

I suppose we had really overreached ourselves in trying to get the dock open to the public so soon. But it seemed terrible to delay when everyone was clamouring to get in. What we were beaten by, apart from the immediately crippling blow of Blake's sudden knock-out illness, was the incredible interest aroused by the *Great Britain*. The sheer tide of numbers which swept in on the dock made everything far more difficult. It was of course immensely gratifying. We had got off to a more wonderful start than any of us had ever dreamt of. But we were throttled by our own success and desperately needed room for manoeuvre to build up our organization, learn the ropes, and complete the necessary preparations in the dock itself. Originally we had thought that 5,000 visitors in the first month would have been quite good going. In fact, 50,000 came in the first three weeks. If Joe Blake had not been ill, there would still have been a crisis. But it would have been more readily contained, and between us we could have coped, as I had always intended, in a more orderly way with the necessary steps to put things right.

Once my wife and I were resident on the spot and had gained the experience of another day or two, it began to be possible to raise one's head for a moment and to take proper stock of the situation. By Friday evening, the end of the third day, I had heard that Blake was better, but that it would still be two or three days before he could possibly be fit enough to join our rat race at the dock. For several months before this, however, he had had a gruelling time, and it soon became obvious that, when he was well enough, he had much better go on to take the leave due to him on leaving the navy, which he had generously agreed to postpone if everything had been normal. In the event, he was thus able to rejoin us for a few days from the Monday and then went on his three weeks' leave.

By Monday 27 July, therefore, though the issues looked harsh they had become much more clear-cut. Though at that point we were not opening to the public on Mondays and Tuesdays there was great pressure for us to do so, and I was very keen that we should as soon as possible. But even with my wife's help I could not do this through August on my own, as I still had certain business meetings to attend to in London, and I had squeezed my own affairs very hard for three months already.

So that morning before I left for London we set some wheels in motion and, with Blake's help, by the Wednesday we were able to start some interviews. As a result, two people joined us in a senior capacity almost at once. The first was Ken Moodie, who has remained with us ever since. With an accounting background, he was able to take over in the office and deal with the cash, which had become an appalling headache.

The other, who joined us the following Monday, 3 August, on one month's agreement only was Lieutenant Commander Gordon Whale. He lived in Bath and had another job coming up in September and it suited him, as it did me, that he should come at once as my temporary stand-in. The arrangement worked to perfection, and once he had found his feet in our rather extraordinary little world his presence changed the complexion of everything.

That first Saturday I had also interviewed and accepted someone else, who had agreed to be what we called our Deputy Project Officer – vital for a seven-day-week operation. This was Tim Webb. He could not actually come until the end of the month, Monday 31 August, but the knowledge that he would be doing so helped to sustain me considerably. And like the other three in the Project Office, he has been with us ever since.

I have said three, because besides Joe, Tim and Ken, the fourth member of our permanent staff in the office, Mrs Joan Andrews, joined us as our secretary. Starting very soon after Ken Moody came, this meant an immediate transformation in the whole position of our paper work. We could even man the constantly ringing telephone! And from the ship's point of view over the years the continuity of these four has been one of the most splendid and helpful developments in the whole life of the Project.

As regards the running of the dock itself, one of the most worrying aspects at the beginning was public safety. It was physically impossible until some days after we opened for Charles Hill's men to get all the walkways on the ship, the railings along the edges of the dock, and the passage across the caisson under the bow wired up with chain link fencing. This meant a real danger of children falling through; and I was acutely conscious throughout that an accident of this kind, for instance from the ship walkways, high up over the three-deck drop to the iron tank-tops below, could have led to tragedy.

On a more mundane plane, however, it was also exceedingly trying. Although I have since seen a much more liberal interpretation of the rules in other places, the visits of the City Engineer's Structural Safety Officer at first produced a ban on our letting more than forty people on to the ship at any one time. As they took a long time gazing about them in the early days, in spite of our efforts to keep them moving, this led to a semi-permanent queue of people waiting to mount the gangway, sometimes nearly the length of the dock, and I was as exasperated as any of them.

Some of our student staff were excellent. Others were less so and were given to going on holiday without notice, or just not turning up when it suited them. In order to add flexibility to our capacity to deal with this fatal modern trend, and also because we needed some additional older people who could cope with the crowds, I came to an arrangement with the Corps of Commissionaires. For some weeks, until our position stabilized itself, two or three of these ex-service non-commissioned officers were usually working for us at any given time, and their characteristic uniforms always added a touch of traditional authority to the scene. They also acted as security guards, and I was grateful to them. To handle the banking of cash we called in Securicor.

Besides being hectic, life at the dock often had its lighter sides. In fact each day produced its own crop of incidents. One was a stall set up outside our entrance by a dissatisfied Bristolian, who started selling prints of the ship in order to raise money for a rival fund. I eventually got him to desist. Another was two small boys, who the harbour police brought in from a dinghy which they had been rowing back and forth beside our towpath, holding a collecting tin out to those on the way to the ship. Ostensibly they were collecting for us, but without our knowledge and certainly without our authority, so that until the police got them to hand over the contents of the tin, there was no telling who might have been the main beneficiaries.

All through August and into September attendances kept up. We passed 60,000 on Tuesday 18 August. By Monday, 24 August, it was 70,000. On Thursday, 27 August, when Joe Blake arrived back, we had reached 75,000. With the Monday, 31 August, a bank holiday, we got beyond 85,000. 90,000 had come by Friday, 4 September and it was on Wednesday, 9 September, exactly seven weeks after we had opened that we had our 100,000th visitor. After that the pressure eased as autumn gradually gave way to winter, and by the end of September the operation of the dock had in any case become much smoother. But in retrospect I am very glad to have been thrown in at the deep end. I have understood the problems ever since.

With the summer emergency out of the way, our thoughts turned with increasing emphasis to restoration. Although virtually nothing had been possible with so many people milling about in the dock, the fact was that we were inhibited from making any striking move even after they had left, because of the need to experiment before committing ourselves. In the most practical terms, we needed to be quite clear about the best methods of descaling the ironwork and repairing the holes in the plating, as well as about the right action to take over the extensive wooden cladding bolted on to the outside of the hull.

'Restoration' is really an omnibus word, which one uses for brevity, a kind of shorthand. Specifically, for us it has three aspects – preservation, restoration proper, and reconstruction. Parallel with them go four overlapping stages of the work – clearing, cleaning, building, and fitting out. In the initial half year up to the end of 1970, we hardly got beyond the clearing stage in any respect.

In order to help us draw up some policy guidelines, Ewan Corlett had originally got together a small group of advisers as an *ad hoc* Restoration Committee. This consisted of Basil Bathe from the Science Museum, L. T. C. Rolt, Brunel's biographer, Grahame Farr, who had written an earlier definitive booklet about the *Great Britain*, and A. D. Sutherland, a Lloyd's Registry surveyor. George Naish was Secretary. This committee held its first and only meeting in Bath on the afternoon of 19 July, the day the ship was drydocked.

I was naturally very dismayed indeed at being unable to attend such a potentially important discussion. But the fact that it was held at such an extremely unsuitable moment did not, of course, prevent any conclusions being reached. What did invalidate its recommendations was that at that point no one could know the timescale on which we would be operating. This would depend both on finance and on our experience of the actual problems of progressing the work in hand.

Thus, although none of its recommendations were ever carried out, the airing of views helped to clear our own minds when we had set up our own executive team for deciding what to do. This was a four-man group which we called the Dock (or, later, Ship) Committee, and it consisted of Corlett, myself, Blake and Goodier, with Corlett presiding and Blake doing the minutes. We held our first meeting on 11 December 1970, and have met three or four times a year ever since. Though naturally responsible to the main Council of the Project, in practice it has been this Ship Committee which has planned, organized, and carried out each step of the actual restoration programme. Blake's full and careful minutes now constitute a well-documented record of how the *Great Britain* is being restored.

Meanwhile, the tackling of our most urgent task, the sheer preservation of the existing structure of the ship – both iron and wood – had to some extent already been pre-empted from the earliest weeks by a succession of business callers at the dock office. They were representatives, or indeed directors, of firms wanting to learn our intentions and whether there was a role for their products or services – at either commercial or reduced rates or sometimes free.

In regard to the iron, quite a number of them were offering various kinds of abrasive descaling treatment, grit or sand blasting, as would normally be applied to modern steel. From the start, however, Corlett had the strongest reservations about the harshness of its effect on the old iron, whether the beams or the plates. We were consequently attracted instead by the offers of three separate contractors in the alternative field of using very high pressure water jetting. So we conducted a series of tests on experimental areas during the autumn and early winter, and the outcome was that we accepted the generous terms of Plant Technical Services Ltd, whose contract gave us their facilities at substantially below commercial cost.

In dealing with the wood, notably the remains of the great gunwale and 1857 keel, we very gladly accepted the services – again with a gift element – of Cotswold Treatments Ltd, under the experienced and expert guidance of the late Nixon Eckersall who had also worked on the preservation of Westminster Abbey.

Plant Technical Services began work early in 1971, and, because one of the conditions was that they could withdraw their men and equipment if these were required for urgent normal business elsewhere, they remained with us for over three years. Their role was accepted by both the management and unions of Charles Hill, since water jetting at between 8,000 and 14,000 pounds per square inch is a highly specialized operation. If mishandled the jets can kill. After the jetting, the procedure was for Charles

Hill to flame-dry the iron and then paint it with old-fashioned red lead, sometimes in practice magenta-coloured. Gas for the drying was given by Shell and the paint by the International Paint Company. By removing all loose scale the jets, of course, made some of the iron plates look temporarily more full of holes than before.

Once descaled and 'cleaned', the platework of the ship had to be made good by the filling in of the holes. At first sight this could obviously be done with replacement iron or steel, and preferably iron. But apart from the cost, as well as the practical difficulty of acquiring enough suitable iron, this would have meant cutting away so much of the original plating, in order to square up for the new insertions, that in practice we would have destroyed an unacceptable proportion of the original ship which we were trying to preserve. We did cast round in any case for old iron plate, and we were eventually lucky in acquiring some contemporary Victorian material, though rather thick, from the dismantled Menai Straits railway bridge, which was destroyed by fire soon after the ship came in. And we will probably use it later on for internal reconstruction, possibly on the transverse bulkheads. But, for the basic repairs to the whole of the *Great Britain*'s sides, we soon came to choose a more modern method altogether. This was glass-fibre lamination. Painted, it looks just like the iron.

The system has been to use glass-fibre reinforced polyester resin in a series of laminates, thus building up to a solid replacement for the original metal. If the conditions of warmth, dryness, and cleanliness are correct at the time of application, the bond is tight and strong. Indeed, with the use of more expensive epoxy resin and lamination from both inside and outside the hull, it became clear that this glass-fibre treatment of the underwater holes would be fully strong enough to enable the ship to be refloated. And throughout our first four years we were under an obligation to the city council to make this possible – a fact which added somewhat to our costs. The resin has been given to us by the Scott Bader Company, and the specialized work carried out on advantageous terms by two local firms, Brensall Plastics and Parglas.

From very early on this question of using glass fibre had brought us straight up against the basic policy decision whether to employ modern materials or whether to try to get back to those put into the ship originally. And our decision of principle throughout has in fact been to use modern materials and modern techniques in the restoration wherever this is practicable, naturally so long as the result can be made to look like the old. We feel that we are building for the next hundred years, and also that we must do so as economically as possible, in terms both of prime cost and of subsequent maintenance problems.

Similarly, the next detailed question we had to consider immediately raised the fundamental issue I have already referred to, namely: which *Great Britain* would we try to restore, Brunel's or one of the later ones? This was the question whether or not to remove the heavy pitch pine cladding with which a large part of the hull – the area 'between wind and water' – had been sheathed in 1882. I think quite a number of people whose opinions I respect had felt, when the ship came in, that it would be a great pity to remove this splendid old timber, weathered and beautifully fitted as it was. Not only had it now formed an integral part of the ship for eighty-eight years, but its removal might seriously damage what was left of the iron hull behind. No one knew exactly why it had been put on in the first place, but there must almost certainly have been a mixture of reasons following conversion of the old hull, forty years after its construction, to carrying heavy cargo. In her later sailing-ship days the *Great Britain* had to float a good many feet deeper in the water than she had originally been designed to do, and in every respect the heavy timber was an important source of additional strength.

Nevertheless – and however all that might be – the moment one started considering the fundamental issue, it became clear that what one must go for so far as possible was Brunel's ship, the original *Great Britain*, the ship whose place in history had led us to her salvage. This was what had inspired the monumental efforts which had already been made. And so the cladding must go.

Removing it occupied many months. Unspectacular in itself, it meant burning off or sometimes being able to unscrew 10,000 bolts, and sawing or breaking up huge, hard planks of quite undamaged pitch pine. Before we did this at the bow and the stern, however, Corlett had further extensive ultra-sonic thickness tests made of the iron beneath, and for a while we delayed progress in these areas in order to allow for other steps to be taken to strengthen the framework there. But when at last the removal was completed we knew that we had been a thousand times right. Most of the metal behind the carefully caulked timber was in quite good order. And above all, as this ungainly shell fell away, the shape of Brunel's original *Great Britain* suddenly emerged with its pristine rounded beauty for all the world to see. When we had got the iron blanking plates off the early sidelights as well, the rows of portholes turned her overnight into the passenger ship she had always been meant to be.

While the priority work on the ship had to be concentrated on the basic clearing, cleaning, and patching of certain parts of the hull, our Ship Committee naturally began considering the realistic steps we could take to move from the strictly preservation to the more positive restoration and reconstruction stage. And here the first items we addressed ourselves seriously to were part at least of the deck problem: the question of masts, any further repair of the starboard crack, and the rebuilding of the Brunel bow.

So far as those first few months in 1970/71 were concerned, however, only three developments took place in connection with any of these items, though each was an important preliminary. The first was a most handsome offer from Henry Elwes in Gloucestershire to give us the wood for the masts and the bowsprit. His family name has been famous in the world of forestry for well over half a century. We were thrilled to accept the promise of six of the finest Douglas firs standing in the woodlands of the timber co-operative of which he was a leading member, five for the masts – we think that the No. 2 Brunel mast, square-rigged, was of iron – and one for the bowsprit. In the event, I went and saw all the trees felled a year later in the autumn of 1971, and the first to be used after a year's seasoning was for the new bowsprit.

The next development led to our obtaining the timber we needed for the vital redecking of the *Great Britain*. One day early in 1971 my telephone rang and I heard Ewan Corlett's voice at the other end.

'You know, Richard,' he said, 'they are pulling down an old naval barracks at Portsmouth. If we act at once, I believe we could get the timber from the floor of the mess hall very cheaply, and it's exactly what we want.'

At that moment we had no cash whatever to spare. But when I approached John Smith he made this his first splendid gift to us, and he paid us the £4,500 for which we got the lot, delivered free. It was a wonderful purchase and a heartening experience.

The third development had a less auspicious beginning. Consideration of the deck had led on to the question of further repairs to the crack, since it would be absurd to build a new deck at the area of the crack, if major structural work were later to be required there. And this in turn raised the point that, before reconditioning and decorating the bow, we must be certain of the strength and stability of the forward end of the ship as a whole.

At our third Dock Committee on 22 April 1971, when the future of the crack was being assessed, I remember taking the view that in all probability the ship would never have to leave the dock, whatever the current cartwheels being turned in the politics both of the City and of the Project at that period – and there had been a development on this front in February which we were yet to hear the last of.

In that case, I was dead against doing anything to the crack, at least for the time being. From a purist point of view perhaps it ought to be done. But I felt above all that we could not afford it straightaway. Secondly, the drama of the *Great Britain* straightening on the pontoon, followed by the welding on of the great steel plate in Avonmouth, was now a positive part of the history of the ship and nothing whatever to be ashamed of. Quite the reverse – so let matters stay as they were.

As a professional naval architect, however, Ewan Corlett naturally started from the opposite point of view, and he would undoubtedly have liked to see the crack properly repaired. To this end he had outlined a plan, which began by actually undoing enough of the emergency strapping to try to pull and push the relevant parts of the structure more completely into their marginally original positions by means of jacks, compressors and tension cables. I was horrified. And when I showed it he came up with a trump card – but fortunately a lesser one.

'From what Joe and I have observed,' he commented, 'I wouldn't be surprised if the bow isn't already sagging a bit on the starboard side.'

'How do you mean?' I asked at once, momentarily taken aback.

'With the very considerable strain the hull has gone through,' came the reply, 'as a result of the crack first of all opening up and then later closing again, there can be no guarantee that the ship will necessarily preserve her shape, particularly when unsupported by water.'

It was to meet this possibility that we did three things. We temporarily deferred removing the timber cladding from the bow because it was a factor of additional strength. For a similar reason we also decided to leave the upper non-Brunel hawse-pipes in place indefinitely, in spite of later uncovering, as expected, the original and remarkable Brunel T-shaped hawse-pipe lower down – a point that has subsequently intrigued our more perspicacious visitors. And, lastly, we set up a plumb-line to check whether there really was any progressive movement or not. If there was, the starboard bow would have to be shored up, at least temporarily – an ugly and degrading performance, I have always felt.

For many weeks through the spring and summer of 1971 this plumb line hung from the top of the bow, its lead weight swinging occasionally in the wind round a datum point in the dock bottom. But of structural movement there was no sign whatever. The ship was more solid than even her stoutest champions had at one time thought.

Assailed again by lingering doubts, four years later we did the same test again. But so far nothing has been proved, except that the undoubted very slight twist to starboard at the bow is a static reality, and not just an optical illusion which at first had passed unnoticed.

11. Ports in a Storm

Occupied though we were by these and other fascinating problems within the *Great Britain* herself, I could never forget that perhaps our most difficult battles were still on other fronts. Apart from – but also very unhappily linked with – the perennial fight for finance, the most important and for the time being the most immediate of these was that of a final permanent site for the ship.

As I have mentioned, the fact that the *Great Britain* was to come into Charles Hill's shipyard from the Falkland Islands did not commit either us, as her owners, or the Bristol City Council, as the responsible local authority planners, to keeping or letting her stay there permanently. Indeed, there were two unanswered questions. Besides the issue of whether she would stay in Bristol at all, it was a wide-open question whether, if she did, she would stay in that particular site, the Great Western Dock. And the bally-hoo of her arrival from the other side of the world had not ostensibly done anything to settle these questions. For a time at least, it seemed, if anything, to have posed them even more dramatically than before.

I was very keen to get both questions answered as soon as possible. For, until they were, we suffered under two considerable handicaps, and these became markedly greater with every few months that passed. First, as is clearer than ever in the light of subsequent inflation, although our money costs were rising, the possibilities of meeting them were steadily being narrowed by a combination of the national economic decline and the transfer of resources from the private to the public sector of the economy. While we really needed to make the maximum possible progress in those crucial early days, however, our handicap was at its worst because many people simply would not look at us, since we could not answer their legitimate, basic question:

'What do you intend to do with the ship?'

At best, if not put off altogether by one's not knowing about a permanent site, they would say:

'Come back when you do.'

Financially, this was crippling.

The second handicap was that, unless and until we knew whether the *Great Britain* would stay in or leave the Great Western Dock, particularly with the added uncertainty of when such an event might take place, one could only feel that anything spent on the amenities in the dock was, as likely as not, money down the drain. Yet it was essential up to a certain point to improve the very skeletal amenities, if we were to attract the public and improve our earning power. Although on a smaller scale than the main fund-raising dilemma, this one also materially hindered our development through the early years.

In the course of the festive contacts when the ship came in, it had been accepted by Gervas Walker that we would all try to hold some kind of set meeting during the autumn, at which the future of the *Great Britain* could be discussed as a matter of policy. And this did duly take place at the Council House on 21 October 1970.

Beforehand, however, and as one of the documents for the meeting, I arranged to accept Stephen Macfarlane's suggestion that a survey should be prepared, which would put down on paper the arguments for and against various alternative possible sites within Bristol itself. That at least, I felt, should help to clarify one of the leading questions. A rising architect in the city, Stephen had recently shown great interest in the ship and had already given much thought to the best Bristol site for her.

As a feasibility study the Macfarlane Report, as we came to call it, had the advantage of being done from outside the Project, not by the Project, and done moreover in Bristol. It was not *our* report and thus stood some chance of being regarded as being objective about us. Macfarlane examined five sites. Common to all four of them, other than the Great Western or Wapping Docks, was the concept that, since there was no other suitable ready-made concrete enclave within the City Docks area in which the *Great Britain* could lie, she should be lifted above the water and be placed on a permanent floating pontoon. The idea, mooted by Ewan Corlett, owed some of its inspiration to her romantic voyage from the Falkland Islands.

This pontoon could be made of reinforced concrete. But, whatever it was made of, an essential point about the concept was that there was nowhere in the Floating Harbour, not even Charles Hill's No 1 drydock next door to us, where it could be constructed in one piece. It would be too big. Nor, for the same reason, could it be brought up the Avon intact – just as the Ulrich Harms pontoon had had to be evacuated at Avonmouth. It would therefore have to be built or brought in in sections and joined together afterwards, a proceeding adding considerably to its cost. Other extra costs would also be incurred not only, of course, by making it submersible, but in dredging a special area in the Floating Harbour where it could be submerged deep enough for the *Great Britain* to float over the top, before being lifted out of the water. The idea of keeping the *Great Britain* permanently afloat had always been ruled out for obvious reasons of age and condition.

The result of all this was a calculation that either to build and adopt such a pontoon, or to create an equivalent new drydock enclave, would cost about £150,000 at 1970/71 prices. This was our estimate, but it was one which I subsequently gleaned from the City Council's staff they had also arrived at quite independently after studying the Macfarlane Report.

The four sites where the pontoon might best be placed in Bristol were listed as Baltic Wharf; Western Wharf opposite the *Great Britain*'s present dock; St Augustine's Reach more or less facing Prince Street Bridge; and – in some ways a magnificent challenge – at the very head of St Augustine's Reach, dominating the traffic right up to Colston Avenue. To cut a long story short, the first was too remote, the last almost too close to the City Centre, and the other two lacking in any special appeal. In all cases the limitations of the pontoon cut down the possible amenities, and there were always car-parking difficulties.

The special challenge of the head of St Augustine's Reach had to be declined for technical reasons alone. It would mean difficult and costly additional work diverting the underground residual waters of the River Frome. And it would almost certainly have to be achieved – so it seemed at that time – before a proposed road bridge was built across the mouth of the Reach, an exceedingly awkward proposition all round. Personally I was always against it too (unless the running expenses of the Project were heavily subsidized from public funds, which in the nature of things seemed virtually out of the question), since I could never quite envisage enough people paying to see over the ship, if so much of her was already so spectacularly on view from public streets and squares on three sides of her.

So the Macfarlane Report came down in favour of the *Great Britain* staying where she was – a unique historic combination with the very dock in which Brunel built her. And by arrangement we sent ten copies to the Town Clerk a week before the meeting of 21 October. We hoped to forward a copy to each member of the City Council after the meeting and to have it published in the local press on 26 October. But, as will be seen, this was not to be.

The meeting lasted for two and a half hours, and Gervas Walker was in the chair. It was formal and matter of fact, and consisted of an extensive enquiry into our views and aspirations, without at the same time anything being given away about the views or intentions of Council members themselves. Personally, I felt that this was a pity and that a special opportunity was being missed. Not only did we for our part leave the meeting almost as much in the dark about the future as when we had entered it, but this was an occasion, indeed the only occasion for several years, on which there were present together in one business session virtually all the people most significantly concerned at that time with the fate and fortune of the *Great Britain*. The Council team included Robert Wall, Bert Peglar, Wally Jenkins and their leading officials, namely the City Treasurer, Town Clerk, City Engineer, Chief Planning Assistant, Port Authority Secretary, and the City Public Relations Officer. With me were Corlett, Strathcona, Anthony Abrahams, and our own helpers Lombard, Blake, a director from our fund-raising consultants, and Stephen Macfarlane.

The basic question put to us of course was: what did we want from the Bristol Council? Was it a site free of rent or rates? If so, was this all? Were we in fact asking for money?

'There are three priorities,' we replied in effect. 'The very first is simply agreement in principle to our remaining here. The second is indeed, if possible, a free berth. And the third naturally is some financial help, if that can be arranged. But this last is essentially number three and we ask it for all the obvious reasons that anyone would. It is not a cardinal request. But the first is. That is vital to us.'

It may be difficult for anyone who has not been involved in responsibility for the survival of a semi-public enterprise to understand how much difference the opposition or sympathy of local government can make. I have mentioned the fact that we could not raise money effectively because of the long-term uncertainty about a site for the ship. But in the short term, as we pointed out on this occasion, the fact also was that, if the authorities turned an entirely deaf ear to us, our position could not fail to be a difficult one. Even in the matter of any planning application at the dock we could not expect to make satisfactory progress. All in all, we felt, it would be better to be told straightaway that from a given date we could not stay in Bristol than to remain frustrated as well as uncertain indefinitely. It was on this basis that above all we asked for some clarification about our position, even if this could only be done informally and without any binding commitment. If nothing else, it was a matter of atmosphere and understanding.

As to the actual site, we said, the Macfarlane Report had shown the merits of remaining in the Great Western Dock and, if that were to happen, we hoped that enough ground could eventually be made available to us, when the City Docks finally did close and begin redevelopment, to allow for car-parking and other facilities.

When it came to the subject of money, I felt that we were in a rather awkward position – as one almost always is. We had sounded out one or two middle-of-the-road Bristol citizens as to what they felt it might be fair and feasible to ask at that time. But I had had no indication from the authorities whether any request for financial aid would be considered at all. And I felt that, whatever we said, we could, of course, be misinterpreted. If we named too low a figure, we risked being regarded as not serious – of which there had been some hint already. If we named too high a one, we could be thought either unrealistically grasping or alternatively so broke already that we could not continue without a massive subvention.

So in our presentation we felt it best to give as much chapter and verse about our financial position as the time allowed, before reaching the point of making any request. Corlett, for instance, summarized the restoration requirements. Blake gave some running costs. Lombard spoke about the long-term significance of our covenanted subscriptions. And on the question of servicing a loan I made it clear that we could do so, though one could naturally not give guarantees beyond a certain point since – to come full circle – our earning power depended in part on knowing about a final site for the ship.

I then named the figure of £25,000 as a possible donation at that stage – in the circumstances a modest sum. If a loan were to be made, our view was that the amount might be larger. I have always felt since that our views on these figures were received sympathetically, it being understood that no decision had been reached about giving or lending any money at all.

Our deposition prompted enquiries about the London alternative for the ship. And here we emphasized the three main points. First, the motive was basically financial – that there would inevitably be the possibility of earning much more money from visitors (and therefore of making faster progress with restoration) if the *Great Britain* were located within easy reach of the well over two million annual visitors to the Tower of London. This has since, of course, been proved with HMS *Belfast* which has had attendance figures around 400,000; her trouble has been her high running and maintenance costs and lack of capital to meet them.

The second basic point was the reality of a potential berth for us in either St Katharine Dock or London Dock next door. The third was that we did not *want* to leave Bristol. It would be costly. It would present serious technical problems. It would put the ship at risk. But in the dilemma in which we found ourselves we would be failing in our duty to those who had already backed the Project, if we did not consider all the options open to us.

The meeting ended without any decisions being taken, or indeed intended. While this was naturally disappointing – since it was above all decision that we needed – what I was particularly sorry about was the request made to us that we should not circulate the Macfarlane Report to the rest of the Council or allow it to be published. We would clearly have been ill-advised not to accede to such a request, but for the time being this inevitably robbed the debate of some useful material – and, as of course one saw, inhibited any wider presentation of our views.

Before noting the decisive move that was to settle the immediate issue just over three months later, a word should be said here about the difficult situation which undoubtedly confronted the Bristol City Council in certain respects at that time. In the eye of history the question is not so much whether the presence of the *Great Britain* presented any special or serious problems for the Council. It certainly did. The question is whether the then leadership found the right answers – and there the judgement must be history's alone.

There were two main aspects of the problem. By the end of 1970 and in the early part of 1971 the necessary steps were already being taken to have a special enabling bill passed by parliament at Westminster, which would give Bristol the power to close the old City Docks to commercial shipping by 1980. Thus, the Bristol Corporation Act, 1971 became law on 27 July of that year. With the development of facilities at Avonmouth and the changed requirements of modern vessels, the docks had begun to lose money at a rate that could only get worse – quite apart from inflation. Amongst other things, however, this involved questions of paying compensation to businesses and the owners of freehold property in the dock area itself, whose otherwise legitimate prospects would be adversely affected by the close down. And the leading firm concerned was the ship-building and ship-repair yard of Charles Hill and Sons.

As subsequent public events have shown, however, an agreement was meanwhile being negotiated between the firm and the city and was signed on 15 June 1971, that is before the Act came into force. This laid down the principles on which the firm's compensation would be assessed; and it specified certain conditions that would have to be accepted by both sides in doing so. But by the very nature of this agreement it had two related features. One was that it would establish certain guidelines which might be applied to, or, conversely, quoted by other neighbouring establishments similarly placed. The other was that it was not in the notable interest of either party to give the agreement any unnecessary publicity before the time came in due course for it to be implemented. Although negotiated through what could be regarded as normal channels on the city's side, therefore, this was done with discretion and, once signed, the agreement itself was filed away until near the appropriate time. Although one could see that there would have to be some such negotiation, I personally never knew what was in the agreement until I read the terms in the *Bristol Evening Post*. In the event, this was not before 1975, when a political uproar took place as a result of trade union hostility to what had been decided.

The injection of the *Great Britain* into the middle of this situation, of course, had understandably been viewed with some concern by the authorities, since no one could quite tell what the effect would be of drawing a great deal of fortuitous public attention to this precise area and its problems. Thus the ship's presence was *ipso facto* an embarrassment, which could be ended most simply by her just going away. Yet none of this was our fault. Nor were the details even known to us. It seemed a little hard, therefore, that we should appear to be blamed for it all.

The second embarrassing aspect for the then political leadership lay in the current proposals for road development. Major plans for a new ring road involved a major bridge being built across the harbour, and the whole concept of the road with its attendant junctions and fly-overs was already the subject of active controversy on grounds of both cost and the destruction of amenities. As ill luck would have it, the key new bridge was to cross the water almost exactly where the *Great Britain* now lay in drydock.

Once again, therefore, she had automatically become a potential embarrassment, and it would be much the best if she would simply go away.

As far as our own future was concerned, matters came to a head on 3 February 1971, that is before either the Hill agreement or the enabling bill came into force. On 15 January Ewan Corlett and I had seen the Town Clerk, William Hutchinson, at his request, in order to answer several further questions which he had been instructed to put to us, mostly relating to the physical and technical requirements for any long-term berth for the *Great Britain*. Then, on 3 February I was called to the Council House. There, in the Town Clerk's office, the Leader of the Council read out to me the full texts of two Resolutions just passed respectively by the Finance and the Planning Committees. The first was brief and clear, the second less so.

By the Finance Committee, February 1st, 1971
RESOLVED
That it is the unanimous view of this Committee that no financial contribution should be made towards the restoration of the *Great Britain*.

Although I had not really expected any financial help at that time, partly because ratepayers were already giving a substantial sum to the Bristol Old Vic's Theatre Royal and had also been called on to restore Ashton Court, the door had now been resoundingly slammed.

Over the very much longer and more thoughtfully worded Planning Committee Resolution which followed, the difficulty lay in its full interpretation. And it was unfortunate that no time had been allowed for effective clarification on the spot, as an urgent appointment had already been made to give out a statement about it on the regional BBC television service. The key passages were that:

(a) the Corporation would 'provide a berth to accommodate a restored *Great Britain* on the clear understanding' that the ship could be moved to another site, the decision 'resting solely with the Corporation';
(b) the costs of any such move would be borne by the Project;
(c) there could be no commitment about any land, though this would be examined after 'the City Docks Closure Bill now before Parliament';
(d) 'for the period of approximately two years during which the ship is to be restored' a nominal rent of the dock would be considered, 'subject to the Corporation accepting no responsibility for the cost of services, amenities or maintenance';
(e) the Project must agree its programme of restoration with the Port Authority,

'in order to ensure that these works do not involve the addition of weight' which might prevent the ship being able to leave the drydock.

It seemed obvious at once that, while the Council had given a very welcome permission for the ship to stay in Bristol, the terms were onerous. It was not the question of the 'two years'; that only arose because at that time we were all talking about the restoration proceeding much more rapidly than proved possible. The really worrying point was that at any moment chosen by the Corporation the Project could be saddled with an immediate extra outlay of £150,000, since there was nowhere else to move to without creating the necessary site.

It was also a measure of the prevailing distrust that our actual programme of restoration must be agreed with the Port Authority. This was a very long way indeed from the approach which we deemed essential if we were to do the best for the ship, and we would never have come into a Bristol shipyard in the first place if we had been bound beforehand to have every step in the restoration subject to veto by the local authority. Fortunately, however, this clause was never applied literally. The overt suspicion that we would trick the authorities into being forced to leave the ship where she was, by rendering her immovable, was in practice allayed by my giving an undertaking that we would not do so. But it was an unpleasant sign of the way the situation had degenerated.

From our crucial fund-raising and general planning point of view, these two resolutions seemed to leave us in some ways even worse off than we had been before. Many people had felt that at least a gesture of financial support from the local authority could have been made – though I personally had not supported this view. But the publicly emphasized 'unanimous' rejection did make others cautious about helping us. And as regards the site we still could not say exactly what would eventually happen to the ship, so that this handicap remained, in addition to the specific further discouragement to potential donors of the extra £150,000 for removal.

Now it may well be that none of this was intended by those who had passed the resolutions in their existing form. It may be – as I think was the case – that some who had agreed to the terms felt that they were being not unhelpful, even generous, towards us. It may well be that in some respects the Council had little enough room for manoeuvre to reach other decisions. It may even be a fact, as a leading councillor once claimed to me some years later (though I genuinely believe inaccurately), that the city would 'naturally' have given consideration to helping us to finance a move, if this had had to take place.

The plain unavoidable fact, however, was that for us on the receiving end this was not how the terms came to look at the time, and it would have greatly helped to smooth the way over the next three years if there could have been some friendly discussion and explanation before matters went any further – or even an expression of regret. But there was none. Nor of course had there been any negotiation as such of the terms. For us it was take it or leave it, and all we could do was to express dismay. The only alternative was to see if better prospects really did exist elsewhere.

Throughout these difficult times one of the most heartening aspects of the whole position was the support from the local newspapers, the *Western Daily Press* and the *Bristol Evening Post*. Under the editorship of Gordon Farnsworth the *Bristol Evening Post* never wavered in its consistent backing for the *Great Britain*. With no axe to grind other than concern for the interests of the city, it always wanted to know the facts. It always gave them coverage. It frequently ran editorials in our favour. And at this crucial period something of our great unhappiness came through in its pages. One felt deeply grateful.

The development of a tragic rift with the current authorities was, of course, the very last thing one wanted, or indeed at the beginning of the great challenge of the salvage had ever for a single moment dreamed would happen. And it inevitably did both parties harm. While some people outside could not quite shake off a feeling that there must be something wrong with us, others kept asking what was the matter in Bristol. In these circumstances the rest of 1971 saw us on the Project anxiously searching for a lasting solution to the problem of the ship's final resting place, and it was unavoidable that we should try to get to the bottom of the London question. In addition, as a result of the publicity about our dilemma we received entirely unsolicited tentative approaches from Portsmouth and Plymouth.

The fundamental problem, of course, was whether there was an acceptable and technically feasible site in London, whatever the methods of financing it. And here the new factor was that the well-known firm of Taylor Woodrow had by now been appointed by the Greater London Council under contract as the commercial developers of St Katharine Dock. They had a resident director in charge, Peter Drew, with offices in a charming little house on the neck of land between the dock and the river. So I went to see him.

At this period, early 1971, HMS *Belfast* had not yet taken up her station on the other side of Tower Bridge. Indeed, Admiral Morgan Giles and his supporters were still actively arguing the toss with the Admiralty about her possible release by the navy, instead of her being broken up. But what everyone at all interested was clear about was that there was great scope for a ship, if not two ships, to form a public attraction in the immediate area of the Tower of London. And it was this concept which also interested Taylor Woodrow, with their bold planning of a proposed hotel – now completed – yacht marina, theatre, and other projects in St Katharine Dock.

Talking to Peter Drew was very stimulating. He himself was facing a task at once imaginative and realistic, creative as well as businesslike. If it failed in any of these things, it risked not being a success over all. And I felt that this also applied to the idea of the *Great Britain* coming to London, just as it had to her original salvage and return to the West Country. The Project had always had to reach for the stars, yet without letting its feet leave the ground. If it was crazy now to try to come to London, it had been crazy to start from the Falkland Islands. And yet with so much already achieved, why risk attempting to get the *Great Britain* down the Avon again, put on another pontoon, towed round the coast to perhaps the Medway, taken off again there, and towed afloat once more, up the Thames and through yet another lock that was really too small? At the same time, why not – after the extraordinary upset that seemed to have lost the ship the chance of a settled future in Bristol? At least, a viable decision must be reached.

Two alternatives emerged from my talk with Drew, and, when I told Ewan Corlett about them, he came and examined the practical problems a few days later. One was to bring the *Great Britain* in through the little lock by removing the necessary stonework; she would then be berthed in a specially built concrete enclave, from which the water would be pumped out. The other was quite simply to put her on a permanent pontoon, moored in the Thames just below the lock entrance and alongside the whole St Katharine Dock development. If a pontoon could be used in St Augustine's Reach, it could be used within hailing distance of Tower Bridge – provided that the Port of London Authority agreed and a minor dredging problem could be resolved, both of which seemed entirely possible.

The problem with the lock was precise. But this time it took two forms instead of one. The length of the ship mattered just as much as the width.

As to the width, the dock was 44 feet 8 inches to the *Great Britain*'s maximum beam of 50 feet 6 inches, though because of her bulbous shape this was not the most relevant figure. It became a question of the draught at which the ship would float and, as in Bristol, of obtaining a high enough tide. Corlett showed that, in the absolute extreme case of the highest recorded tide on that part of the Thames, and given a feasible degree of extra buoyancy to the empty hull – so long as it was empty – the *Great Britain* could just float through without the walls of the lock being altered in any way. But to achieve this, he declared, was to make the operation 'become impracticable'. On the other hand, since it then became a question of how much masonry would need to be removed from the top of the lock walls to make it more practicable, the problem could be contained within limits that were soluble, given the expenditure of enough money. It was in fact more like Brunel's difficulty in getting the *Great Britain* out of the Floating Harbour in 1844 rather than ours at the Great Western Dock in 1970.

The length of the St Katharine lock was only 200 feet compared with the *Great Britain*'s waterline length of 289 feet. But here the nature of the difficulty was different. Provided she was brought in on a reasonably high tide, there was enough depth of water for the gates at both ends of the lock not to need closing at the same time; the gates behind her from the river could be closed the moment her stern had cleared them, by which time her bow would be projecting into the inner water of St Katharine Dock. The real difficulty then lay in the fact that the ship was too long to be able to swing either way without hitting the wall on the opposite side of the fairly narrow waterway leading on into the West Dock proper. With money, however, this was not too serious a problem. Again stonework could be removed. The easiest way would be to take a chamfer on the starboard side, running 25 feet each way from the lock corner and extending 6 feet below the waterline. The *Great Britain* would then enter the main dock stern first.

Although all this was possible, it was not easy. And so, compared with any such antics, the pontoon on the Thames came to be regarded as a better bet – though personally I always felt that there would have been something much more complete and satisfying about being properly inside the dock rather than lying outside it. Corlett drew up a design for a special pontoon suitable for the Thames site, which in due course with the supporting evidence about the lock, together with our calculations about attendances and day-to-day financial viability, went up to the Taylor Woodrow board.

After examining in detail the figures for visitors to the Tower of London, the *Cutty Sark*, and the *Victory*, we estimated that we would start off with half a million visitors a year, and that this should produce a minimum turnover of more than £100,000 a year, from which it seemed reasonable to expect a net contribution to restoration funds of at least £20,000 a year. Subsequent practical experience at the dock in Bristol, though on a smaller scale, has since substantiated the line of argument.

The reinforced-concrete pontoon was an extremely ingenious affair. It would be 320 feet long and 64 feet broad, recessed down the middle by 8 feet in order to lower the *Great Britain* by that amount owing to the required amenities for the proposed theatre, alongside which she would lie. It would be constructed of 8 separate units, each to be 64 feet wide, 40 feet long and 12 feet deep at the sides. Fabricated on one of the quays within the dock area, these units would be launched individually into the water, taken out one by one through the lock, and joined together by normal pre-stressing concrete techniques, preferably in a drydock somewhere on the river.

When completed, this pontoon would be towed to a suitable rendezvous with the *Great Britain* on her ordinary sea-going *Mulus*-type pontoon, probably in the shallow, sheltered waters of the River Medway. There it would be sunk and the ship also de-pontooned. Then, when the *Great Britain* had been floated over the top and brought to rest by a falling tide, special submerging holes would be permanently blocked up, the water pumped out, and the whole combination brought to the surface, finally being towed back up the Thames with the *Great Britain* riding high on top. If the concrete had been properly pitched, both inside and out, and received proper maintenance, the structure should last for a hundred years. And it would be large enough to provide quite serviceable office and other accommodation inside the two edge sections running along the ship. The plan was as bold as it was succinct.

Although all this is now past history, so much water, as it were, under a non-existent pontoon, I have given an account of it because a great deal of serious work went into it, and the pontoon did receive approval in principle from the Taylor Woodrow board in June 1971. It was agreed at the time that nothing would be announced publicly until more specific progress had been made.

While all this was very heartening so far as it went, the fact was that the sources of finance for such a major undertaking were still unclear. And until they became more tangible, the essential background on which any sensible decision could be taken about the long-term future of the ship remained lacking. I felt acutely conscious throughout this difficult period that, as a Project, we were face to face with having to decide on something real, and that sooner or later a decision could not be put off any longer. We had brought the *Great Britain* back to Bristol for restoration. But would we, or would we not, wish to leave her there? While it seemed terrible to embark on another move, we might be in a much deeper hole financially if we stayed where we were, than if we went in for something on a bigger scale altogether.

There were three potential sources of finance. If we came to London, our greater prospective revenues might enable us to borrow on a larger scale. If Taylor Woodrow really wanted to include the ship in the amenity plans for their prestigious development, it was not unreasonable to suppose that they might share part of the burden, which could in any case be only chicken feed compared with their total costs. And the fact that we would be almost literally on the doorstep of the City might improve our chances of receiving appreciable donations.

As things turned out, events took a hand in bringing matters to a head, since it soon became apparent that the position was too inherently unstable to last. Interest in the *Great Britain* in Bristol was immense and, with the ship already the virtual centre of a political storm, reporters from the local press and media were constantly on the look-out for new angles. Thus they soon got to know that there had been developments in London, with the result that on 26 July a joint release was issued by Taylor Woodrow and the Project.

In view of all the possible innuendoes we had some difficulty in agreeing on the wording. But the simple facts were plainly stated. We said that a firm offer had been made in principle of a site at the St Katharine Dock which was under development by Taylor Woodrow, and that the Project was consequently preparing a detailed feasibility study, going further than it had already into questions of cost and into the technical problems of taking up such an offer.

All hell then broke loose. Although the position was too complex for simple treatment in headlines, the love–hate relationship in Bristol made sensation inevitable. Everyone got very cross with everyone else and we were caught in the middle. I naturally became the villain of the piece, since it was to me that the questions of the press were directed.

To decline to say anything at all would have led to suspicions that there was something to hide – which there was not. To say, as was true, that Bristol was still the most desirable site for the ship – if she could be adequately financed and cared for there – could be made to sound insincere in one's attitude to the serious and imaginative offer from London. Yet to suggest that we were about to go ahead with the London offer was to beg many questions not yet adequately examined, and to cast stupid aspersions on Bristol. Both parties resented any idea that we might be trying to put the *Great Britain* up for auction. No one in Bristol seemed willing to believe that the facts were as they were. And certainly no one at the London end was prepared to have any kind of wrangle with Bristol as such, nor to be thought – as would have been quite inaccurate – to have launched some kind of take-over bid for the ship. I may be forgiven, perhaps, for having thought for my part that no one – 'but no one', as the saying is – had ever stopped to look at *our* very real problems from our own beleaguered point of view.

There was no simple way out of the impasse – except, I suppose, if the London offer had been withdrawn, which it never was. Fortunately the August holiday season intervened, so that the heat could be allowed to die out of the immediate dispute. Meanwhile, however, we were left with the situation that we were to go into matters further in the autumn and Taylor Woodrow were to review progress as soon as we had done so. This became complicated by two foreign visits that I was to make in September and October to Italy and the United States respectively, both on business of my own. It was therefore left that we would not be looking for any real change in the situation till nearer the end of the year. And by then, as it happened, a factor was to emerge which was to settle everything.

This period of delay had two effects. One was to leave an impression with many people up and down the country that the *Great Britain* was definitely being moved to London – which never was the case. Even some years later there were still people who thought this. The other effect was to arouse active interest in two other cities in the possibilities of the ship finding a permanent home with them. Of these the Portsmouth enquiry went much further than the one from Plymouth. We wondered whether Liverpool might also enter the fray, as the ship's main home port historically. But it never did.

My own difficulties had been enormously accentuated during the summer by no less than two changes of the Project's General Secretary within a couple of months, together with the move of our London office from Chancery Lane to Cannon Street. This upheaval, which naturally took up a great deal of time and effort, came about for reasons basically concerned with our fund-raising. After a year and a half with us the time had come for Fitz Lombard to hand over to a retired naval officer, based in London, who was to combine being General Secretary with a specifically fund-raising role, in which he had considerable direct experience; at the same time, our agreement with our fund-raising consultant firm ended. Unfortunately, this officer was then unexpectedly selected for a job abroad before he had had time to settle down with us, and I had to recruit at short notice Group Captain Peter Gibb, who took the whole thing on and stayed for a year. With Peter I moved from the little office in Chancery Lane, since Anthony Abrahams rather wanted it back, to premises in Swire House in Cannon Street, which Adrian Swire and his brother John most generously let us have for no immediate payment. It was sad parting from Fitz. We made him our first formal 'Life Governor' of the Project.

The fact that all this had happened, and that on 30 October I returned from America with a renewed determination to settle the site for the ship, whatever the answer might be, made the enquiry from Portsmouth almost symbolic of a fresh start, coming as it did almost the moment I got back to the office. Entirely unsolicited and out of the blue, it was from an acquaintance there who told me that, if the future of the *Great Britain* was not yet settled, a number of city councillors would like to talk to me about having the ship in Portsmouth – the birthplace, I was reminded, of her designer, Isambard Kingdom Brunel himself. Peter Gibb and I duly spent a day with them, but the discussion came to nothing as there proved to be no adequate way of financing it. When I accepted a similar discussion at the House of Commons with Dame Joan Vickers, at that time one of the Plymouth MPs who was acting on behalf of certain interests in the city, the outcome was the same.

There remained the London question, and there the new factor in our relations with Taylor Woodrow in London was that of timing. The dénouement, which began to emerge as I renewed active contact with them, was curiously unspectacular, considering all that had happened during the year. Instead of any drama, the die was cast in an almost routine telephone conversation I had with Peter Drew shortly before Christmas. It was now well over a year since Taylor Woodrow had moved into St Katharine Dock, and their work was progressing well – while ours was not. I was not altogether surprised therefore, when he made the point that, if the *Great Britain* was going to come, it would probably have to be during 1972.

It was perfectly obvious that, considering the actual condition of the ship at that moment, this would not be possible. She would have to be in a much more advanced state of general restoration than anything which experience with our existing resources and circumstances now permitted. I had always considered that restoration would continue after any move, but a certain minimum was essential beforehand and we were nowhere near it. Nor did it now look as if any major fresh financial support was likely to be forthcoming in time from Taylor Woodrow or any other source, to make it feasible to put work in hand on the proposed permanent pontoon, (if that indeed was to be the preferred solution – which had also not yet been finally decided). So I said at once on the telephone:

'I'm afraid that we couldn't possibly be ready by then.'

And that really was that. The two parties were engaged in operations on different time scales, and, while they had started from a common point, they were now already too far apart to have any significant contact. So the *Great Britain* would never go to London. I knew, too, that come what might, she would now never go anywhere else either. Enough is enough. So I thanked the developers very sincerely for all that they had done, and we agreed to drop the matter.

Curiously enough, it was only a very few days after this, when it had finally become certain that our future lay in Bristol, that word reached me indirectly from the Bristol pilots. They would never, it was reported, take the *Great Britain* out of Bristol. She belonged in Bristol and so far as they were concerned, having brought her in so successfully, whatever plans anyone else might have to take her out, they would never have anything to do with them. In its way this loyal gesture was one of the most genuinely encouraging things that had happened in our whole long story.

With London settled, it now only remained to redouble our efforts to get straightened out in Bristol. And the first step, considering the mountain of cross-purposes, indignation and misunderstanding which had by now developed, was to take our own formal decision and make as sure as we could that it was known outside. So when the Project's next Council took place, which was on 25 January 1972 in the boardroom at Swire House in Cannon Street, we all came to it, I think, with our minds made up. The decision to declare for Bristol was unanimous and, with Adrian Ball's help, we prepared a press statement which was issued the following day.

In it we said that we would keep the *Great Britain* in Bristol, and would do all in our power to try to see that she remained for ever in the historic Great Western Dock where she now was. We would do nothing, and would take no part in any discussions with anyone, to consider any other site unless and until our Bristol aims might finally prove unattainable.

It was just on a year since the City Council's last announcement. Though we could not know it then, it was to be another three years before their next one. But slow and difficult though this extensive period was sometimes to be, it was also one in which the light did finally prove to shine brighter and brighter at the end of the tunnel.

12. Costs and Achievements

The worries about a permanent site could not be allowed to become the be-all and end-all of our existence, and during the years from 1971 to 1975 a mass of other things was always happening. Life with the *Great Britain* has never lain down quietly and probably never will. Thus, one of the events towards the end of Fitz Lombard's time with us in the spring of 1971 was great fun, as well as quite useful. He and I, with our wives and with Lady Gladwyn, a direct descendant of Brunel, were invited up to County Durham for the launching at Swan Hunter's yard on the Tyne of the 250,000-ton supertanker *Texaco Great Britain*.

It was some measure of the status the Project had reached by this time that, when Texaco proposed to include this country among the names of their supertankers, following the *Texaco Denmark*, their public relations team thought it would be nice if this could also be linked in some way with the Brunel ship. So, besides making a generous contribution to our finances, Texaco had a hundred thousand little medallions stamped out with an impression of the huge new tanker on one side and the original *Great Britain* on the other. These were then mounted in stiff cardboard with appropriate wording, and fifty thousand were handed out free at Texaco garages in the North East, with fifty thousand similarly in the West Country. It was a splendid advertisement and no doubt brought quite a few visitors to our dock.

A special train-load of guests was brought up to Durham from London for the great occasion. Before the launch itself I stood for a moment beneath the incredibly oppressive and seemingly endless, totally flat bottom of this gigantic vessel. I felt numbed by her immensity, while also struck by what seemed in comparison her paper-thin steel plates. The idea that this vast city block of a structure could slide down the slipway, let alone float, seemed as preposterous as the seaworthiness of Brunel's 3,000 tons of iron must have done to many observers in 1843. But of course it did, and all went well.

That evening, when it came to my turn to say a few words at the official dinner, I was much aware of the American attitude about things old and new, and that, while Texans particularly might venerate the old, it was the new that they admired. So I put it to them.

'We of the SS *Great Britain* wish God speed to the fine vessel that has been launched today. But there is one thing I would ask you not to forget.' I sensed a flicker of awakened interest.

'When this great ship is scrapped and gone, ours will live on.' I paused. 'She is already a century and a quarter old. Now, we are building for the next hundred years.'

There was a second's hesitation. Then the apparent impudence of it sank in. And with these friendly Americans laughing and applauding, I knew I had got a part of our philosophy across. Until the train left next day I was conscious of a faintly unusual approval of what we were doing. Later we gave a print of Keith Griffin's striking painting of the *Great Britain* at sea to hang on board the *Texaco Great Britain*, framed in wood from the timber cladding.

It has been a feature of life with the ship that there are always lectures and informal talks to be given, speeches of thanks or welcome or celebration to be made; and like one or two of my colleagues I have taken part in a good many over the years. One occasion which I will always particularly remember was a set lecture that I gave, with slides, to a packed audience at the Royal Society of Arts in London on 13 January 1971. The chair was taken by Earl Jellicoe, at that time in the cabinet as Lord Privy Seal. Not only did it reflect the type of considered and serious interest which the ship was arousing, but the enthusiasm for the subject was so great that the Society printed the lecture as a separate publication, and later gave me one of its now discontinued annual silver medals to mark the event.

On another occasion a paper was presented by Ewan Corlett at a meeting of the Royal Institution of Naval Architects on 27 April 1971. It was entitled 'The Steamship *Great Britain*' and he had taken great care to see that it gave a full technical account of the ship's construction and place in history, as well as a professional outline of the salvage. Accompanied by drawings and photographs, it was published as the authentic statement of our work and was only superseded in a sense by his book *The Iron Ship*, which came out four years later.

Most of the meetings in those days were connected with trying to raise money. My third particular memory is of one that, while not attempting to do so in itself, marked the start of others that were. It was an evening sponsored by the Institute of Directors at the Grand Spa Hotel in Bristol, at which Euan Strathcona and I were both invited to speak. Arising out of it, George Ross Goobey joined in to help us over the next three years or so. On the board of Imperial Tobacco and Hill Samuel, he had a considerable national reputation in business and financial circles, and was dubbed by the press 'the man who invented the cult of the equity', because of his success in that direction as a pension-fund manager.

For some months before that we had had a special staff member seconded to us from our financial consultants, and it was part of his job to guide us into setting up a fund-raising organization, as well as holding the appropriate types of meetings. This also involved drawing in people from outside our own group to form, first, a Fund Raising Policy Committee and then our main – as we called it – Foundation Fund Committee. The first committee met about half a dozen times either in the City or at our consultants' offices during the early part of 1971. When its work was done, the main Foundation Fund Committee took over, holding its inaugural sessions, thanks to George Ross Goobey, at the Imperial Tobacco Group's London offices near Hyde Park Corner. My own colleagues most concerned in these operations were Eric Custance, Euan Strathcona, Maldwin Drummond, Adrian Swire and George Naish, while from outside our circle we drew on the support of a wide spread of business knowledge and interest.

Meanwhile, I had embarked upon a series of three general presentations of the *Great Britain* story to invited audiences drawn predominantly from business and finance. The first was held specifically in the City at the Great Eastern Hotel, and the second at Shell Centre on the South Bank of the Thames opposite Westminster, by courtesy of the company. The third was in Bristol at the Grand Hotel. At each I gave a talk, with slides, and included information about our financial position, the chair being taken by an appropriate business figure. At this period a good many other meetings also took place in the form of much more intimate slide shows on the premises of particular firms and partnerships. They were usually limited to one hour at 5.30 or 6 pm, just as the offices were closing, and with audiences of between six and twenty-four people. Although brief, these were the occasions when one could really get across to significant individuals what one was doing, and invariably some of them agreed to help us. Most of these meetings took place in London, but as part of this opening series we also held at least one respectively in Birmingham, Manchester, Glasgow, Bournemouth, and Bristol itself.

I have sometimes been asked over the years, particularly in Bristol, when we were going to launch our appeal for funds. The general answer, of course, is that we launched it long ago by the methods chosen above, which were regarded by our consultants as the most likely to succeed. But the answer locally is also that, because the *Great Britain* had become such a problem, we found it impossible to make much financial progress there. We even met this special difficulty in near-by Cheltenham, where people who at one time had looked like helping us suddenly withdrew, quoting the Bristol situation. It was all very sad. But the result was that the restoration fund for the city's own ship was mainly built up through the early and perhaps most significant years of the Project without as much support in the surrounding area as it obtained elsewhere.

There were naturally many aspects of the question of presenting our proposals in the most effective way for fund-raising purposes, and we used to go through the figures and projections at our Fund Raising Policy Committee meetings again and again with the utmost care. But one, of course, was of fundamental importance. How much were we trying to raise? What was the target figure?

To determine this was more difficult than might be supposed, not because we did not know what we were trying to do, but because even in those days it was obvious that inflation would change everything – though one still hoped that the national collapse of the currency would not go as far as in fact it did. So there were always two other cardinal unknowns, in addition to the uncertainty about the site. The first was the costing of the programme at the time, and the second was the number of years it would take to carry it out. The latter will, as I have already mentioned, have a huge effect on the eventual total nominal cost.

The costing at the time was also greatly affected by the degree to which we could, and would, receive gifts in kind and services below cost. We could of course calculate a value and then regard as a bonus anything given or done for us below that cost. But we had no means of knowing what proportion of our restoration might come into this category. And whereas, in looking back on the total value put into the ship, we have been able to assess money equivalents for items given, and thus arrive at some reasonably accurate overall 'cost' of the restoration already completed, to do this forward leaves room for widespread error. And here as usual our local critics were already accusing us, even before we launched our fund-raising, of not knowing what we were doing.

'It will cost three million pounds,' one of them announced publicly. In those days that was a great deal of money. 'They might as well build an entirely new ship,' chimed in another. And so the ceaseless carping went on. Perhaps in view of this I may be excused if I list some solid facts in the next few pages.

In reality, once we had got the *Great Britain* safely back into drydock and had had an opportunity of taking a hard look at the situation, we settled on our restoration aims and these have never varied. As we have put it ever since in our literature, we seek 'to create the external appearance of the original Brunel ship and enough of the interior to show what life on this Victorian liner was like.' That, we have always said, basically means restoring the upper 'tween decks promenade in the after section of the ship; the main dining saloon on the deck below; a few cabins leading out of these two areas, including the captain's accommodation (there was no bridge on the *Great Britain* in the sense that one means it today); and the officers' and crew's quarters in the forecastle. We have, of course, always said that we would also recreate the engine room and the great driving chain to the propeller shaft, together with the operational fronts of the boilers. And I have throughout made a very positive point that this should leave the whole of the forward half of the ship, apart from the forecastle beyond the forward bulkhead, to be retained exactly as it is, apart from its being cleaned up and the ironwork fully painted.

Thus, to return to the vital question of the target figure to be named for our approach to the public, there were plenty of grounds for discussion, and to set it either too low or too high could be equally counter-productive. In the end we settled on an initial target – hence the word 'Founding' in our expression 'Founding Fund' – of £650,000 at 1970 prices. Later, as we gained experience both of the actual way restoration was working out and of the accelerating pace of inflation, we decided to speak of separate 'phases' of the restoration, and in 1973 we named the three of them as Phases I, II and III.

Phase I was from 1970 to the then current date, namely 31 July 1973. We showed that, in round figures, if one included the period up to the drydocking of the ship, we had spent £165,000 on the salvage and put in a further £135,000 afterwards, making a total of £300,000 for Phase I.

This latter sum had covered all the waterjetting and removal of timber cladding; the strengthening of the forecastle structure; the decking of the forecastle and mounting of the bowsprit; the repair of the bow, and creation of the decorative trailboards and coat of arms; the temporary installation of the propeller (itself a gift); and repairs to some of the plating and gunwale.

Phase II was then named as running for the six years to the end of the seventies, that is the rest of 1973 to 1979, and was estimated to require at the current 1973 prices a sum equivalent to £320,000. This would cover further work on the hull and main structure of the ship; the decking, deck fittings, masts and rigging; the funnel, with its necessary underlying structure; the stern windows and the stern frame and rudder – though the whole question of this frame was subsequently expected to be put back to a later stage.

Phase III consisted of the longer term, and covered future completion of the officers' and crew's quarters, the cabins, the dining saloon and promenade, the reproduction engine and engine room, and adequate ventilation and lighting to cater for modern requirements. We stated that in view of the national circumstances it would be idle to pick a figure out of the air to cover these costs at that stage.

As regards the actual income and expenditure of the Project, by 1973 we were in a position to show that against our total outgoings of £300,063, we had received £307,134. We estimated that to meet the requirements of £320,000 for Phase II we had an already foreseeable income of £68,000. This left our fund-raising target for Phase II at £252,000 – or a round figure of a quarter of a million.

By 1975, or to be more precise by the end of our financial year on 31 January 1975, we were able to show that we had by now financed a total expenditure of £332,056. And, in view of the radical uncertainties introduced by the raging inflation, we set a limited target for fund-raising over the next two years of £100,000, which would go towards whatever the final costs of the planned Phase II might in the end prove to be. Physical progress on the ship has in fact been maintained and from year to year has never so far been halted, in spite of the mounting difficulties on the national scene.

Part of our financing has naturally consisted of money we could earn from the opening of the dock to the public. And on the advice of the Charity Commissioners, when in January 1971 we finally incorporated the charity company, SS *Great Britain* Project Ltd, (with the new charity number, 262158) we also incorporated as a wholly-owned subsidiary another company of an ordinary standard type, which we called SS *Great Britain* Trading Ltd. This has covenanted its annual profit to the parent charity company, thus benefiting from tax concessions. The entire income and expenditure arising out of the operation of the dock in all its forms goes through the books of the trading company – admission, souvenir sales, restaurant commission, car-park fees, and any other earnings, being set against salaries and wages, general administration costs, maintenance of the property, advertising and promotion, and so on.

Thanks to the devotion of all who work at the dock, this operation has so far always made a profit. The 1975 turnover had reached approximately £60,000, which produced a net contribution to the restoration fund of rather more than £13,500 – vital in terms of our cash flow and viability, though not, of course, more than a fraction of the requirements of the capital fund as a whole. All this naturally depends on the number of visitors, and that in turn means keeping up our advertising and the effort constantly made over general promotion. But, if recent trends continue and the problems of maintenance do not multiply unduly, the whole enterprise should at least sustain itself.

The British habit of understatement, inhibitions about pushing oneself forward, and an instinctive distrust of the press have combined in some quarters to make 'publicity' rather a dirty word. Until recently at least it was apt not to be used in the navy without the automatic prefix 'undesirable'. Accordingly, in view of my emphasis throughout our story on publicity, promotion and presentation, I hope that no one will accuse the Project of simply looking for sensation or notoriety – we have had our fill of both. The fact is that publicity to keep the Project in the public eye with the right sort of image is the lifeblood of a business such as ours, depending as it does on an essential flow of visitors and of donations. And with this in mind, I have always done all I could to ensure an adequate supply of photographs and colour slides of the progress of the Project.

It was against this background, therefore, that my distress over the question of that other crucial medium, a film, deserves to be judged. Once we had got into our stride after the ship came in, I knew that disenchantment with the BBC had to be put to a decision. Would they, or would they not, honour their implicit promise of help with material for a suitable film of the salvage itself? They had broadcast a documentary which most people regard as giving a marvellous impression of that stirring event. But would they allow this to be translated into a film for everyday use – of a suitable shorter length, with a balance of forward-looking reality, with distortions of fact ironed out, and with appropriate additional material since the homecoming?

On their first promise, a free copy of film of the salvage, they did indeed present us with a 16-millimetre print of the version which they finally edited, I believe, for their commercial sales abroad. But this was very unsuitable for our own purposes, since it ran for almost an hour and said virtually nothing about the Project as such – almost useless for fund-raising. We were forbidden to cut, edit or add to this film in any way. To do so, I was given to understand, would infringe BBC copyright. This was in no sense the approach we had been promised at the start. It also served to impose on posterity the specialist producer's interpretation of events, as if this was an accurate record.

The Corporation used a similar argument on the second point, left-over material. Copyright was again invoked to claim that it was impossible to let this material out of the BBC. The next thing I heard, however, was that they had actually offered it themselves to the National Maritime Museum. No word of explanation, let alone of apology, was even offered to the Project. Naturally the Museum accepted this unique and valuable material, and there it rests. But the let-down still appears in retrospect as even worse than the worst one might have expected. I was personally the more sorry about it because, for the very many years in which I used to appear on dozens of BBC radio and television programmes, I never dreamed that outsiders could be treated in this way.

All this left us high and dry without any background film. It was therefore not until an independent director came along, Mr B. L. Burgess, who in addition to his own support secured the generous backing of the Phoenix Assurance Company, that we were able to envisage the eventual composition of a film based on other historical material, and on the gradual shooting of sequences covering the restoration as it takes place. And this is now being done. Also, since the *Great Britain*'s return to the drydock both Harlech TV and the BBC's current news and documentary coverage has been excellent – which has certainly helped to heal the need-less wounds of the past.

One of our happiest general relationships has been with our commercial publishers, Macmillan. Early on we reached a carefully negotiated agreement about editorial control, and they have not only produced our guide-book and some of our other literature, but have done so on a deliberately favourable financial basis, with a donation to the restoration fund as well.

Since the abrupt start in July 1970, we have done what we could to improve the amenities at the dock. But I find it intensely regrettable that we have never felt justified in doing a very great deal more. Joe Blake, Tim Webb, and their staff have had only the most cheeseparing sums to spend on the amenities, and – as I have discussed earlier – over the years we have held back because we could not be certain of staying in the dock to reap the full benefit. Nor was the site the only problem. It was only after a tacit understanding with the unions that we felt we could touch any of the dock structure ourselves – the ship herself continuing to remain outside our jurisdiction. By the end of 1975, however, settlement of the detailed terms of our lease at last meant that, in the dock at least, we could make substantial improvements once we could find the money for them. And I greatly hope that this will not now be too long delayed.

The feature of attendances at the dock, of course, is that they are very seasonal, though from Easter through to October is all quite good. The lowest months are December and January. In our first winter we had to decide whether to stay open or not. As a certain nucleus of staff would be needed anyway for security and maintenance, we decided we might just as well go on letting the public in, and we have done so ever since. The only day in the year we normally close is Christmas Day. We received our 200,000th visitor within twelve months of opening, that is on 29 June 1971. The half millionth came on 29 July 1974, and by the spring of 1976 we had reached 700,000.

Although this is far below the two ships in London, the *Cutty Sark* and the *Belfast*, and the very long-established *Victory* in Portsmouth, it is a long way above our original estimates and the trend is upwards each year, the current annual figure approaching 130,000. It is also well above all but the topmost stately homes, and it has held up in spite of the national economic crisis.

One of our mainstays has been the growing number of organized parties which come on visits, many of them from schools and colleges, but others from bodies as varied, for instance, as the British Society for Strain Measurements, the Canadian Cadet Rifle Shooting Team, and the Rolls Royce Foremen's Association. From 1971 to 1975 the number of parties booking in to see the ship during the year rose from 171 to 629, of whom the students showed an increase from 6,669 to 19,805. There were also a rising number of coaches which came without booking. We invariably give them a welcome, though we could sometimes do more for them if we knew beforehand.

When I study our statistics, I think of the official difficulties we originally encountered and I sometimes recall the remarks made quite early on by a distinguished local citizen, who claimed to be speaking as a friend. If he had classed himself among our opponents, I shudder to think how he might have put it.

'The trouble with you,' he said, 'is that you are like a cat with a mouse. Like the cat which rushed off to catch a mouse, you went and brought this ship back here. But, like the cat after she had caught it, what you've got is a dead mouse. And it's no use now fawning and laying it at the master's feet expecting to be stroked!'

So friendly – and some mouse.

The seasonal nature of the work with the public meant that Blake built up a small nucleus of permanent staff, taking on extra people for the summer only. Thus we have created quite a number of new jobs in Bristol. By and large the nucleus consists of older men, some in their sixties, and this is the way it should be with our kind of occupation. Over the years a number have been with us a long time and the Project has had much to thank them for. In the first instance our two supervisors were Alf Warren and Jim Charlesworth – though everyone shares in most of the duties, particularly at the admission kiosk and in the souvenir shop.

Taking tours round the ship is rather a special art and two who have guided many thousands in their time are John Allen and Carl Harrell – who is also a paid-up Member of the Project. Other old hands have been Jack Stokes, Fred Studley, Frank Thorpe and Fred Stephens. Partly because winter conditions in the docks are sometimes difficult, few women have been on the more permanent tasks. But we have had one marriage – in 1972, Ann Locke and Keith Boyes, who first came to work on the *Great Britain* as a water jetter for Plant Technical Services. And I would like to think this may have greatly pleased the famous old ship that all the fuss is about. She saw a good few others in her heyday.

A hundred years ago, moreover, Anthony Trollope wrote the whole of one of his novels, *Lady Anna*, while on the *Great Britain* on a two-month voyage to Melbourne in 1871. She sailed from Liverpool on 27 May and he had a special desk put up in his cabin before coming on board. He wrote something every day except one, when he was ill, covering sixty-six pages of manuscript each week with, as he records, an average of 250 words on each page. The work was published as a book in 1874.

All this raises the legitimate question of what we are aiming at with the dock. My own view has always been that we should create a centre of good design, with the twin objects of enabling people of average means and range of interest to spend a pleasant half-day there, and at the same time to come away having absorbed knowledge about the life and times of Brunel's most successful ship. I see this combined entertainment and educational purpose as being achieved by means of a skilfully arranged exhibition hall or small museum building; a miniature cinema; a comfortable medium-grade restaurant, with a self-service counter from which the ship herself would be visible, preferably in silhouette from the south, or port side; a set of administrative offices, a storeroom and a shop, all accessible from the street; and a lecture or reception room available for meetings or parties, which might eventually be on board the ship.

This would require a rather larger area than we have access to at present, particularly as the car park ought to be immediately adjoining it. It would mean pulling down the old corrugated-iron buildings on the north side, which would also make the *Great Britain* a splendid sight from across the water; and the whole public entrance arrangements would then best be changed to the other side of the ship, with direct access from Gas Ferry Road. The south side of the dock would be sloped back so as to allow a better view of the hull as a whole, and the main block of buildings would be constructed just beyond the edge of this new arrangement.

A glance at the present dock will show that nothing of this general plan has so far been achieved – except in so far as we have been able in a skeleton way to set up a souvenir shop, an embryonic little 'museum', and an outside restaurant by the car park. The shop premises have gradually been created by the efforts of our own staff, and Tim Webb has skilfully masterminded the contents. We first opened the existing museum in April 1973 and with the help of the Bristol City Museum have been able to improve it a bit since then. The present *Great Britain* Restaurant came into existence early in 1974, as a result of an approach from a catering subsidiary of the Falkland Islands Company and our own application to the Port of Bristol Authority for the lease of the building, when it was closed down as a port workers' canteen. The restaurant was much improved during 1975.

Naturally, there can be no question of carrying out the main scheme until any final proposals for redeveloping the City Docks have been agreed, since major questions of land use are involved. It would also probably require adequate overall financing in its own right, whether by a private contractor or under a public authority. But some concept of this kind one hopes may receive sympathy and support in due course – whether or not a major Bristol maritime museum is eventually created and the *Great Britain* becomes, as I am sure it should, very closely associated with it.

In trying to add to the historical items that people might like to see, I feel that we have naturally had to take account of two aspects – what fate puts in our path, and what we ourselves would wish to do. On the first question, one of my own growing worries during the first few months was the fact that cost and technical difficulty had forced us to leave behind at Avonmouth the two great 20-ton masts taken out of the ship in Sparrow Cove and brought back on the pontoon. Out on the open dock they were at risk from weather and vandals, and they clearly could not stay there for ever anyway. So, early in 1971 we arranged for the National Maritime Museum to collect the foremast – on permanent loan from the Project – and it has established this historic piece of timber as a separate exhibit in the grounds at Greenwich. The mainmast we brought up the river, to be dumped temporarily in Charles Hill's yard, together with the 4-ton iron spar that used to hang from it. Then, on 18 February 1972, we moved them into their present positions in our own dock.

Another addition to our exhibits was a particularly welcome one. This was the original ship's bell of the *Great Britain*, which had been on board when she arrived in Stanley for the last time in 1886. As visitors to the ship will know, this now hangs temporarily on board, having been presented to us at a little ceremony by the chairman of the Falklands Islands Company, Maurice Waldron. We had obtained it by sending out in exchange another bell, presented to us for the purpose by a Bristol businessman, Roger Marcus. A subsequent surprise gift was the bell of Brunel's first ship, the *Great Western*, which had come into the possession of the Southern Electricity Board some years previously. Delighted to have it, we then explored the possibiity of also acquiring the bell of Brunel's third and last ship, the *Great Eastern*, thus creating a uniquely interesting joint exhibit. But, although we located it in private hands, negotiations have not so far been fruitful.

This brings me back to the other historical aspect of the problem and the question of how far we should go out to acquire things not directly linked with the *Great Britain* herself. In the early years we were in no position to do much about it even if we had wished. But I quite soon came to realize that, to make the exhibition of the *Great Britain* herself as instructive and attractive as possible, we would need eventually to include at the dock not only reproductions of the shore-establishment machinery used at the time of her building, but also a limited number of other items relevant to illustration of the Victorian age in which she operated.

Just what these should be it is hard to say until one knows more about the availability of funds and suitable accommodation. But it was when considering this kind of problem that I had always wanted to see more of the way the Americans tackle these and other ship preservation questions. And I had them very much in mind during a visit to the United States in our formative period of 1971 when I was able to visit Mystic Seaport in Connecticut and then to make my own somewhat deferred visit to the San Francisco Maritime Museum, where I met Karl Kortum, its distinguished director. The main lesson borne in on me by both places, particularly Mystic, was that almost everything which helps to illustrate the contemporary background of maritime life – buildings, tools, equipment, people's customs – against which a vessel operated is likely to make a visit to her in the present day more interesting and comprehensible, provided that its proper significance is brought out by the way it is shown.

During that trip I also went to see Bill Swigert in Oregon and Scott Newhall again in San Francisco. From talking with Swigert I came to realize that his years of deep interest in the *Great Britain* had left him with probably the most extensive collection of memorabilia to do with the ship that exists anywhere in private hands, including the captain's desk, several original prints and historic documents, and five-foot models of all three of Brunel's ships, together with a beautiful Bassett Lowke working model of the *Great Britain*'s engines like the one in the Science Museum at South Kensington in London. From my talks with all three – Kortum, Swigert and Newhall – I came to the conclusion that, quite apart from our British group being formed to salvage the *Great Britain* in 1968, they were already meeting a number of problems which might well have frustrated them in the end anyway.

It was soon after my return home from that trip late in 1971 that I was able to be present at two occasions which, each in its own way, heralded some of the first breaks in the clouds that hung over the ship locally. One was a meeting of what came to be called our Bristol Committee. Formed spontaneously some weeks before by a group of young and active local citizens under the sponsorship of Stephen Macfarlane, it began to hold monthly meetings to see how support on the spot could be rallied for two propositions – that the *Great Britain* should stay in Bristol, and that she should stay in the Great Western Dock. This was a very welcome development from our point of view, and the Bristol Committee gradually brought us the backing of almost all the independent societies and bodies in the area, from such organizations as the Bristol Civic Society and the Cabot Cruising Club to the Senior as well as the Junior Chamber of Commerce. The Junior Chamber of Commerce had in fact been outstanding in its support for us right through from the start. In 1970 it produced a very timely booklet about the ship, which we were extremely glad to sell at the dock and which gave the Project an invaluable profit of several hundred pounds.

The other occasion, I confess, had its humorous side. Sir Hugh Casson, the distinguished architect and designer, who knew Bristol well, had recently been appointed to carry out an enquiry and give advice on the redevelopment of the City Docks after their closure to commercial traffic, then scheduled during the nineteen seventies. Obviously what he said would have great, possibly crucial, bearing on any official decisions that might finally be taken about the *Great Britain*. And the whole forward planning of the area was destined to pause for over a year, while he produced his Report.

It so happened that early in his career Sir Hugh had been in partnership with a relative of my wife's, and I knew how very much aware he was already of the existence and great historic interest of the *Great Britain*. Early on he thus asked me to have lunch with him at the Royal College of Art in London, where he had an appointment as Senior Tutor in the School of Environmental Design. And amid these highly suitable surroundings, after we had been joined by his colleague who would be involved in the Report, Michael Cain, we reviewed together very thoroughly the whole position of the ship, on which we saw eye to eye.

A couple of weeks later I was having one of the talks with the Town Clerk which we both found useful from time to time in order to keep in touch with developments, when he mentioned to me the undesirability of my talking to Sir Hugh Casson at that juncture. I saw how he had come to say this. But happily there was absolutely nothing I could do about it – and everyone else soon began lobbying like mad anyway.

13. Pushing on with Restoration

I was always rather depressed by the amount of time taken up by the two long slogging jobs of water-jetting the ironwork and removing the heavy wooden cladding from the ship. Between them they absorbed over 12,000 man hours during our first two years. But by quite early in 1972 I felt that we were beginning to see daylight, and in retrospect I think that the period between mid-1972 and mid-1973 was the most encouraging we had in terms of getting ahead with the *Great Britain*, in spite of several postponements. At any rate this helped to offset the frustrations of waiting to see whether, how, and when our long-term position in the City Docks might be resolved.

One simple but important problem at least was settled fairly readily. The timber cladding had been held in place by just over 10,000 bolts and nuts. However, the question was what we were to put in their place, since their removal had, of course, opened up 10,000 fresh holes in the old iron plates. We did consider glass-fibre filling, but this seemed a rather costly nonsense. So we put another 10,000 bolts and nuts back in the hull, but this time holding only neoprene waterproof washers. The steel company, GKN, gave them to us, a gift worth many hundreds of pounds. As can be seen today, the result is very effective. It gives an appearance of riveting throughout the hull, and is quite distinct from the original flush-headed rivets.

As part of the water-jet cleaning being done by Plant Technical Services, an interesting question had arisen. They had opened and begun scouring out the tanks between the double bottom and the keel, a slow, difficult, and in some ways dangerous process, owing to the cramped space and the large quantities of congealed Falklands mud inside, which necessitated specially powerful equipment. But one tank near the stern proved to contain rather dirty, though nevertheless fresh, water. Was it 1886 water?

The exciting event at the dock which gave us a special send-off for 1972 was the arrival of the replica six-bladed propeller. Weighing four tons, it was 15 feet 6 inches in diameter; this was an exact copy of Brunel's original, except that it was made of steel instead of iron. It was manufactured in Glasgow to Corlett's drawings and presented to us by Stone Manganese Marine. Symbolic of everything the *Great Britain* stood for, we were highly delighted to receive it, even though the ship was not yet ready for it to be mounted.

Technology in Brunel's day was not far enough advanced for him either to cast the blades in one piece with the shaft or to weld them together. So instead they had been bolted on. Copying this method in 1972 had the advantage that the blades could be taken off temporarily for travel; and the whole propeller thus came on a lorry by road without any trouble – or a police escort. I was only disappointed that I was unsuccessful in my efforts to get a sign put on the vehicle saying what its load was; all the way down the motorway this would have been a fine advertisement for everyone concerned. When the propeller duly arrived, we lowered it carefully into the dock to the accompaniment of press and TV photography, and leant it against the side wall. And there, unfortunately, it had to remain for over a year, though at least I got the blades screwed back on and we put a notice on it to tell visitors what was happening.

We had no immediate prospect of mounting the propeller properly, since the stern would have to be reconstructed first. But, as it lay there, I felt increasingly that we really must connect it to the ship in some way. Almost the whole point of reiterating that the *Great Britain* was the first propeller-driven ship was being lost on visitors to the dock, if this fascinating replica was only to be seen mouldering in a corner. But here we were up against several technical problems and at first there seemed little to be done, unless we were to upset our carefully calculated priorities and spend money on a major temporary step that we would later have to retrace.

Given that we could not run to the major stern reconstruction for the time being, there were two lesser problems. As the propeller is too big to revolve in the present aperture on the ship, we felt we ought really to do part of the later job anyway, which would be to cut away at least a section of the lifting trunk and perhaps the bottom horizontal of the non-Brunel stern frame. But, if we did, there might not be enough strength in the rest of the ironwork to carry the weight of the propeller, until structural repairs had been carried out above and, preferably, the weatherdeck also put on. The other problem was how to take the four-ton weight, while the propeller was actually being swung across into position. No crane could get a purchase on it owing to the overhang of the ship. As was done eventually, the move could be made by shifting in stages from one set of transverse ropes or chains to another. But this also brought in question the strength of particular parts of the old ironwork to which they would be attached.

I feel it of some interest to record all this for two reasons. First, this kind of situation arises all the time in the reconstruction, and the fact that no action can be seen to be taking place is no evidence that quite hard work may not be going on in the background. On the positive side, for instance, we are continuing to stockpile draughtsman's detailed drawings for items quite a long way down the pipeline – and this came in very usefully in 1975, when we were suddenly offered the gift of No. 2 steel mast and could produce the technical papers at once. Secondly, of more importance to the general concept of restoring the *Great Britain*, the issues surrounding the propeller dramatically raised major questions of public relations. In particular, when should money be diverted from long-term restoration to keeping the current image of the ship alive?

We debated the point at more than one Ship Committee meeting towards the end of 1972. Ewan Corlett and Joe Blake naturally wanted to press on with every bit of restoration we could manage. So did I. But to the case that what mattered in the long run was the final restoration, I could not help making the standard reply:

'In the long run we are all dead.' And I added 'What matters quite as much is how we get there.'

So we took a policy decision to cut away in due course the top section of the lifting trunk only at the upper 'tween deck level. This would be necessary anyway, in order to recreate the beautiful stern gallery at the after end of the famous promenade saloon; meanwhile, the stern structure as a whole would not be weakened. And, making good photogenic material for the media, the propeller itself was successfully moved on 22 May of the following year, 1973, to hang for the time being in the aperture as it is now, the cost being £460 (at current prices).

Although in 1971 we had decided to concentrate our major efforts on the bow, the following year it became clear that the stern windows themselves must be made an exception, as well as the external decorations above them. I had thought for many months that it was becoming more and more unsuitable and degrading that the first view of the ship, which visitors obtained from the car park, should be the rough and wasted top of the stern as seen over the brick wall of a timber yard. So, beginning in the winter of 1971–3 we embarked on the task of removing the sailing-ship timber on the windows; straightening out their frames; descaling, repairing and laminating the delicate transom; clearing the inside of the stern gallery, including lifting out the great spare tiller still lashed to the deck and probably never used; and, by no means least, carving and moulding the gilded coat of arms itself with its decorative surrounding cornucopia. Triplex gave us the heavy-duty glass for the windows, each one slightly different in shape from all the rest.

The main restoration feature of the whole of this period, however, was the bow, that is the external appearance of it and the general reconstruction of the forecastle behind it. And with inevitable pauses, sometimes agonizingly long ones, this went progressively ahead. Started in 1971, it was completed as regards the external appearance by the summer of 1973. Unfortunately the basic work on the forecastle was then delayed by the effects of the nation's oil and power crises on the Project as a whole.

Since the main achievements really belong to 1973, however, perhaps a word should first be said to complete other aspects of our story in 1972. Away from the dock the year began with a bang – and a great deal of work. In January Sir Max Aitken had given us a free stand at the Boat Show at Earls Court, sponsored by the *Daily Express*. This was a splendid way of helping us, since it drew the attention of tens of thousands of people to the *Great Britain*'s existence. Peter Gibb, as General Secretary, arranged a roster of some thirty volunteers so that for the eleven days of the show two of us were on duty there from 10 am to 9 pm. Seven of the volunteers came by courtesy of the National Maritime Museum, which we particularly appreciated. Notable parts were played by the Custance and Naish families, as well as by Lombard and by Gibb himself.

We had quite a big stand, enclosed and with a single entrance; the main feature was the set of special panels produced by the *Daily Express* and mounted on the interior walls, part of which is now in our museum. Designed to tell the story of the ship and the Project, we had started work on these panels together four months beforehand. We also sold souvenirs, exhibited the Charles Hill model of the *Great Britain* in the centre of the stand, and ran an automatic, continuous, ten-minute set of slides with a recorded commentary, which I had found it a considerable challenge to write and dub to the best advantage. At the end of the Boat Show we were allowed to keep all the panels so long as we removed them personally between 9 pm on the last Saturday and dawn on the Sunday morning. So we filled a car and trailer and in pelting rain I drove them through the night to the country.

The late winter of 1972/3 and early spring were marred by the first of the bitter national coal strikes. The year before at the same period during the postal strike, I remember trying to conduct *Great Britain* business at home for nearly seven weeks without a telephone, as we were on a manual exchange. This year it was the power cuts, sometimes stopping electricity for nine hours in the twenty-four. At the dock this was cruel for the staff in the kiosk and the shop; like so many others up and down the country they were dependent on electricity, and it was a cold winter. The following year there were the late winter railway, gas and hospital strikes, which indirectly reduced the possibilities of work on the ship just at a moment when we were trying to get things done before the spring season started. But then a year later everything came to a dead stop altogether, when the miners struck again and the new crisis forced a general election.

With the United Kingdom's spiral of lowering standards and hopes, it was natural to cast one's mind to the other areas in which the ship had operated, and where there might be potential financial support. The problem of trying to get started in Australia, where the *Great Britain* had spent a quarter of a century in and out of Melbourne from 1852 to 1876 on her runs from Liverpool, took a fresh turn in April 1972, when Group Captain Gibb flew out to his daughter's wedding in Sydney. Although he was able to forge some new personal links for us, nothing more positive could be done immediately. This was partly because of the inherent difficulties, partly because it was just at the height of Australian indignation about Britain entering the Common Market, and partly because Australians were just starting two notable ship-preservation projects of their own with the *Polly Woodside* and the *James Craig*. Nevertheless, we have continued to make a little progress there since then.

It was during 1972 too, that our relations with the now well-established Maritime Trust became more firmly based. The Trust had found that so much needed doing in the maritime field as a whole, that it very much welcomed the various other ship-preservation bodies maintaining their own independent viability if they were able to do so. We for our part were glad of this and welcomed its aim of trying to ensure that the limited national resources available were used to the best advantage.

The execution of the Trust's policies was now in the hands of its distinguished new Director, Vice-Admiral Sir Patrick Bayly. And with regard to the SS *Great Britain* Project as such there were three particular angles which I had discussed with him. The Trust would promote our interests whenever it could; it would at any time listen sympathetically if we asked to be taken over; but it would meanwhile not go out of its way to enlist any special financial aid on our behalf until the Casson Report had been published and our position in the port of Bristol had become clearer. In all of this I spontaneously concurred.

For this and the other vital reasons on the spot therefore, one of the constant anxieties of the year was the continual postponement of the publication of Sir Hugh Casson's findings. He and Michael Cain had first told me that they hoped for publication in May. Then the word in Bristol became September, and later November. Yet it was not until 24 January 1973 that the Report finally did appear – but more of that later.

On the second anniversary of the ship's drydocking, 19 July 1972, we held the first Annual General Meeting of the incorporated charity company. This was not only historic in its way, but there were assembled in our chartroom at the dock offices for the first time ever a number of our formally elected 'members'. They were people who had qualified either by covenanting £5 a year to the Project, or by paying a minimum of £100 (the rates have since been raised by inflation), or by doing something of that or greater equivalent value. But they were also the people who had the power, like shareholders in an ordinary company, to throw us all out if they wanted to. Fortunately they seemed to approve of what we spent so much time and effort trying to do.

Every August, when colleagues are apt to be away, some blow has normally fallen on our enterprise – or at least so it has seemed – and 1972 was no exception. Just when everything appeared to be going rather well, Peter Gibb handed me his three months' notice as General Secretary. He had been with us for a year, but an opportunity had arisen for him to take up an interesting appointment in government service, and the advantages to him were so overwhelming that one could only wish him the very best. The particular importance to the Project of this development, however, was that it became the catalyst, which led to the closing down of our London office and the final concentration of our whole base in Bristol.

The General Secretary's role was primarily to administer our fund-raising. That was the main reason why his office had been in London. But I now had to ask myself two questions. Was it worth immediately going through the arduous personal search again to find someone else, so long as the deadlock persisted in Bristol? And, on the more fundamental aspect, with the country already clearly moving towards economic and political crisis, could we really afford to take someone on full time to struggle against the tide?

I had not, and have not, the slightest doubt that the Project is doing something in the national interest, which will also be of value to future generations everywhere. And that, as I have said earlier, will be true whatever form of society emerges in Britain. The Russians put enormous emphasis on the preservation of national treasures from the past, and I have myself seen some of the results of the very large sums they have spent since the war on reconstructing damaged structures from Tsarist times. But whether, considering the nature of this country's present crisis, the Project could expect ever to be wholly completed under private enterprise alone had already become a valid question by 1972. Since then this has only been underlined more sharply.

So, to cut a long story short, on 23 October 1972 we finally closed the London office, which we had maintained for nearly four years, first in Chancery Lane and then in Cannon Street; and the next day Peter Gibb drove the contents in a hired van to Bristol. Our occupation of the Cannon Street premises had involved an element of generous gift by John and Adrian Swire. But I was also particularly sorry to lose the close contact it had meant with Adrian, whose balanced advice as one of our Council members I had only had to walk down the stairs to seek.

Peter Gibb and our secretary, Mary Carslake, handed over to Joe Blake and Joan Andrews in the Bristol office, and in a few days both were gone. Peter we made a Life Member of the Project. We were now more visibly connected and committed to Bristol. And that was a good thing.

Naturally we had to go on seeking funds, but this was now to be in a different key and with a changing emphasis at various times according to the fall of events. To look after this vital aspect of our affairs, therefore, I found and arranged for Captain Colin Shand to help us on a part-time basis. Coming over from his home near Bath, he was able to see us through the fairly momentous first half of 1973 before in turn handing over to Captain Douglas White, owing to the pressure of his several other interests. White then held the fort for us for the next couple of years.

There was one other short, but very significant, chain of events which took a fresh twist before the end of the year. On 9 November 1972, Blake and I attended a meeting with the local leadership of the Transport and General Workers Union at Transport House in Bristol. A number of members from Charles Hill's shipyard were present, and Alec Foulds was there as managing director of the firm. Lamentably enough, this was the first proper discussion of common problems that we had ever had with the trade unions, though it was not for want of trying.

As I have mentioned previously, with the *Great Britain* we were always in the difficult position of not employing labour directly on the ship ourselves. This arose because we were in theory – even after it had ceased to be the precise case in practice – just another ship in a working shipyard for the purpose of being repaired. And we were not supposed to do anything direct. In September of the previous year, we had made a serious effort to meet the District Committee of the Confederation of Shipbuilding and Engineering Unions. But in spite of negotiations through the summer, the prior circulation of subjects to be discussed, and a willingness in principle on their part to meet us, this very regrettably indeed had come to nothing. The meeting was fixed for 14 September and I returned from a conference in Italy specially to attend it. But, when Blake and I got there that morning, they told us that they were too preoccupied with a strike at Rolls Royce to be able to discuss anything with us, and when we remonstrated, they gave us ten minutes to state our case. This was so unsuitable and so very much what I did not want, quite apart from the disappointment and discouragement, that, as I had feared, the relationship proved too lukewarm to be sustained.

The atmosphere at our discussion at Transport House, on the other hand, was generally quite good, even though there were moments when it looked like getting a little heated. But enough people present wanted to cool it for me to feel when we left that quite a favourable start had been made. One member commented at the end that he felt the *Great Britain* ought to be given a donation from union funds.

As was to be shown later, nevertheless, none of this was quite good enough to carry us much further. I had opened with a general statement explaining how far we felt we had got in the immediate programme of work on the ship and what we planned to do. In this way I hoped that we would not only be telling union members something of genuine interest to them, but would also be able to spell out to them the rather unusual and charity nature of our particular undertaking.

When it came to discussion of the specific points of concern to the Project, Blake and I raised the four topics to which we attached primary importance, just as we had set them out in the agenda proposed for the abortive meeting with the craft unions the previous year. We wanted to be free, so far as the unions were concerned, to employ the most suitable contractor for any particular job. We similarly wanted to be able to employ our own skilled labour – the point being taken that, if they were members of a union, they stood in a different position from non-union labour. We wanted general union acceptance of the special nature of the *Great Britain*, so that members might become sufficiently interested, if not enthusiastic, to consider how demarcation rules might be made more flexible in given circumstances. And, above all, we wanted sanction to have volunteers help with appropriate tasks on the ship, particularly as this became more suitable in the later stages of the restoration.

What emerged from the meeting, however, was first and foremost the fact that, in spite of all the publicity given to the *Great Britain*, even men on the spot in Charles Hill's shipyard knew very little, if indeed anything at all, about our aims and objects. This was tragic proof that communications really had failed. And, while those listening were quite interested in what we could tell them at the time, it was natural that they absorbed it with some caution. The only specific point on which any tangible progress could be made was about our own employment of labour on the ship. We had so far not been able to sweep up the dirt, let alone do any skilled work. In fact, when a volunteer party of naval ratings from HMS *Fearless* had once come for half a day to help clear up and make things look a little more shipshape, we had learned that this could not be repeated. Now, however, if we wanted to take any union members into our own employment for work on the ship, we were given to understand that this would be negotiable.

As regards volunteers, the answer was an unqualified refusal. This was disheartening, because its total rejection without discussion seemed so unreasonable in terms of the future. All over the world ship preservation depends on harnessing the active help of its supporters, and yet here it was to be banned entirely, simply because we had started life in a shipyard. Obviously being in the yard did lead to complications. I could see that to allow volunteers would affect the whole basis of our ostensible status there. In the early, heavy construction stages volunteers would also be unsuitable. This was obviously shipyard work. But we had a huge and varied restoration programme to complete eventually, and parts of it would take for ever if voluntary work was excluded. It was, and is, essential to the interests of the ship that sooner or later this should be hammered out and appropriate understanding reached.

What it all came down to, of course, was jobs. And beyond these basic terms we could not go. Napoleon may or may not have been right to call Britain a nation of shopkeepers. But today, when there is already something faintly unaccepted about being a shopkeeper at all, we seem to have become a nation of job-keepers – regardless of whether the job is worth doing or even really exists.

There was one sequel to the Transport House meeting, though it did not lead anywhere. Three months later, on 21 February 1973, after a good deal of preparatory arrangement, Blake and I were happy to be invited to attend one of the regular monthly meetings of the shipyard's Joint Shop Stewards Committee, which was held on that occasion at Avonmouth. The idea was to explain and discuss our plan of work and generally to create a better understanding all round. I was also given the opportunity of out-lining again the charity aspect of our operation, as well as the rather special problem of admitting the general public to the dock while restoration work was going on. One or two of the men we knew to be good friends of the Project were there, while others, who were not, were not. All in all it seemed a step forward.

Nothing further happened, however, and as guests there was nothing more we could do. Although it was later suggested that we might be invited again, first, on 21 November, and subsequently on 16 January 1974, in each case the state of the nation overrode the idea. For by then the oil and coal crises had thrown all previous assumptions overboard. In any case to achieve a closer liaison we all needed to meet a good deal more than just once or twice a year, and that seemed impossible. So there matters rested, and everything carried on very much as before without any agreement being arrived at. It was a position which I felt would certainly change one day, but no doubt not until some of the background factors had altered.

One of the people, who had no difficulty in seeing the *Great Britain* from our point of view, started some lectures for us in various parts of the country at about this time. He was Geoffrey Marr, lately retired as Com-modore of the Cunard Line, having commanded no less than thirteen of the company's ships in a period when Cunard was still second to none and passenger liners were still passenger liners. A born raconteur, he was a most welcome addition to our small band of lecturers. But what enchanted me was the way he would express his special role in the Project's public image.

'The *Great Britain*,' he put it, 'was the first of the true Atlantic liners. The *Queen Elizabeth* was the last. And as her last captain, now that we are in the air age, I can look back over this whole great line of ships and say with very special emphasis that this first ship above all others should be saved and restored.'

At the end of 1972, I flew to Teheran and then on to Pakistan, where I found myself up on the famous Khyber Pass on the old 'North West Frontier' of India. And as we drove across the arid plain from the historic cantonment of Peshawar and approached the low, dun-coloured hills of the Khyber, I reflected on one of the unusual roles which the *Great Britain* had twice played in her long service at sea, when she was a troop ship first for the Crimean War and then in the Indian Mutiny. A hundred and fifteen years ago under her regular and best-known commander, Captain Gray, she had left Cork on 24 September 1857, with some 1500 men on board. By the Capetown route she had arrived in Bombay on 17 December, returning to Liverpool by 10 April 1858. And now, well over a century later this same hull lay in Bristol docks, its restoration a monument in some small way to the history of the Victorian era in Asia, as well as to Britain's relations with the new worlds of America and Australia.

From the winter of 1972-3 on into the summer of 1973, much of our restoration was geared to a special event. This was Prince Philip's proposed second visit to the *Great Britain*. The occasion was to be his presence at a reception at the dock given jointly by the Maritime Trust and the SS *Great Britain* Project, the first that the Maritime Trust had held outside London, the previous ones having been at Buckingham Palace.

To begin with, a date in July had been suggested and we had put forward 19 July, which had already played such a part in the life of the ship. But in the end July proved impossible and the only suitable date that could be slotted into the Duke's heavy summer engagement list was 9 August. He would be in Bristol on that day accompanying the Queen on her visit to celebrate the 600th anniversary of the city's Charter, and he would break away from the royal route to come to us. As soon as I heard of the plan for this date I kept my fingers crossed, since I felt sure that all would not be plain sailing – and nor was it.

As far as our restoration programme was concerned, we did not undertake any special work, but I did feel strongly that we should make great efforts to complete what we could by this target date, so that we could put on as good a show as possible for the several hundred VIPs who would be present. And having this spur was no bad thing anyway.

When we surveyed the scene in January 1973, there were three major items potentially in hand. The most important as well as the largest and the most advanced was the external work on the bow as a whole, involving as it did the final repair and painting of the plates, the decorative trailboards, and the bowsprit. The other two were the possible installation of the funnel in time for the great day, and the erection of a mast – presumably, as we saw it then, the wooden No. 1 mast, which would be one of the Douglas firs now felled, seasoned, and ready in Gloucestershire.

During the previous few months all the planning for this had been processed through our increasingly effective little Ship Committee – Corlett, Goodier, Blake and myself – and a number of preparatory steps were already well under way. But what had worried me personally more and more since October was that, having at last got past the purely rescue stage and started positive reconstruction, we risked dispersing our limited resources too widely. Above all, I felt, we needed to concentrate on one particular area and to achieve publicly visible progress there. Obviously this was now the bowsprit.

For over a year by this time a young Bristol sculptor, Brian Rothnie, had been working part-time for us on moulding the gilt decorations for the trailboards and the royal crest. He did this in plasticine from drawings and diagrams largely produced by Ewan Corlett. These mouldings would then be set in rigid polyurethane, painted, and mounted on the ship. We had all agreed that this highly modern process would be hard wearing and, when done, indistinguishable from Brunel's wood. Fortunately we had one quite large piece of the original lion and unicorn crest, which had come home with the ship and which gave us the scale and depth of the carvings to go by. There had been a disastrous moment earlier on when it had dropped out of the back of a van during transit and been lost. But the publicity given to the incident by the *Bristol Evening Post* had been so considerable that it was found and safely handed in.

Rothnie was by now well advanced in his task. As a studio for him we had rented some accommodation in the Grove, and he promised that all would be ready in time. The key point therefore became the bowsprit. The first of the beautiful, straight Douglas firs given by Henry Elwes and his Woodland Owners Co-operative had arrived in Charles Hill's hands on 24 October 1972. During the following weeks it had been cut to the precise measurements and painted the yellowish buff of the original. It now lay waiting in a shed. But how were we to get it into position? Owing to its weight and size there was no crane in that part of the dock which could lift it.

Before we could settle this problem, however, we had the pressing basic questions to decide about the funnel and the mast. Would we be able to go ahead in time to get either up by 9 August?

In its way the funnel was the most significant, since like the propeller it symbolized the early steamship aspect, and to have it mounted on the ship would be a striking testimonial to our progress. There was, moreover, an actual funnel already in the offing. As far back as 1971 we had started drawings and contingency plans. And in the summer of 1972 we had been truly delighted to receive an offer from Mr Beaumont of F. E. Beaumont Ltd of Gravesend and near-by Warminster to make and give us a replica funnel. So by early 1973 they were already in the process of manufacturing it.

As with the mast, a key question was the amount of structural under-pinning that would be needed within the ship to carry the weight of the 38-foot funnel. And here, whatever the gift element might be in the item itself, the work had to be done by Charles Hill. At that time, however, the news from the yard was bad – from our point of view. Business was booming and they were terribly busy. In these circumstances we always came off second best. Management naturally had valuable contracts to try to finish on time, and the unions disliked working for us anyway.

So I appealed to the chairman, Richard Hill, for the special limited priorities we needed if we were going to achieve any – or all – of our purposes by August. And Joe Blake backed this up in his almost daily liaison meetings with Michael Hill – without whose unvarying good humour and good sense many things on the *Great Britain* would often not have got done at all. The firm undertook to do what it could. And, without their generosity in stretching a number of points, we would never have scraped through in that high-pressure year, even to the extent we did.

By the spring, nevertheless, I was quite clear that the funnel was simply not on. Hill's had not yet been able to give a date for starting work on it, and Beaumont's for their part were meeting special difficulties with the details of the design for this uniquely old-fashioned smokestack, particularly the ringbands. And it was not until two years later, in May 1975, that the funnel was completed, installed, and painted. But then it did indeed do everything we had hoped for the ship's public impact.

The mast came unstuck for partly similar and partly a very different reason. It was a curious story. Everyone with any interest in the ship had always tended to ask us:

'When are you going to get a mast up?'

No ship, or at any rate no ship in the age of sail or early steam, was felt to look like a ship if she had no masts. Brunel's *Great Britain* had been particularly famous for her six original masts. And some people seemed to think that we could not be getting anywhere until we had re-installed at least one of them. It became the hallmark of our good intentions.

We had been keen to get No. 1 mast up, and we had already integrated into the strengthening of the forecastle bulkhead the previous year a steel tube – given to our measurements by British Steel – that would in addition carry the weight of this mast. We had also arranged with Avonmouth Engineering Ltd that they would provide for us the large steel replica hinge on which Brunel had mounted it.

It was at this stage, however, that we would have to tackle the question of holding the mast in place with wire-rigging – as Brunel had originally done. Mounted only on a hinge, the mast after all would have no stability at all on its own. This entailed not only a supply of suitable wire ropes, but what was far more to the point a series of strong points on the hull, to which they could be fastened. And these did not exist without further structural work being done – which it was hardly worth doing on a purely temporary basis. It called in question the completion of the forecastle deck and its surround. And it was when we came to examine these implications seriously that we realized that No. 1 was not necessarily the best mast to put up first.

'If we put up No. 2 mast,' Corlett observed at the relevant Ship Committee meeting, 'being made of steel and the only one to be stepped down to the keel, it would also be tremendously useful as a Sampson post. We could use it for heavy lifting work at the forward end of the ship – including hoisting up No. 1, which would otherwise present us with a problem anyway.'

Thus it was that by early on in 1973 we had in fact come to adopt the view that, other things being equal, No. 2 should go in before No. 1, instead of the other way round. But in the circumstances this was asking a great deal. Not only was the area round No. 2 far from ready to receive it, but we also did not yet have any mast sections. Steel tubing of suitable dimensions would have to be obtained for welding together. And all this would take time. It became clear that, if we were to bring everything to a head for 9 August, we had better forget about the masts – both of them. And so with regret we did. Even three years later, by the beginning of 1976, there was still no mast up, but we had been given a firm promise of No. 2 as a gift during the next few months.

As for the bowsprit, there were three possible ways of getting it into position. Weighing nearly a ton, it could be lifted by a hired mobile crane, or hauled up with scaffolding and manpower – or it could be lowered into position by a helicopter. On going into the question of a crane, it soon emerged that the considerable range and height required, given the weight, would need such a large vehicle that the edges of the dock would be at risk. It would also be difficult to get the vehicle there by the available access. And as for the scaffolding, the cost and complexity of a whole special structure from the dock bottom seemed at first undesirable, if we could think of a better alternative.

I came to favour a helicopter, and the others went along with me on the idea. I felt that a good photograph of it lowering the bowsprit would go round the world.

During April 1973, I approached Westland Aircraft in Yeovil, fortunately not very far from Bristol. They were so interested that they sent their chief test pilot, John Morton, almost at once on a reconnaissance. He was at first a little worried by the possible effects of the downdraught from the rotor blades on all our old currugated-iron buildings, particularly the roofs which would be hit by the strong upward blast bouncing off the ground in the confined space. The danger of loose bits of detached corrugated iron flying about would not be too healthy for the chopper either. But on going into the relevant distances with careful measurements and inspecting the buildings closely himself, Morton decided that our proposal, though difficult, was feasible. And, as with all men of action, once the decision had been taken he was full of enthusiasm. It was a splendid tonic to be dealing with this kind of approach again – more like the great days of the salvage than the endless haggling over restrictive practices to which we had now become accustomed.

'I'll recommend it,' he declared. 'In fact it'll be good training for someone.'

But this was not to be. At that moment Westland had no helicopters big enough. So they put me in touch with the Royal Naval Air Station at Yeovilton. The navy did have suitable machines. They too were very interested. They too sent a recce team to the dock. They too said with equal enthusiasm:

'It's on.' And they added very truly: 'The publicity would be good for naval recruiting.'

With them, however, the snag was different. They could not do the job without clearance from the Ministry of Defence. They hoped it would be forthcoming without too much difficulty. The commanding officer's recommendation went up to the Flag Officer, Naval Air Command.

From our point of view, however, as I knew only too well, this was a blow because it was obviously a question not only whether the Admiralty would sanction the operation, but whether it would do so in time. And the delay soon began to look serious, rising first in days and then in weeks. The trouble was that Rothnie could not complete his work till the bowsprit was up. And even once the helicopter had been authorized our room for manoeuvre was limited. If a flight on a pre-arranged day had to be cancelled because of bad weather, for instance, the shipwrights necessary to receive and secure the bowsprit could not be whistled up again at short notice. Cancellation could put us back several days straightaway.

So, when by the first week of June still nothing had been heard, with some hesitation I took it on myself to write to the Minister, whom I did know. We had known each other for over twenty years. But in retrospect I think this was probably a mistake, since it meant that Lord Carrington did become personally involved and that the papers had to go all the way up to him. And the wheels of government ground terribly slowly. It was only on 20 July that, subject to certain conditions, I heard that permission had been given for a Royal Navy helicopter to be used.

By that time, however, as with Captain Scott reaching the South Pole, Roald Ammundsen had just got there before him. It was a Friday. But with August now just upon us, it had been the previous Wednesday, two days earlier, which we had finally had to decide upon irrevocably as the very last day to which we could afford to wait. Then we would simply have to lay on the alternative plan which we had thrashed out during the weeks of more and more anxious waiting.

Moreover, the conditions were that we would have to pay for the helicopter at £147 per flying hour – a normal proceeding – but that we would also have to take out an appropriate insurance to indemnify the Ministry against accidents, and certify in writing that the trade unions, as well as any employer involved, had agreed to the Navy doing the job. Even if we had felt we should reverse plans to try to meet these conditions in the non-existent time still left, it would in the circumstances have been impossible. So we thanked the navy with very real regret, as well as not a little embarrassment, and reluctantly pushed on with our alternative plan.

This was to do what Brunel and Patterson may well have done, namely to adopt the time-honoured method of running the bowsprit out from the forecastle deck. And we finally achieved it on Wednesday 25 July, a day ahead of the schedule. We lifted the bowsprit on board where the crane was located further aft and manhandled it forward with a team of eight men from the shipyard.

This was no easy task because there was only the narrow walkway to do it on; and then the great beam of wood had to be raised several feet up to the new forecastle deck – which by now was fortunately in place. The final problem was to push it out gradually over the beak of the bow, without letting it tip and drop into the dock when its point of balance went beyond the support of the ship, as it had to do. For this very tricky operation, which had never been performed before by any of those handling it, a narrow tower of scaffolding had been built up from the dock bottom, anchored back to the ship, and fitted with rollers on top. Finally, the bowsprit had to be pulled back a few inches into the specially reconstructed bitts to hold its squared foot firmly and permanently in place.

I watched the whole of the manhandling on board and everything went extraordinarily well, in fact too well. We had anticipated that it would take two days and had invited press and television to see the final tricky part over the dock on the Thursday morning. But it suddenly became evident on the Wednesday afternoon that everyone was working with such a will and so successfully that it would be madness to stop. So we went on and by 4 o'clock the job was done. On the Thursday morning, therefore, we had to grovel to the media who could only photograph some finishing touches; and in fact only one or two pressmen came. We felt proud but sheepish, and there was an atmosphere of morose anti-climax. So much for making a big splash with a helicopter.

The one and only thing that really mattered, of course, was that our great new bowsprit was up and in place at last. Rothnie completed his decorations on time and by 9 August the whole new bow looked wonderful. The *Great Britain* had been transformed.

Meanwhile, back in January of 1973 the Casson Report with recommendations about the redevelopment of the docks had duly appeared at last. And what it said about the *Great Britain* was first class. But, as I had begun to suppose might happen, the delay had been such that we were now running into the period when the forthcoming changes in local government encouraged even further postponement of difficult issues. That of letting the *Great Britain* stay in her dock was as difficult as any, and nowhere in the whole country was the effect of the Local Government Act, 1972, more marked than in Bristol.

With the creation of Avon County, Bristol City was to be reduced to a

District and truncated. And although fresh elections for the new county had been held in April 1973, and for the city in May, neither council took office until April 1974. It was a complete recipe for further delay.

The old City Council had invited comments on the Casson Report from all and any interested parties – ours were among many sent in – and in practice this took up the whole of 1973. It then made a statement early in 1974 which was described in the press – understandably enough from several different points of view – as being 'of Byzantine ambiguity.' And after that everything was deferred again, at least until the new council could get into its stride. History has not been kind to Casson. His report as such became submerged in the tide of events. By three years later, indeed, the whole position about the City Docks looked like changing yet again, and it seemed possible that they would not be entirely closed to commercial shipping after all.

For the record, however – and the record certainly did not go unnoticed in regard to the *Great Britain* – the Report made two splendidly categoric observations. As item 8.2 it asserted:

With the closing of the Floating Harbour to commercial shipping, the presence of the *Great Britain* resting in its birthplace at Wapping Dock is an invaluable reminder of a passing age. Of all the possible sites this is the best, providing as it does, security without concealment.'

Earlier, in its first introductory page, it had declared:

The waters of the harbour, used to unify and to separate, to enliven and to relax, should return to the citizens for their enjoyment; the wharves and banks to be opened up for boatyards, marinas and waterside promenades, with the restored *Great Britain* as the magnificent centre-piece.

Even we could not ask fairer than that. To be candid, however, I should perhaps also add that there were in any case two most valid reasons for whatever authorities were in power to defer taking positive action on the Report. It would have cost a very great deal of money. And the road assumptions, which had unfortunately been included in Sir Hugh's brief, were politically obsolete by the time his Report came out.

For my own part the early summer of 1973 became nearly as hectic as that of 1970, when the ship came in. We were at absolutely full stretch at the dock, and this absorbed more than every second of time and effort that I could possibly give to the *Great Britain*, getting the great reception of 9 August securely launched – in which Colin Shand, to whom we had now given the slightly Buchanesque title of Secretary to the Project, played a major part – drafting a new fund-raising booklet to be entitled 'Report on Progress', and tying up the restoration work. We were greatly assisted by Ben Thomas on the financial side.

There were also two significant visits to the ship. One was by Chay Blyth, about to start out on the round-the-world yacht race in *Great Britain II*, which Jack Hayward had sponsored and which I went and saw launched by Princess Anne at Ramsgate. We had had to give our formal agreement to the use of the name – and I have only been so sorry since that almost no one has ever referred to the *Great Britain* in connection with the *Great Britain II*, or indeed the *Great Britain III*. I gave Chay Blyth a painted and mounted bolt from our ship as a talisman.

The other visit was a brief transit of the dock and ship on 23 June by Wally Jenkins, as Lord Mayor of Bristol, on his way to attend the opening of the city's Water Festival farther up the harbour. That he should embark from our dock for the first time was a significantly friendly gesture which we all appreciated in terms of a rapprochement between the authorities and the Project, particularly in view of his own original stand.

Into the intense pressure of events immediately after this, however, there dropped from the blue a domestic crisis in our own ranks, which for a few days demanded my own absolute attention to the exclusion of everything else. This was the dispute about our immediate amalgamation with the Maritime Trust – to which I have briefly alluded earlier.

The basic cause was the immense and unnerving delay in any solution being reached about a long-term site for the ship. My colleagues were certainly as anxious about this as I was. Accordingly, when it was privately suggested, I believe, to one or two of them by contacts in the city that the Maritime Trust should forthwith take over the *Great Britain* lock, stock and barrel, they seemed to take this as a prelude to an immediate promise that the ship could stay in the dock, if this course were adopted. Accompanying the suggestion, it appeared to have been hinted that this would avoid any eventual so-called settlement with the Project as such, which as an organization was held to be too unsubstantial, as well as disliked, for the city to deal with.

That this was essentially a political move struck me at once, and possibly – as I later discovered to be the case – from only a minority interest. It was perfectly clear to me that the City Council was really in no position to make any final declaration about the future of our dock in the middle of 1973, whether to us, to the Maritime Trust, or to anyone else. I also discovered that, so far from placing all their faith in the Trust, most leading councillors had never even heard of it. And I further found that the policy of the Trust itself had in no way altered. It neither wished to take over immediate full responsibility for the *Great Britain* nor had the resources to do so. The whole thing was in its way a plot, in which, as is often the case in matters of this kind, questions of personalities also entered into it.

The fact that the proposal was inherently nonsensical, however, did not detract from its being dangerously explosive and disruptive. In the Project we had never had a row like this before. The situation was also desperately urgent, if we were to settle everything before the joint reception with the Maritime Trust on 9 August – when it had even been suggested that an announcement of the shotgun marriage should be made. For it would be a recipe for disaster that we should be joint hosts at a royal reception, if some of the individuals most directly concerned were going round stabbing each other in the back over the vol-au-vents and champagne.

Five of us therefore held an emergency meeting at Ewan Corlett's offices near Basingstoke on 6 July. Besides Ewan and myself there were Euan Strathcona, Maldwin Drummond and Colin Shand. It was a difficult but important occasion in the *Great Britain* saga, and it led to the circulation to all our colleagues of papers setting out the issues, so that when a full Project meeting took place on 19 July everyone would be able to talk the same language.

By this time we had made several significant additions to what we called our Project Council, and the two arguments which settled the question were succinctly put. Speaking as a Bristolian, Stephen Macfarlane made the fundamental point that for a London-based organization to be called in to take over just at the very moment when we were at last beginning to be accepted as committed to Bristol, would create a singularly bad impression. And David Owen – between ministerial appointments at that time – put it that, since no decision could now be expected from the authorities until the new Avon and Bristol councils had come into effective operation the following year, this was precisely not the moment to burn all our boats by integrating permanently into the Maritime Trust. We should wait and see.

The case was overwhelming. Fortunately this became obvious, and we closed ranks once more. We would work as closely as we possibly could with the Maritime Trust, whose help and support we greatly welcomed, but neither we nor they wanted constitutional amalgamation. All was set fair again for 9 August – but the *Great Britain* had lived up to her reputation of never giving one a dull moment.

14. The Site - at Last

The object of a reception, such as the one we held with the Maritime Trust on 9 August 1973, is basically to spread the word about the ship and to interest a wider circle of significant people in her future. But it is not possible to have a party of this kind without also inviting some of those who have helped in the past and those who feel that their links with the Project entitle them to be present. The inevitable result is a tremendous pressure on the numbers that can be accommodated – under cover if it rains, as well as for reasons of cost. So, when we came to take stock of the position a month beforehand, on 9 July, we found that with the absolute maximum of 350 guests to which our limit had inexorably been raised, we already had 301 acceptances and 175 replies still to come. In spite of this being the middle of the summer holiday period, we obviously had a delicate situation on our hands.

We had also come through exactly the difficulties I had foreseen about holding the reception at all. It had proved unwelcome to the city authorities – which I was sorry about, but was powerless to avoid. And there had been an effort to get it quashed on the grounds that the day of the Queen's visit was unsuitable. But those who took this line were not I think aware, initially at any rate, of quite what they were up against. It was not just our SS *Great Britain* Project which was the issue, but the whole year's programming of the Maritime Trust. And the decision to hold a reception at the *Great Britain* fortunately proved unshakeable, since Prince Philip was coming as the Trust's President.

Just before the great day itself there was one further distracting but wholly delightful development. Late in the evening two days beforehand, my telephone rang at home. The operator asked me to stand by for a call from the royal yacht, *Britannia* – which was at that moment in the Solent. Major Benjamin Herman, Prince Philip's Equerry, came on the line and told me that it had just been suggested that the two younger sons, Prince Andrew and Prince Edward, might like to see the *Great Britain* while *Britannia* was in Avonmouth for the centenary celebrations. I felt a bit stunned, partly because I did not at first recognize the names of the two others who would be accompanying them, the Marquess of Milford Haven and Lord Ivor Mountbatten. And it dawned on me only after a moment or two that these were their cousins, two boys of about twelve and ten years of age like themselves.

'All right,' I heard myself saying on the telephone, 'we'll be very happy indeed to see them. I'll lay on a car and make the arrangements and then let you know.'

This was not quite as simple as it may sound. But fortunately all went well. Charles Hill very kindly provided a car, the police sprang into action, and in the event *Britannia* arrived at Avonmouth on time in spite of the gales, so that they reached the Great Western Dock about an hour before the Duke of Edinburgh was due to land on Wapping Wharf by helicopter. As I had to be there to meet him, after welcoming them I asked Maldwin Drummond to show them around. And my wife gave them tea in a small staff room at the back of our office block – the only room we had available and not required for the main reception. Their father greeted them before they returned to Avonmouth.

My wife and I had driven over for this considerable occasion in our motor caravan, and we spent two nights on the dockside, the one before and the one after, so that I could see for myself how all our planning worked out. Amongst other arrangements a special marquee had been constructed between the entrance and the ship, in order to give more room in the event of bad weather. Volunteers from our Bristol Committee came in to clear, clean, and straighten all they could in the dock the evening before. Our own staff did a great job carrying this endless task through on the day. Immediately beforehand the police went round with Blake to search for bombs. Two of our failures were to arrange any tea for visiting chauffeurs and to make it easy for VIPs coming by helicopter to get landing permits.

Special notices were put up and cloakroom arrangements made, food and drink brought in – the latter mostly a gift from Harvey's – the car park organized, particular gates and doors locked and unlocked, the shop

and our offices put in order, the furniture in the chartroom cleared, the
museum polished up, the warehouse checked, press and TV personnel
lists gone through for the last time for accreditation, literature assembled,
briefing of visiting Project helpers organized, the microphones tested for
the three short speeches that were to be made, the places selected for the
Royal Marines band to play, the temporary radio hut on the weatherdeck
manned by the amateur Radio Society of Great Britain – from where they
linked us up with the Falkland Islands – and, most important, the timings
of our whole programme were reviewed and, where necessary, rehearsed
yet again.

The one thing we had to leave to chance was the weather – vital though
it was. When Colin Shand, Joe Blake and I had mentioned this problem to
Sir Patrick Bayly earlier on, however, he had given us the blue-eyed, deep-
water assurance that only an admiral can. So I was never really worried.

'On 9 August,' he had told us, 'it will be fine.' And, mercifully, he proved
right.

Our many guests started arriving in good time – which they had been
asked to do. The Duke of Westminster came, as Chairman of the Maritime
Trust. And shortly before 5 o'clock Sir Patrick Bayly – as Director of the
Trust – Ewan Corlett and I moved out to the spot on the concrete beyond
our car park where Prince Philip's red helicopter was due to land at
1710 hours. And in view of all that was at stake or could go wrong, it was
with no small relief that bang on time I saw the helicopter swinging over
the harbour from Durdham Down to land with a roar of wind a few paces
in front of us.

There was a sudden stillness as the jet engine was switched off and the
rotor blades came to a halt. We all moved forward. The figure one had
come to recognize so well and with so much regard climbed down from
his seat by the pilot, came over and shook hands with the official civic
welcoming party beside us, and then with ourselves. When I invited him
to get into the first of the line of cars – provided by the city – he asked
how far it was. I said, off the cuff:

'Four hundred yards, sir.'

He chose to walk instead, and we all set off – between the ranks of
assembled guests, local residents and near-by office workers, holiday
makers, officials, and police. Arriving in the dock unexpectedly on foot
meant that we were curiously and suddenly there, without people being
quite aware of it. But in a moment we had slipped into the pre-arranged
programme – every stage of which has to be sent in beforehand – and we

toured the ship and dock before arriving finally in the marquee, by now packed tight with the assembled company.

From a small wooden stand, I was to speak first. I summarized the Project's efforts and emphasized the ship's historic link with Bristol. It took 4 minutes and 29 seconds, which was 29 seconds too long. Corlett followed with a little more time in which to state the case for the ship's unique maritime and national importance. Then Prince Philip stepped to the microphone and spoke quite informally of his own involvement.

'The first time I saw the *Great Britain*,' he said, 'was when I went to the Falkland Islands in 1957 . . . If anybody had told me then that there was a chance of getting her back to Bristol I would have suggested that they should try something else . . . (But) as you have heard, I was myself on board when she was put back into this dock. You can see how she fills the dock now, and you can imagine we had some exciting moments wondering whether she would in fact go in at all . . .

'When I went on board and had a look round, the mess was indescribable, as you can imagine after nearly forty years (partly) under water. Inside the hull everything had rusted and fallen in. There was mud everywhere, and barnacles. Today you can buy the barnacles in the souvenir shop.

'To come back after three years and see the work that has been done is really tremendously encouraging . . . The present generation will be able to watch the exciting programme of rebuilding, and to future generations she will be a source of endless fascination . . . I sincerely hope that you will all become as interested in the restoration of this ship as I am.'

In October we had another royal visit. On the sixteenth the Prince of Wales came to see the *Great Britain*. I had known about this from just before the August occasion and we had felt honoured by his own wish to do so. Compared with the Duke of Edinburgh's visit, this was to be much more private. Prince Charles was with us for just on an hour one afternoon at the end of a brief West Country tour. Again, he arrived and left by helicopter – and the corporation water lorries again had a field day jetting and sluicing every stone and speck of mud from the surface of Wapping Wharf before the helicopter arrived. And once again all the precautions were taken, with special police, thorough bomb searches, and a strict programme – so much so that, when the inevitable crank phoned in at the moment of arrival to say that there was a bomb on the ship, we all knew very well that there was not.

This time I went out to meet the helicopter alone, apart from the civic party; and as the little red speck lowered itself, flashing from the sky, I felt how strange this life had become – and how even stranger it must seem to the proud and brooding spirit of Brunel himself, watching us all no doubt from somewhere in the background. Once inside the dock, Prince Charles met our main party in the museum, after being greeted by Ewan Corlett beside the ship. We managed to keep the numbers down to about a dozen, and, besides members of the staff, this included Jack Hayward, Jim Goodier as a member of our Ship Committee, and Richard and John Hill. Euan Strathcona was scheduled to return to London in the royal helicopter.

One of the things we all regret on this sort of occasion is that the dock has to be closed to the public. But there really is no alternative for security reasons. It does also mean, however, that the best use can be made of the time available. We followed the same route through the ship as in August, which also meant climbing up all the forecastle decks. Prince Charles came through alone with just Corlett, Blake and myself and we did our best to answer his many questions. It was an encouraging and very special experience.

After all these adventures, life moved on into the winter in a lower key – at least so far as the *Great Britain* was concerned. No work at all could be done during the power crisis, and as 1974 opened, black and forbidding with soaring interest rates and roaring inflation, we had to take stock of our own prospects. And in terms of restoration, as well as improvements to the dock itself, I felt it prudent to cut back severely. Money which we might have expected would not after all be coming in, and in the end we had no alternative. At best we could hope only to complete those items which had already been started. As with every other business up and down the country, our first task in the face of the onslaughts on the nation's economy was, I felt, to survive.

This left us, however, with quite a good residual programme from the public point of view, and during 1974 we completed almost all of it. We gave top priority to plate repairs on the upper port side by Parglas Ltd – fully painted finally in black and white – and to the major task of finishing the erection of Beaumont's great funnel, which had by now lain on board in three sections for quite some time, awaiting Charles Hill's ability to complete the underpinning and skirting.

We also mounted the rigid polyurethane castings of the Bristol coat of arms, the unicorns and the cornucopia on the stern. And we continued to receive transportable items of future equipment such as the magnificent deck fittings from the Royal Engineers of Central Engineer Park near Stratford on Avon, the wood for which was donated by the timber trade.

We also set in motion the design work which was to lead in due course to gifts of portholes by Delta Metals and to the construction of the ship's docking 'bridge' by English China Clays.

The fact remains, nevertheless, that the decisions we had to make to cut back on the rest of the programme marked a change of gear, and, while we have continued to make progress ever since, the specific directions have had to be carefully chosen and limited. Thus in 1975, for instance, we went on to do rather more on the starboard side plating than on the port side the previous year. But we left the crack repair and the completion of a mast till 1976. All in all, however, each step has done much to enhance both the physical and the public relations image of the ship, and already people can imagine quite readily what the final restoration of the whole will be like.

The one really major item for which we could set no date was the decking of the whole ship. It is extremely important that this should be completed by 1980 at the latest, if further deterioration of the ironwork is not to reach disturbing proportions. This is because even in the semi-industrial climate of Bristol rain contains some element of sulphuric and hydrochloric acid, which was not the case in the remoteness of the Falklands. And every time rainwater collects in the crannies of the interior a trace of acid remains when the water evaporates. The pace of corrosion is thus quickened. We bought the timber back in 1971, but the task is a major one and by 1976 we had not yet seen our way to tackling it.

Until a weatherdeck is on, of course, the ship has no proper interior, and no work can be done to fit her out even on a minor basis. It was partly to create an 'interior' in the limited area of the forecastle that, as long ago as 1973, we decked the forecastle as a pilot operation. And with the later work done on the scuppers and bulkhead we began to be able to dry it out. The only significant setback was the fiasco, whereby the unions declined to let us accept the offer which we had had of a package deal to caulk the deck the same year by an outside contractor. Then they said they could not do it themselves straightaway, as they had no experience of the necessary technique with the material to be used. The shocking result was that this new deck went right through the winter without being caulked until the spring of 1974.

I have left our main story – the question of a site – at the opening of 1974, and it only remains to conclude with the steps which led to the settlement of the very unhappy differences of view with the city of Bristol. For settled it was. The key, as I have mentioned, was a change in the balance

of power as a result of the local elections. These not only brought new men
to the positions of authority, but also enabled those who had had to bear
the long-standing burden of the *Great Britain* trouble to bow out grace-
fully. No one had to unsay anything that had been said, and no one from
the previous administration could be held responsible for what might
come next.

The new City Council had a Labour majority, and a fresh and younger
wave of leaders rose to control it. The first step was to meet them. I began
doing this soon after their electoral success in 1973, as a favourable opportunity occurred during the festivities associated with one of Bristol's most
adventurous developments of recent years – international power boat
racing in the harbour. For three days each year, incidentally, these machines
hurtle past the old *Great Britain* in a flurry of spray and noise. Surprisingly
enough, our own attendance falls off because most people only come into
the dock to watch the races, and sit all afternoon like starlings on the great
white 1857 spar – the one that was cut down in Sparrow Cove – now
mounted on blocks on the towpath.

The second development came rather unexpectedly in the dark days of
January 1974, when the Planning Committee was able to address itself
officially to the Casson Report for the first time. Our own comment from
the Project, as also from our Bristol Committee, sent in as asked for the
previous year, had been to make two requests, and two only. We had
requested that a decision about the Great Western Dock should now be
taken in principle independently of the rest of the Casson Report. And we
asked, of course, that it should be in favour of allowing the *Great Britain*
to stay in the dock permanently. Then, on the sixteenth of the month, I
suddenly heard that the Planning Committee had officially minuted its
view, that it had 'no objection' to the *Great Britain* remaining in her
existing drydock.

This negative may not sound much, but considering how local government works, we realized that it was something of a breakthrough. And I
concluded that, although it might still take some time for the new council
to turn this negative into a positive, port was in sight at last. From
that moment on, I felt that a fresh stage had been reached, and that our
primary task was to help to make the ship as acceptable as possible to all
Bristolians.

Then in April came the news from the city authorities that our rates
would be reduced by 40 per cent, which is the maximum they do for any
charity. And on 9 May for the first time we had the genuine pleasure and

interest of being able to hold an informal exchange of views in our chart-room, looking out on the *Great Britain*, with three key men in the new leadership, the Leader of the Council, Charles Merrett, the Chairman of the Planning Committee, Brian Richards, and the local Secretary of the Labour Party, the late Roy Willmott, whose early death came as a shock to us all. With me were Joe Blake and 'Knocker' White, and together the six of us reviewed the entire situation. One's only regret was that this had not been possible years before.

During the summer and early autumn of 1974, we had two more dis-tinguished visitors to the dock. The first was Lord Mountbatten on 14 July, and then on 28 September the new Lord Mayor, the late Bert Peglar, who came to unveil the Bristol coat-of-arms on the stern. I mention this here, both because of the way it reflected the new standing of the *Great Britain* and because of what was said during the ceremony. Some-times these occasions may sound platitudinous, but for those involved the titular head of any administration represents the mood of its governing body, and the actual atmosphere is a political reality – which is why one attaches importance to people like Lord Mayors.

The *Great Britain*, Peglar said, was ... 'the most important ship, the first screw-driven ship, and the direct forbear of modern shipping. She is here back in the place where she was built after a most remarkable career and perhaps the most remarkable salvage operation of all time.'

'I would congratulate most heartily those who conceived the idea and had enough drive to inspire such an operation, for few in those days thought it was practical or indeed even possible to see the ship back in Bristol.'

He concluded by saying that I had 'made the impossible possible' and by again congratulating all concerned. Coming when and how it did this was a genuine comfort and of genuine value to us – particularly as he him-self had been a leading sceptic in the earlier years. Stephen Macfarlane had paid tribute to his presence in an opening speech, and in my own reply I ended with words which I firmly believe:

'The crest unveiled today is not only a tribute in itself to Bristol's own great sea-faring past. It is also something which, when visitors see it on the ship, will help them to appreciate the *Great Britain*'s deep association with Bristol.'

In the eye of history there were to be four months yet before the final settlement. And some weeks later I was away on a visit to South America, in the course of which I travelled by ship through the Straits of Magellan from west to east. Discovered in 1520 by the Portuguese explorer, Ferdinando de Magalhaes (Ferdinand Magellan), this forbidding waterway cuts the corner at the very tip of the continent and avoids the passage round Cape Horn. While making this famous and remote traverse, the life of the *Great Britain* seemed very near. For she had rounded Cape Horn thirty-three times from west to east, and twice the much harsher way, from east to west. But had she ever been through the winding 300 miles of the straits? I found the question intriguing, and have done so since. As we have never been able to trace any of the *Great Britain*'s official logs, no one seems to know. It appears that she may have done so just once. But in general she stood off to the southward and made the maximum use of her sails with the westerly gales. For similar reasons she never went through the Suez Canal, but always took the Cape route when outward bound to Australia, although the Canal was opened some years before the end of her service life.

When I returned to England in November I obtained my colleagues' agreement to take a step which, however logical, had previously been impracticable for us. This was to invite two members of the City Council to join our own charity company board, that is the Project Council, one from each of the main parties, Labour, and the Citizen Party, the Conservatives.

It is simpler in such cases to start with the people out of power, since they are more available. Moreover, there was a clear candidate from the Citizen Party, who in normal circumstances we would have invited to join us on personal grounds anyway long before this, because of his known interest in the maritime history of Bristol, and who had spoken up for the ship's admission back in 1969. But the political situation had made this impossible. This was Councillor, previously Alderman, Robert Wall. Although now the leader of the Conservative opposition in the newly constituted City Council, he accepted our invitation after consulting his party and we were delighted to co-opt him on 10 December 1974.

There was no obvious Labour choice, and so I consulted the Leader of the Council, Charles Merrett. It was not long before a very satisfactory solution emerged. This was the nomination of the new chairman of the Finance and Land Committee, Councillor John McLaren, who had entered local politics from schoolmastering. When he came to the dock early in January, we told him everything we could think of about our affairs, and by 18 February 1975 he too had been co-opted. With these two additions to our own council we were on a new leg of the course.

Meanwhile, Charles Merrett and John McLaren, together with their supporters and in concert with the opposition, had been moving actively to resolve the longstanding issue of the site for the *Great Britain* once and for all. And, as is the way when what everyone wants is no longer in dispute, this traumatic question suddenly seemed to lose the terrors it had held for so long. At a stroke, the drama was ended.

For us the decision came in what was almost an anti-climax – though nothing whatever could dim the relief and appreciation one felt that the seemingly endless nightmare was at long last over. It was arranged that the final settlement should take place by resolution of the Finance Committee on the morning of Thursday, 23 January 1975. And I was assured that this was the equivalent of committing the Council as a whole.

As these committee meetings are held in public, it was suggested that Blake and I should come in and hear the final proceedings. When we went up to the Council House at about ten o'clock, we found to our surprise, in view of the previous interest, that the only other person on the public benches was a press reporter from the *Bristol Evening Post*. And we had not been there more than a moment or two before the City Public Relations Officer, Anthony Buckley Trott, very kindly came over and offered us a cup of coffee. The *Great Britain*, I felt, really was accepted at last.

As decisions had already been reached in private, there was almost no discussion when the item came up on the agenda, and the emptiness of the press and public benches mirrored the fact that all contention had gone out of the issue. For the record John McLaren, who was in the chair, gave a brief outline of the problem about the last lease of the Great Western Dock having run out in June 1970. Then he made the two announcements which I had lived the past five years to hear.

The *Great Britain* would now be entitled to remain in the Great Western Dock in perpetuity.

Secondly, the SS *Great Britain* Project would be charged a peppercorn rent for the Dock – that is, nothing.

On this basis, a direct lease would be granted to the Project, initially for three years. It was explained that, when the lease came to be renewed at the end of that time, it might be possible to review the delineation of the area, if sufficient progress had been made by then with redevelopment plans for neighbouring parts of the City Docks.

This gave rise to the only substantial discussion in the Finance Committee, and there were chuckles all round when one of our former doughty critics could not forbear a parting shot. This underlined the point that the peppercorn rent covered only the dock itself.

'They must pay for the car park and restaurant at commercial rates.' And so we have to. This clarion call having been made, the deal went through unanimously.

Thus ended the long-drawn-out fight for a permanent site for the *Great Britain*. She had already become part of Bristol's life, but now she had also come to be recognized as part of Bristol's future. It was very nearly seven years since I personally had first heard of her existence in Sparrow Cove, and five years almost exactly since we had commissioned our salvage expedition. As Joe Blake and I left the Council House that morning and stepped into the brisk air of a winter's day, I also recalled the occasion six years before when I had had my first discussion in the same building with the authorities of that time, and they had asked me what I wanted.

'Well,' I had said, 'what we would really like is a free berth.'

I doubt if any of them had any more idea than I did what we would all go through before this came to pass. But the fact remained now that this was wonderful news. Nor was it quite all. In addition, the city let us off the payment of any back rent for the dock, refunding certain sums which had already been paid to cover the period since our arrival. So we will have had a free berth throughout after all. This generous gesture and the tenure of the Great Western Dock are of immense value and importance to the whole prospect for the *Great Britain*. Above all, having this site has added to the very stature of the ship herself by automatically creating this unique combination unequalled anywhere else in the world – of a historically important, ocean-going vessel and the special, intrinsically interesting dock expressly made for her original construction. While we on the Project are immensely grateful to the Bristol government of 1975 for what they have done, they have also unquestionably struck an inspired blow for the world prestige of their own proud city.

With all this behind us, of course, it still remains to finish the fight for the restoration of the *Great Britain* in the image of Brunel. At the time of writing, as 1975 gives way to 1976, one can but look back on 1975 as a year in which the national crisis compelled everyone to do no more than tread water. With firms going bankrupt at an unprecedented rate, with the richer classes silently cutting living standards to a degree unrecognized outside their own ranks, and with the prospects of inflation still riding high on a falling pound and mounting government debt, it was quite impossible to launch into the new round of fund-raising which the settlement of the site should have demanded.

A little private money continued to come in, of course. We had some further financial help from the Maritime Trust. Our own earnings at the dock held up promisingly on a bigger attendance than ever. And I managed to get us started into a wider campaign of small-scale individual subscriptions by means of our 'Friends of the *Great Britain*' membership. But all this did no more than enable us to repeat the experience of the previous year, 1974, in carrying out certain limited, though positive, restoration aims – finishing the funnel, completing the upper starboard side, and doing sundry weather-proofing to the forecastle. On a similar basis for 1976, we entered the year intending to erect No. 2 mast, carry out the final proper repair to the starboard crack, and put the 'bridge' across the weather-deck. For more than that, for a fresh surge forward in general it seemed that we would have to wait for better times for the nation as a whole.

Meanwhile, compared with the top fifty stately homes all over the country, only ten had more visitors in the 1975 season than we did. But while we would never be able to operate on the scale, say, of Beaulieu with its magnificent motor museum, which comes at the head of the list, there is no reason why progress in our own restoration should not enhance our earning power. Perhaps one day, after all, hard-pressed shipping interests might also even see in us the sort of worthwhile public relations cause that the motor industry has seen in Beaulieu.

It was with thoughts of improving the quality of our own dockside presentation, as well as spreading personal knowledge of the ship to suitable people, that I tremendously welcomed an approach by the Director of the Design Council, Sir Paul Reilly, early in 1975. Long a supporter of ours, he proposed that, since the annual design awards were being presented in Bristol that year, everyone concerned should be invited to come down and visit the ship. If we had been further advanced with the restoration of the *Great Britain*, he would have proposed that the presentation ceremony should actually be performed on board. Instead, it was to be done in the *Concorde* hangar at Filton.

These awards are presented every year by the Duke of Edinburgh, and when the arrangements were being planned he said that he would like to lead the party down to us – for what would be his own third visit to the ship. So the occasion was fixed for the afternoon of 28 May, and we laid on a tea for some 300 people, again having a marquee put up on the dockside.

Again we were lucky with good weather and everything went off well. I was allotted a few minutes to give an outline of the Project while tea was being served, and one of the star attractions was a beautiful replica bronze porthole, one of several given to us by Delta Metals. Afterwards everyone toured the ship.

Prince Philip went on board as soon as he arrived. As we walked round, I realized that there were now few people outside the Project itself who knew as much about the *Great Britain* as he did. And while we seemed to have come a long way since that far off July evening five years before, when he had been on board for the historic docking, I was only too conscious of how much more we might have done in the time, if conditions had been more propitious. I resolved that, come what might, this really was a job which one day we would well and truly finish.

On the broad question of state help for the *Great Britain* I feel that this is perhaps the right note with which to end an account of the Project so far. For, as 1975 drew to a close, it was evident that a new attitude to the maritime heritage of the nation was beginning to emerge at last, and not least in some of the corridors of power.

The reason is twofold. During the past few years there has been far more interest than ever before in the preservation of the records of the past. Secondly, concern for our great maritime history has come just at the moment when there has been a massive shift of control of national resources from the private sector into public hands. It has therefore become manifestly impossible to do all that is required from private sources alone. In the age of the mixed economy, the rescuing of the past is a mixed responsibility too.

Our maritime heritage is the Cinderella of the business, in that only during the last few years has there really been any widespread popular concern about it. The period of development has in effect been very much that in which the rescue of the *Great Britain* was planned and achieved – thereby contributing in some measure to what has taken place. And yet, as I wrote in a letter in *The Times* of 22 April 1975:

> If one had to single out any particular feature of British history which has been predominant in shaping our whole development, it is that we have lived by means of the sea. It is therefore surely absurd that our maritime heritage should be treated as a poor relation. Since the Maritime Trust was formed a start has been made with public opinion and with a factual assessment of the priorities. But there is a long way to go. . . .

Something like £11·5 million was spent by the state on historic buildings and ancient monuments under the 1974–5 Estimates of Public Expenditure. But ships are not included. Part of that sum went in matching grants pound for pound against what had been found from private sources. And this surely is the way at least to start. Even that, however, needs the support of an informed, interested, and concerned public opinion. And with the tide of views now just beginning to move towards this only sensible, yet critical development, one of the great functions of the Maritime Trust, as in its way of the *Great Britain* Project, too, is to do everything possible to help with information, example, and the right sort of public relations.

For, when all is said and done, we come back to the original question I used to ask myself in the early days of our own grand design. What is it all about? Why try to save the *Great Britain*? And, while there is a wider truth, part of the answer is like that of the mountaineer who, when asked why he climbed a mountain, replied:

'Because it is there.'

The wider truth, however, is that, whatever may be the fashionable thought in any changing age, the human race today is inseparable from its own past. It is what it is, because of the way it has come to reach the point that it has. And, in the age of the *Concorde*, knowledge of the industrial steps to the summit are essential to an understanding, as well as an appreciation, of the current achievement in itself. The *Great Britain*, we somewhat tritely observe in Bristol, was the *Concorde* of her day. Just as bold, just as revolutionary, just as challenging to the doubters, she represented one of the supreme engineering and industrial steps ever taken in this country, or indeed in the world. It would be a crime against future generations, if what has already been achieved with her restoration were not to be carried through to its final conclusion with public and private support alike.

Index